# Directions in Australian Electoral Reform

Professionalism and Partisanship
in Electoral Management

# Directions in Australian Electoral Reform

Professionalism and Partisanship
in Electoral Management

Norm Kelly

Australian
National
University

E PRESS

**ANU**
**E PRESS**

Published by ANU E Press
The Australian National University
Canberra ACT 0200, Australia
Email: anuepress@anu.edu.au
This title is also available online at http://epress.anu.edu.au

---

National Library of Australia Cataloguing-in-Publication entry

Author:         Kelly, Norm

Title:          Directions in Australian electoral reform : professionalism and partisanship in
                electoral management / Norm Kelly.

ISBN:           9781921862878 (pbk.) 9781921862885 (ebook)

Notes:          Includes bibliographical references.

Subjects:       Elections--Australia--History.

                Election law--Australia--History.

                Law reform--Australia--History.

                Voting--Australia--History.

                Representative government and representation--Australia--History.

                Australia--Politics and government.

Dewey Number: 324.60994

---

Cover design and layout by ANU E Press

# Contents

# Abbreviations

| | |
|---|---|
| 2PP | two-party preferred |
| AATA | Administrative Appeals Tribunal of Australia |
| ABS | Australian Bureau of Statistics |
| ACE | Administration and Cost of Elections Project |
| ACT | Australian Capital Territory |
| ACTEC | Australian Capital Territory Electoral Commission |
| ADI | Australian Defence Industries |
| AEC | Australian Electoral Commission |
| AGPD | Australian Government and Politics Database |
| ALP | Australian Labor Party |
| ATSIEEIS | Aboriginal and Torres Strait Islander Election Education and Information Service |
| CLP | Country Liberal Party |
| DoFA | Department of Finance and Administration (Commonwealth) |
| ECQ | Electoral Commission of Queensland |
| EFA | Election Funding Authority (NSW) |
| HCA | High Court of Australia |
| HoR | House of Representatives |
| ICCPR | International Covenant on Civil and Political Rights |
| IDEA | Institute for Democracy and Electoral Assistance |
| JSCEM | Joint Standing Committee on Electoral Matters (Commonwealth) |
| JSCER | Joint Select Committee on Electoral Reform (Commonwealth) |
| LSI | least squares index |
| MEC | Minter Ellison Consulting |
| MHA | Member of the House of Assembly |
| MLA | Member of the Legislative Assembly |
| MLC | Member of the Legislative Council |
| MP | Member of Parliament |
| NSW | New South Wales |
| NSWEC | New South Wales Electoral Commission |
| NK | Norm Kelly |
| NT | Northern Territory |
| NTEC | Northern Territory Electoral Commission |

| | |
|---|---|
| PVA | postal voting application |
| SA | South Australia |
| SAS | Save the ADI Site Party |
| SCEPPF | Select Committee on Electoral and Political Party Funding (NSW) |
| SCETYP | Standing Committee on Education, Training and Young People (ACT) |
| SCLA | Standing Committee on Legal Affairs (ACT) |
| SEO | State Electoral Office (South Australia) |
| SOC | Statutory Officers Committee |
| TEC | Tasmanian Electoral Commission |
| VEC | Victorian Electoral Commission |
| WA | Western Australia |
| WAEC | Western Australian Electoral Commission |

# 1. Introduction

A democracy's electoral system is fundamental to its legitimacy.[1] From the electoral system flow the form and style of representation, the relative strength of political parties, the formation of government and the development of policy positions. In a representative democracy, the structure of a state's electoral system plays a critical role in determining the nature and form of political discourse and parliamentary representation. The electoral system establishes who may vote, how many representatives are to be chosen from which areas, who is in charge of the conduct of elections and how votes are counted. Because adjustment or manipulation of these elements can have severe positive or negative consequences for the viability of political parties, attempts to make changes are often fiercely debated. Electoral system reforms can also impact strongly on the ability of citizens to participate in a state's general political discourse and democratic processes—as voters, candidates or as members of political parties. Beyond any formal barriers, the perceived fairness or unfairness of the electoral system can also affect citizens' willingness to engage in democratic processes.

Australia has been at the forefront of electoral design and innovation over the past 150 years and, with nine legislative jurisdictions,[2] there is ample opportunity for experimentation and diversity. Australia is one of the oldest continuing democracies in the world and the first to introduce the modern form of the secret ballot, the first country to vote itself into existence through popular referenda, and the first country in which women could both vote and stand for parliament.[3] In the nineteenth century, Australian colonies introduced democratic innovations such as the use of government-printed ballot papers and written nominations for elections. By the late nineteenth century, Tasmania had pioneered the single-transferable-vote form of proportional representation for its lower house.

Since the 1980s, significant electoral reforms have continued at the national and sub-national levels; however, while nineteenth-century innovations such as the secret ballot, independent electoral officials and standardised ballot papers were seen as measures to improve the fairness of elections, reforms can often be viewed as providing a partisan advantage for the political parties in power. For example,

---

1   In this book, the term 'electoral system' is used in a holistic sense to refer to all aspects of an electoral regime, including the voting system, electoral regulation, administration and management. The term 'voting system' is used to refer to the method of voting, such as proportional representation or majoritarian single-member electorates.

2   Norfolk Island is an external Australian Territory with a legislature smaller than many Australian local councils and does not operate on party political lines, so is not considered in this assessment.

3   Australian women (except Indigenous women in some States) were entitled to vote and stand for parliament from 1902. While New Zealand was the first country to give women the vote in 1893, women in that country were not entitled to stand for parliament until 1919.

political scientist David Elkins argues that recent electoral experimentation, while promoted as improving democratic outcomes, is primarily designed to provide partisan advantage.[4]

This book looks at Australian electoral reforms from a political science perspective; however, the author's experience as a parliamentarian and party administrator provides further insight into how and why reforms occur. The author was a Member of the Western Australian Legislative Council from 1997 to 2001, representing the East Metropolitan Region for the Australian Democrats. During most of this term, the Democrats held the balance of power in the Council. After leaving parliament, he became a member of the party's national executive, including a term as deputy national president.

Much of the information in the following chapters is derived from the author's doctoral study, when, as part of his research, he interviewed ministers and shadow ministers, electoral commissioners and others from all Australian jurisdictions. The institutional structures of Australia's electoral administration are considered and, in particular, an assessment is made of the independence of the nine electoral commissions around Australia. A case study approach is then taken to assess several areas of electoral law. Reforms over the past 30 years have generally served to tilt the electoral playing field in favour of one of the major parties or, at times, in favour of the major-party cartel against other players. Some areas that receive specific attention include entitlement to vote, closing of the electoral roll, political party registration regimes, public funding, malapportionment and postal voting.

# Background briefing

Australia, with the rich diversity of electoral systems in its nine legislative jurisdictions (comprising the national federal—also referred to as Commonwealth—level, six States and two Territories), provides excellent material for comparative analysis. Most of these jurisdictions have long-established representative democracies of more than 100 years. Only the two Territories—the Northern Territory and the Australian Capital Territory (ACT)—have achieved self-government comparatively recently. Their first legislative elections under self-government were in 1980 and 1989, respectively. While there are many similarities between these nine jurisdictions, there is also significant diversity in their electoral systems, histories of reform and administrative procedures. This variation warrants detailed analysis. Australia is often held up as a shining example of electoral best practice, so it is worthwhile

---

4   David J. Elkins. 1992. 'Electoral Reform and Political Culture.' In *Comparative Political Studies: Australia and Canada*, eds M. Alexander and B. Galligan. Melbourne: Pitman, p. 68.

examining whether that remains the case. This can be done by comparing Australian systems with each other and assessing them against internationally accepted norms for electoral management and fair elections.

At the Australian national level, there have been two significant instances of electoral reform in the past 30 years. The first occasion followed the 1983 general election, when the incoming Hawke Labor Government initiated sweeping changes. These included the introduction of ticket voting for the Senate; party identification on ballot papers and ballot order decided by lot (replacing alphabetical listing); the adoption of a modified Gregory system for the Senate count; public funding; party registration; and the establishment of a statutory electoral management body—the Australian Electoral Commission (AEC)—which replaced the Australian Electoral Office.

The second major set of reforms occurred in 2006 under the Howard Liberal–Nationals[5] Coalition Government, which was finally able to implement significant changes that it had pursued from the time it first won office in 1996. Having won a Senate majority at the 2004 election (taking effect from July 2005), the Howard Government enacted reforms in 2006 that impacted on many facets of electoral administration. These reforms included the disenfranchisement of all prisoners, the earlier closure of the electoral roll,[6] more stringent proof-of-identity requirements, increases in donation disclosure thresholds and an increase in the level of tax-deductible donations.

Electoral systems at the sub-national level have similarly been subject to significant reform and amendment during this period. Queensland and Western Australia have moved to reduce malapportionment, Western Australia and Victoria have replaced legislative council single-member elections with regional proportional representation, Queensland and New South Wales have moved to optional preferential voting, and all jurisdictions have introduced and/or tightened party registration criteria. Tasmania has significantly reduced district magnitude in its house of assembly electorates—changing from seven-member to five-member seats. As a result, the assembly has been reduced in size from 35 to 25 members. Even in Australia's newest legislative jurisdiction, the Australian Capital Territory, the modified d'Hondt voting system of a single Territory-wide electorate that was originally used has been subsequently replaced with a system based on three multi-member electorates using the Hare-Clark form of proportional representation. The Australian Capital Territory's parliamentary terms have also been extended from three to four years.

---

5   The National Party, formerly known as the Country Party, changed its name to The Nationals in 2003.
6   The disenfranchisement of all prisoners and earlier closure of the electoral roll were subsequently found to be unconstitutional by the High Court.

It can be argued that in electoral democracies there is an ongoing tension between voting systems and political parties, with each attempting to exert dominance over the other. This tension is explained by Ken Benoit as the mechanical functioning of voting systems against the psychological behaviour of political parties. Benoit argues that voting systems place mechanical restrictions on how votes are distributed and seats are awarded, while political parties use psychology to shape campaign strategies and thereby maximise results within the voting system's constraints.[7] Arend Lijphart assesses the institutional consequences of this tension, arguing that proportional voting systems produce stronger electoral institutions due to the tendency towards non-majority governments in such systems.[8]

The ongoing tension referred to by Lijphart and Benoit is described by Claus Offe as competing forces of institutional change and stability. Offe argues that there is an inherent institutional tendency to remain stable. Importantly, however, he also identifies the capacity for institutions to change from within, through legislated powers for institutions to alter their own lower-level operational and administrative mechanisms.[9] This is pertinent for Australian electoral system design, where there can be tension between electoral commissions seeking to act independently in accordance with professional norms and governing political parties attempting to assert a preferred electoral regime for identified or perceived partisan advantage. Administrative changes that do not require legislative approval might have significant partisan impacts and the Australian experience has generally been that the governing political parties keep tight controls over this area of electoral regulation.

There exists a large disparity in the capacity to contest elections, which is determined by access to incumbency benefits. The disparity between incumbents and contestants without access to incumbency benefits has developed in recent decades. Incumbency benefits include parliamentarians' travel, staffing, printing and communication entitlements, media coverage (such as involvement in televised debates), publicity resources (including access to public service resources) and voter databases. There is a hierarchy of incumbency advantages (depicted in Figure 1.1), ranging from those enjoyed by the party in government and those enjoyed by parliamentary parties, by parliamentarians without party status and by parties without parliamentary representation to the relatively limited benefits available to Independents. While this skewing of the electoral playing field through incumbency advantages is mostly separate from Australian electoral system design, it is important to acknowledge the impact it has on the fairness of Australian elections.

---

7   Ken Benoit. 2004. 'Models of Electoral System Change.' *Electoral Studies* 23(3): 363–89.

8   Arend Lijphart. 1994. *Electoral Systems and Party Systems: A Study of Twenty-Seven Democracies 1945–1990*. Oxford: Oxford University Press.

9   Claus Offe. 1996. 'Designing Institutions in East European Transitions'. In *The Theory of Institutional Design*, ed. R. E. Goodin. Cambridge: Cambridge University Press, pp. 207–9.

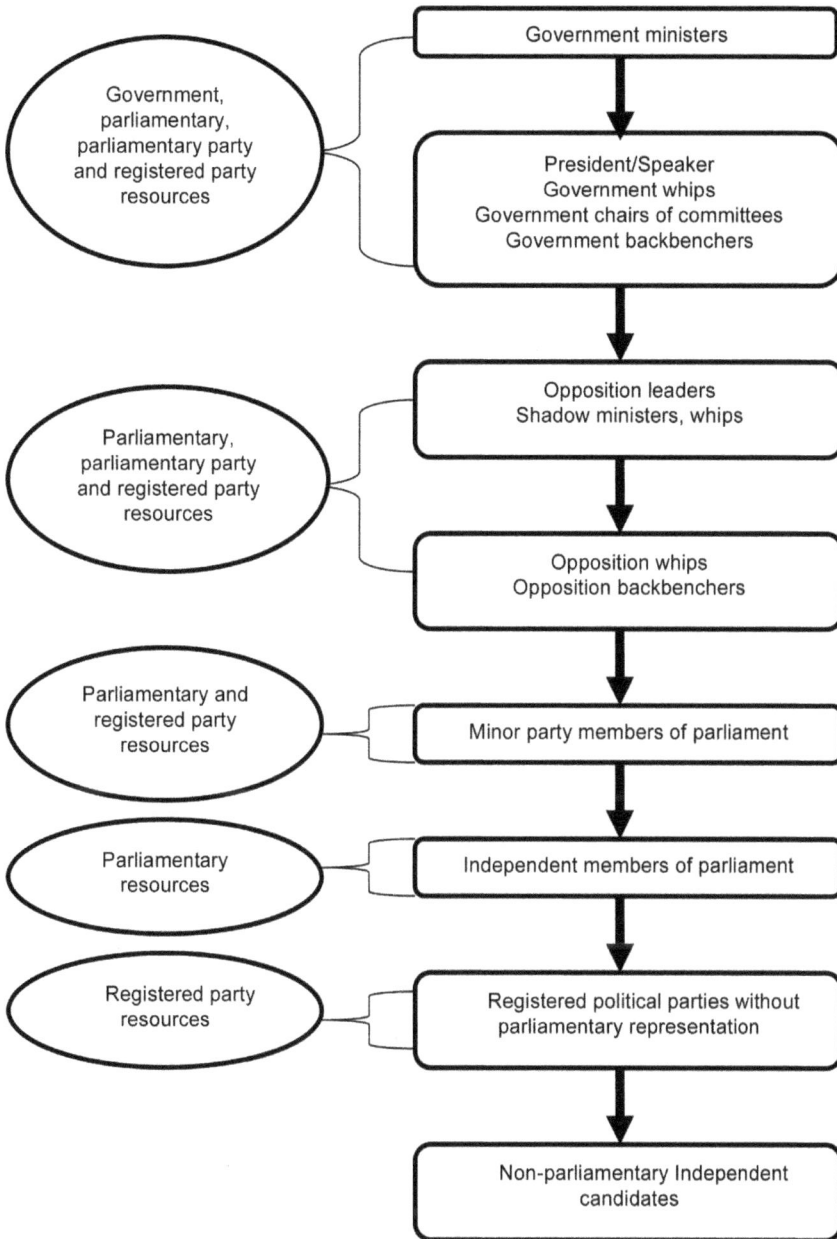

**Figure 1.1 Hierarchy of Incumbency**

The fact that the current two-party system has now been in place for more than a century[10] suggests an entrenchment of the perception of the voting public that there are only two parties to choose from. This perception is reinforced by the two parties' control of the political agenda, campaign funds and the electoral system itself, despite the occasional opportunities that arise for smaller parties, as previously mentioned. Minor parties can win more support at the expense of the two major parties where proportional representation exists.

**Table 1.1 Support at Federal Elections: House of Representatives versus Senate (per cent)[11]**

| Election | Labor | | Coalition | | Democrats | |
|---|---|---|---|---|---|---|
| | HoR | Senate | HoR | Senate | HoR | Senate |
| 1983 | 49.5 | 45.5 | 43.6 | 40.0 | 5.0 | 9.6 |
| 1984 | 47.6 | 42.2 | 45.0 | 39.5 | 5.5 | 7.6 |
| 1987 | 45.8 | 42.8 | 46.1 | 42.0 | 6.0 | 8.5 |
| 1990 | 39.4 | 38.4 | 43.5 | 41.9 | 11.3 | 12.6 |
| 1993 | 44.9 | 43.5 | 44.3 | 43.0 | 3.8 | 5.3 |
| 1996 | 38.8 | 36.2 | 47.3 | 44.0 | 6.8 | 10.8 |
| 1998 | 40.1 | 37.3 | 39.5 | 37.7 | 5.1 | 8.5 |
| 2001 | 37.8 | 34.3 | 43.0 | 41.8 | 5.4 | 7.3 |
| 2004 | 37.6 | 35.0 | 46.7 | 45.1 | 1.2 | 2.1 |
| 2007 | 43.4 | 40.3 | 42.1 | 39.9 | 0.7 | 1.3 |
| 2010 | 38.0 | 35.1 | 43.6 | 38.6 | 0.2 | 0.6 |

Source: Australian Electoral Commission.[12]

To illustrate this, on a national basis in the past 11 federal elections, Labor and the Coalition have always received a lower level of primary voting support in the Senate than in House of Representatives seats. In comparison, the Australian Democrats—successful at winning Senate seats from 1977 to 2001—have consistently received a higher vote when contesting more winnable positions in the Senate (see Table 1.1). Despite the growing success of the Australian Greens in recent elections, both in the Senate and, in 2010, in the House of Representatives, Labor and the Coalition continue to garner more than 80 per

---

10   The development of a two-party system originates from 1909, when the Protectionist Party merged with the Anti-Socialist Party, creating the Commonwealth Liberal Party, also known as the Fusion. The party (not to be confused with the current Australian Liberal Party) opposed the Labor Party.

11   Percentages are national averages, therefore they under-represent Democrats support when the party did not stand candidates in all House of Representatives seats. An accurate example of increased voter support in the Senate can be seen in the 1998 figures, when the Democrats stood candidates in all House of Representatives seats.

12   This book sources its election data from official electoral commission publications and web sites, as well as the Australian Government and Politics Database (AGPD), based at the University of Western Australia. Due to the number of sources used, only the organisations are listed.

cent of the House of Representatives vote. The only time that the two major parties' combined vote has dropped below the 80 per cent mark in the past 30 years was in 1998 (79.6 per cent), when Pauline Hanson's One Nation was able to attract votes away from the Coalition, winning more than 8 per cent of the vote.

The history of Australian electoral institutions indicates that path dependency plays a critical role in electoral design and, as a consequence, impacts significantly on the representative nature of the democracy. For example, the Northern Territory's self-governing legislation—the *Northern Territory (Self-Government) Act 1978*—stipulates single-member electorates for a unicameral assembly. As a result, there has been only one change of government in more than 35 years, with the government always having an assembly majority. While the NT Labor Government's electoral reforms in 2004 were extensive, the Commonwealth legislation prevented it from considering changes to the single-member majoritarian voting system, demonstrating that electoral reform is restricted to a particular path.

In comparison, the Australian Capital Territory's voting system, which was designed less than 15 years after the Northern Territory's first election under self-government, is regulated by the Commonwealth's *Australian Capital Territory (Electoral) Act 1988*. This Act specifies a proportional representation system for a unicameral assembly. In the 12 years from 1989 there were four changes of government (including two changes of government between elections). In addition, only one government has held an ACT Assembly majority since 1989 (the 2005–08 Stanhope Labor Government). When the Australian Capital Territory considered electoral reform in the early 1990s, a referendum was held to determine voters' preferences for single-member electorates or proportional representation, with two-thirds of electors supporting the latter. The original Commonwealth legislation had set the Australian Capital Territory on a path of proportional representation. The reasons for such different approaches to the voting system design for the two Territories can be found in the timing of the legislation—for the NT legislation, the Fraser Coalition Government had control of the Senate. For the ACT legislation, in contrast, the Hawke Labor Government had a Senate minority, and therefore needed to negotiate with the Australian Democrats—a minor party that benefited from proportional representation. These brief examples are indicative of the importance of path dependency in the evolution of electoral systems.

The next two chapters look at the administrative structures for conducting Australian elections, including electoral commissions and parliamentary oversight committees, and the degrees of independence that Australian electoral commissions operate under. From Chapter 4 through to Chapter 10, a case study approach is taken in assessing reforms in several contentious areas of electoral law. Chapter 4 considers the voting franchise—for non-citizen permanent residents (specifically, British subjects); and for prisoners. Chapter 5 assesses enrolment procedures, turnout and informal voting; combined, these three factors influence how many eligible Australians actually make a formal vote in elections. Chapter 6 looks at the various party registration regimes operating around Australia, and how these regimes impact on who contests elections.

Three specific political finance issues are addressed in Chapter 7: public funding, donation disclosure regimes and the tax deductibility of political donations. The issue of malapportionment (vote-weighting) is analysed in Chapter 8, using the recent history of Western Australia's move to 'one vote, one value' as the main study. Chapter 9 illustrates the ways in which the major political parties have been intricately involved in postal voting processes, and finally in Chapter 10, issues relating to increasing the size of parliaments are discussed, using examples from the federal, Tasmanian and ACT jurisdictions.

# 2. Australia's Electoral Administration

The institutional structure of an electoral system provides the environment in which electoral laws are administered and amended. An understanding of this environment is necessary to evaluate the fairness of a system, in terms of both democratic behaviour and electoral outcomes. Australia's electoral management bodies have an international reputation for their professional, non-partisan and independent performance. Yet how strongly entrenched are that integrity and independence? Is the reputation deserved? Australian electoral administrations are relatively similar in terms of structure and responsibility; however, their powers vary depending on their enacting legislation. In most cases the legislation also limits the ability of commissions to act independently in the interests of best electoral practice and in providing a level playing field for election participants. In addition to their regular interactions with the government of the day, as in negotiating budgets and liaising with the responsible minister, electoral commissions are subject to different levels of parliamentary oversight, in terms of inquiries into the conduct of elections and other electoral matters.

## Australian electoral management bodies

The origins of Australia's professionalised and independent electoral administration lie in nineteenth-century colonial society, with a lack of strong local authorities or precedent, which enabled professional, efficient and non-partisan electoral systems to develop. As Marian Sawer describes, administration was initially the responsibility of public servants working in a government department, with greater independence later being achieved through the use of statutory bodies, or 'offices', and finally with the removal of ministerial direction and the establishment of commissions.[1]

At the federal level, the Australian Electoral Commission (AEC) was established in 1984 by Section 4 of the *Commonwealth Electoral Legislation Amendment Act 1983*. The AEC replaced the Australian Electoral Office, a statutory authority founded in 1973. As former electoral commissioner Colin Hughes notes, although the 1983 legislation effectively removed the minister from the principal Act for all matters except the tabling of reports in parliament, the government retained control over budgetary and legislative matters.[2] At the State and Territory levels, all electoral administrations are commissions.

---

1   Marian Sawer. 2001. 'Pacemakers for the World?' In *Elections: Full, Free and Fair*, ed. M. Sawer. Sydney: The Federation Press.
2   Colin Hughes. 2001. 'Institutionalising Electoral Integrity.' In *Elections: Full, Free and Fair*, ed. M. Sawer. Sydney: The Federation Press, p. 156.

There are strong relationships between electoral administrations at the federal, State and Territory levels, and innovations in the management of electoral systems are regularly disseminated between the jurisdictions. The commissions regularly assist each other in the conduct of elections by, for example, providing pre-polling facilities and specialist staff, and exchanging information on technological advances, such as electronic voting. The names of the nine Australian administrations, and the years the administrations were established as commissions, are provided in Table 2.1

**Table 2.1 Australia's Electoral Management Bodies**

| Jurisdiction | Electoral management body | Commission established |
|---|---|---|
| Commonwealth | Australian Electoral Commission (AEC) | 1984 |
| New South Wales | New South Wales Electoral Commission (NSWEC) | 2006 |
| Victoria | Victorian Electoral Commission (VEC) | 1995 |
| Queensland | Electoral Commission of Queensland (ECQ) | 1992 |
| Western Australia | Western Australian Electoral Commission (WAEC) | 1987 |
| South Australia | Electoral Commission of South Australia (ECSA) | 2009 |
| Tasmania | Tasmanian Electoral Commission (TEC) | 2005 |
| Australian Capital Territory | Australian Capital Territory Electoral Commission (ACTEC) | 1992 |
| Northern Territory | Northern Territory Electoral Commission (NTEC) | 2004 |

# NSW Election Funding Authority

Typically, the commission is the sole institution with responsibility for the conduct and administration of elections in their jurisdiction (except for the drawing of electoral boundaries, which is determined by a separate statutory body administered by the commission); however, whereas other jurisdictions entrust their commissions with the task of administering party registration, public funding and other political finance matters such as financial disclosure, New South Wales in 1981 established a separate authority under the *Election Funding Act 1981* for these purposes. This is the three-member NSW Election Funding Authority. While the establishment of a separate agency for political finance purposes is not in itself a problem in terms of fairness, the membership of the authority is problematic.

Briefly, one of the authority's responsibilities is the administration of public funding to parties and candidates, including the provision of public funds for 'electoral education'. New South Wales is unique in Australia in providing funds to the parties for the production and dissemination of information about policies and party-related work. This expenditure may be used exclusively for providing services to party members, if the party chooses. Funding is calculated on the results at the previous general election, with six of the 16 parties that contested the 2007 election receiving funding based on their 2003 election results.

The electoral commissioner sits as the chair of the authority, with the other two members nominated by the premier and the leader of the opposition. The current members are Kirk McKenzie, a lawyer and Labor branch president who was nominated by the Labor government, and Ted Pickering, a former Liberal parliamentarian and minister nominated by the then Opposition Leader, Barry O'Farrell. The ability of the two major parties to nominate members of the authority makes New South Wales the only Australian jurisdiction in which appointments to an electoral management body are made on a partisan basis. This appointment process impacts on perceptions of the independence of the NSW Electoral Commissioner, who is required to preside over this authority and yet is outnumbered by political appointees.

The authority has the power to initiate legal proceedings against candidates who do not comply with the requirements of the Act. This places the authority's two nominated members in a position of potentially starting action against their own party colleagues—a clear conflict of interest. It can be argued that having an independent chair holding the casting vote might prevent blatantly partisan decisions that favour one party over the other; however, there is also the capacity for the two party appointees to act in collusion, as a cartel operating against fairness principles and against the interests of other parties and election candidates. For example, the two party appointees could support each other to avoid actions against their party colleagues. The authority's 2006–07 annual report lists (mostly local government) candidates against whom proceedings were initiated. Of 47 separate actions, 43 were against Independent candidates, with the remaining four candidates representing minor parties (the Unity Party and the Christian Democratic Party).[3]

The fact that no candidates from the appointees' parties were subject to proceedings against them might simply indicate the report's focus on the local government level, at which party campaigning is less overt, or that the parties' candidates had all complied with the law. The perception of a lack of independence remains, however, due to the presence of political appointees. In 2008, the NSW Select Committee on Electoral and Political Party Funding (SCEPPF), which included Labor and Liberal party representatives, recommended that partisan appointments should cease, *to remove any perception of bias*.[4]

---

3   Election Funding Authority. 2007. *Annual Report 2006–2007*. Sydney: Election Funding Authority, pp. 13–15.
4   Select Committee on Electoral and Political Party Funding. 2008a. *Electoral and Political Party Funding in New South Wales*. Report no. 1. Sydney: Legislative Council, New South Wales Parliament, p. 213.

It would appear to be a simple exercise to incorporate the functions of the authority with those of the Electoral Commission, as in other jurisdictions. At an administrative level, this would be a seamless transition, as the authority is essentially subsumed by the commission in any case; the authority does not employ any staff, with the commission providing all staffing and administrative resources. The fact that the corporate plan for the commission and the authority is a joint document is another indicator of the symbiotic nature of the relationship. The closeness between the two institutions is highlighted by a comment from the Commissioner that 'it was very unclear to me, when I came into the position of Electoral Commissioner, who was running and administering the Election Funding Authority provisions'. The Commissioner has, however, expressed opposition to the commission taking on the authority's responsibilities, stating that 'I do not think it would be in the public interest to have one person effectively dealing with all of this'.[5]

One official, however, stated in an interview that it would not be a major problem to integrate the authority's functions with those of the commission, at the same time overcoming the commissioner's concern about having one person responsible for funding and disclosure issues:

> One of the things that in time might eventually happen is the Election Funding Authority would get subsumed into the actual commission, with probably some sort of similar model to what Queensland has, where you have an augmented commission when you're dealing with the funding stuff. So you could have a nominee of the auditor-general and a nominee from somewhere else.

As the SCEPPF found, there is merit and support for removing partisan appointments, based on internationally accepted norms for electoral management and concepts of independence (discussed more fully in the next chapter). At present, neither the Labor nor the Liberal leadership has expressed a willingness to give up their right to nominate members of the authority. The possible integration of the authority with the commission is less contentious, because in its current form the authority is essentially administered by the commission. Despite the partisan appointments, no allegations of corruption or partisan bias have been made, but the concern remains that the principle of fairness is diminished by the perception of partisan behaviour.

---

5    Select Committee on Electoral and Political Party Funding. 2008b. Hearing Transcript, 3 March. Sydney: Legislative Council, New South Wales Parliament, p. 21. URL: <http://www.parliament.nsw.gov.au/prod/parlment/committee.nsf/0/02C2B246F4664981CA2573D8000D1077>

# Parliamentary oversight of electoral matters

Parliaments are made up of election winners. As the beneficiaries of the electoral system, parliamentarians have a clear vested interest in maintaining (or changing to their own further advantage) a system from which they have benefited. Therefore, their parliamentary activity requires close scrutiny to determine whether their actions are based on principles of fairness or on their own self-interest and partisan considerations.

**Table 2.2 Parliamentary Oversight Committees**

| Jurisdiction | Committee established | Committee name |
| --- | --- | --- |
| Commonwealth | 1983 | Joint Standing Committee on Electoral Matters (JSCEM, formerly the Joint Select Committee on Electoral Reform, 1983–87) |
| New South Wales | 2004 | Joint Standing Committee on Electoral Matters (NSW JSCEM) |
| Victoria | 2007 | Electoral Matters Committee |
| Queensland | 2011 | Legal Affairs, Police, Corrective Services and Emergency Services Committee |
| | 2009 | Law, Justice and Safety Committee |
| | 1990 | Legal, Constitutional and Administrative Review Committee (LCARC, formerly Parliamentary Committee for Electoral and Administrative Review) |

Four Australian jurisdictions have parliamentary oversight committees with a distinct role in overseeing and inquiring into electoral systems and the conduct of elections (see Table 2.2). As the larger parliaments have more members to draw on for issue-specific committees, it is not surprising that the three largest jurisdictions (in terms of parliamentary size) have committees dedicated solely to electoral matters. These three jurisdictions are the Commonwealth, with 226 parliamentarians (150 MPs, 76 Senators); New South Wales, with 135 (93 MLAs, 42 MLCs); and Victoria, with 128 (88 MLAs, 40 MLCs). In Queensland (with a parliament of 89 members), currently the Legal Affairs, Police, Corrective Services and Emergency Services Committee (LAPCSESC) has responsibility for inquiring into electoral matters, among its many other portfolio responsibilities including justice and policing matters.

The remaining jurisdictions, with parliaments ranging from 17 (Australian Capital Territory) to 95 (Western Australia) members, tend to use their legislative or other committees to conduct inquiries into electoral matters. The issue in question often determines to which committee such matters are referred in these jurisdictions. For example, the Australian Capital Territory's Standing Committee on Legal Affairs (SCLA) inquired into possible changes to the overall size of the assembly and electorate magnitude in 2002, while in 2006–07, the Standing Committee on Education, Training and Young People (SCETYP) inquired into a proposal to lower the voting age. In Western Australia, the Standing Committee on Legislation inquired into the Gallop Labor Government's 'one vote, one value' legislation in 2001. The larger jurisdictions also send certain electoral matters to other standing committees. The following sections explain the inquiry activity of these committees, with a focus on partisan influences at work. Four standing committees with specific references for electoral matters are examined, as well as two examples of other committees that have received electoral matter referrals (a Commonwealth Senate standing committee and a NSW upper house select committee).

## Commonwealth

The oldest Australian electoral committee is the Commonwealth's Joint Standing Committee on Electoral Matters (JSCEM), formerly the Joint Select Committee on Electoral Reform (JSCER). The Commonwealth committee has developed a substantial history of conducting inquiries, with a total of 37 reports published in the past 29 years (a list of the committee's reports is provided in Appendix A). The committee's main focus is inquiring into the conduct of each general election. Additionally, the committee conducts inquiries into specific electoral issues, such as levels of representation (1988 and 2003), the integrity of the electoral roll (2001 and 2002) and political finance issues (2006).

The depth of the committee's election inquiries has grown in the 25 years since its inception. The growth in the number of submissions it receives after each election is evidence of this increasing depth, with 129 submissions for the 1987 election inquiry, increasing to 221 submissions following the 2004 election. As Colin Hughes notes, the JSCEM election inquiries, which include extensive public hearings after initial submissions have been received, is possibly the best existing form of scrutiny into the electoral system, adding transparency that is lacking elsewhere.[6] Being a joint committee—that is, drawing on members from both houses of parliament—means that there is some representation available for minor parties, with the Australian Democrats having a member on the committee from the initial formation of JSCER in 1983 through to 2008. From July 2008, the Greens have provided the minor party/Independent representative. The membership of the committee is currently made up of five Labor, four Liberal and a Greens member; however, for the inquiry into the

---

6    Colin Hughes. 2001. 'Institutionalising Electoral Integrity', pp. 153–4.

funding of political parties and election campaigns (current at late September 2011), the membership has been enlarged to accommodate a Nationals member and an Independent representative (Tony Windsor).

In interviews, members of the committee expressed the view that the regular election inquiries are very important to the overall administration and conduct of elections. One member noted:

> You get a good spread of witnesses. You get good opportunities for scrutiny and debate around the circumstances of what's occurred in an election. In respect of reports, you get issues pretty reasonably canvassed in the body of reports. The report normally gives you a pretty good account of what's occurred, the points of differentiation.

Concerns were raised, however, that the committee operates on an extremely partisan basis that is largely unavoidable, as in this observation from a committee member:

> People should have no doubt that it is the most political of committees, given the nature of what it's looking at, and so its recommendations are invariably often political. Invariably you end up with dissenting reports, practically more than any other committee that I'm aware of. The government of the day has a significant influence on the outcome.

An electoral administrator commented on the partisan nature of the committee, noting the difference in approach when the Howard Government had a Senate majority from 2005 to 2007:

> It's in an environment where the government has a majority in the Senate and that changes the dynamics greatly because there is less need to come to a compromise, because the government members feel they've got their senior colleagues behind them. They can go for broke.

It is understandable that there would be a close relationship between an electoral matters committee and the elections administrator. The JSCEM holds regular (twice yearly) private hearings with the AEC. Although these hearings are recorded by Hansard, the transcripts are not released to the public; they are regarded as briefings and an opportunity to discuss the mechanics of electoral administration away from public scrutiny. The AEC also provides substantial submissions to JSCEM inquiries—for example, more than 1000 pages of information and comment were submitted following the 2004 and 2007 elections. Typically, the AEC's submissions present data on the conduct of the election, as well as providing information and comment on specific electoral issues that have been raised through the media or might have been foreshadowed or requested by the committee.

# The 2004 federal election inquiry: the Richmond result

One example of the partisan nature of the JSCEM is contained in the inquiry into the 2004 federal election. The issue was the outcome in the Richmond electorate, where the sitting member, Nationals Minister Larry Anthony, was defeated by the Labor candidate by 301 votes—a margin of 0.19 per cent. Significantly in such a close contest, the Liberals for Forests candidate received 1417 votes (1.8 per cent). The 10-member committee, with five government members, including the Liberal Party chair (who resolves any tied vote), decided to investigate this outcome in Richmond. The investigation was based on complaints from The Nationals and the Liberal Party on election day that the design of the Liberals for Forests' how-to-vote cards, which gave preferences to Labor ahead of The Nationals, misled voters into thinking that Liberals for Forests were connected to the Coalition parties.[7] The AEC provided advice to both Coalition parties on election day, based on legal advice from the government solicitor, that a breach had not occurred.

In July 2005 the committee held a public hearing in the electorate and used some of the evidence given to this hearing in its final report. There appeared to be a clear intention by Liberal members of the committee to gather evidence that the Liberals for Forests' how-to-vote cards were deceptive. The leading nature of the questioning, and the subsequent report, is typified by the following exchanges at the hearing:

> *Senator BRANDIS (Liberal):* In any event, there is no doubt in your mind that you are not alone in being misled—that there were a substantial number of other people misled in the same way as well.

> *Bronwyn Smith:* That is right.

In reference to this exchange, the committee report stated that 'Ms Smith characterised the number of people who were misled as "substantial"'.[8] Although Ms Smith agreed with the comment, she did not use the word 'substantial'; this was suggested by the Liberal senator.

> *Senator BRANDIS (Liberal):* What was it? Tell us.

---

7   Section 329(1) of the *Commonwealth Electoral Act 1918* states that '[a] person shall not, during the relevant period in relation to an election under this Act, print, publish or distribute, or cause, permit or authorize to be printed, published or distributed, any matter or thing that is likely to mislead or deceive an elector in relation to the casting of a vote'.

8   JSCEM [Joint Standing Committee on Electoral Matters]. 2005. *The 2004 Federal Election: Report of the Inquiry into the Conduct of the 2004 Federal Election and Matters Related Thereto*. Canberra: Commonwealth of Australia, p. 119.

*Mrs Flower:* It was a bogus party, set up to steer votes away from the National Party.

*CHAIR (Liberal):* To deceive people.

*Mrs Flower:* To deceive them. Although someone in the room has another theory.

The report printed the majority of this exchange, except for the final sentence referring to another theory. The committee's report found that 'Ms Elliot [the Labor candidate] was elected as a result of preferences on the basis of deceptions by Liberals for Forests'. The Labor members of the committee, however, included a minority report, attacking the majority report for its 'inflammatory allegations', concluding that 'the allegations made in the Majority Report are nothing more than a political stunt on behalf of the Coalition'. The regular insertion of minority reports in the JSCEM reports indicates the political nature of the committee. The report was subsequently referred to in parliamentary debates on the Howard Government's 2006 electoral reforms, which included the deregistration of parties such as the Liberals for Forests. The investigation into the Richmond result demonstrates inherent partisan biases in the inquiry process and committee reporting.

# NSW Joint Standing Committee on Electoral Matters

The NSW Joint Standing Committee is a seven-member committee that was established in 2004. Its terms of reference require it to have a majority of government members. The current membership is made up of four government members (two Liberal, two Nationals), two Labor members and one Shooters and Fishers Party member. Like its federal counterpart, the committee is developing a practice of inquiring into general elections, having conducted inquiries into the 2003 and 2007 elections. It has also inquired into voter enrolment issues (partly in response to reforms at the federal level). Unlike its federal counterpart, however, the NSW committee has not developed a partisan culture of majority and minority reports. Nor does it appear to have a comparable level of public interest in its inquiries, with only 14 submissions received for its 2003 election inquiry, and 19 in 2007. Two days of hearings were held for each inquiry.

# Victorian Electoral Matters Committee

Victoria's Electoral Matters Committee was formed in mid-2007 and completed an inquiry into the State's November 2006 general election. The inquiry received 28 submissions and held two days of hearings. Between 2008 and 2010 it also conducted four other inquiries—into: political donations and disclosure; voter participation and informal voting; misleading or deceptive electoral content; and the administration of voting centres. The committee is currently inquiring into the 2010 general election, for which it has received 19 submissions. The five-member committee has a government majority, with three Liberal and two Labor members. The other parties in parliament, The Nationals and Greens, do not have representation.

Although it is difficult at this early stage of the committee's work to determine a particular culture of reporting, its first report is encouraging. The 269-page report provides an extensive analysis of various aspects of the 2006 election, including enrolment procedures, party registration, electronic voting and ballot paper design. It is interesting to note the absence of dissenting (minority) reports and the fact that, of the report's 72 recommendations, 56 are directed to the Victorian Electoral Commission, with only 11 recommending legislative action.[9] Two later inquiry reports included relatively minor dissenting reports. This might indicate an emphasis on administrative detail rather than electoral system reform, but could also allude to the greater powers that the Victorian Electoral Commissioner holds in comparison with his Commonwealth counterpart.

# Queensland's various electoral-related committees

Queensland has a history of including electoral matters inquiries in the ambit of a committee with other justice-related portfolios. About 1990, the Parliamentary Committee for Electoral and Administrative Review (PCEAR) was created, in response to the recommendations of the Fitzgerald Inquiry. PCEAR quickly became the Legal, Constitutional and Administrative Review Committee (LCARC), which was in place for almost two decades, before evolving into the Law, Justice and Safety Committee in 2009, and, from 2011, the Legal Affairs, Police, Corrective Services and Emergency Services Committee (LAPCSESC). These committees examine electoral matters as part of their remit to inquire into broader issues of a legal and constitutional nature, not all of which are related

---

9 Electoral Matters Committee. 2008. *Inquiry into the Conduct of the 2006 Victorian State Election and Matters Related Thereto: Report to Parliament Electoral Matters Committee.* Melbourne: Victorian Government Printer.

to the electoral system. This wider focus is likely a reflection of the smaller size of the Queensland Parliament compared with the above three examples, rather than a lack of interest in electoral matters. As LCARC is easily the longest-formed of these committees, the following paragraphs concentrate on its performance.

Queensland's LCARC was a seven-member committee, with a government majority and representatives of the other parties in parliament. LAPCSESC has six members: three from the Labor Government, two Liberal National Party members and one Independent. The intention to hold regular election inquiries is clearly evident in the case of the three largest jurisdictions; however, the situation for Queensland is not as clear. LCARC's remit was centred on reform, with four areas of responsibility: administrative review reform, constitutional reform, electoral reform and legal reform. Of the 66 reports published since 1996, only nine specifically dealt with electoral reform issues: truth in political advertising; electoral legislation; how-to-vote cards and appeal processes; electoral fraud; young people engaging with democracy; and Indigenous participation.

Because LCARC was concerned with issues beyond electoral matters, it was difficult to establish regular election inquiries, with only one report on the 1998 election (receiving 25 submissions). In August 2008, however, the committee announced an inquiry into 'Certain Contemporary Electoral Matters', with a focus on the 2004 and 2006 general elections. Unfortunately, this appears to have lapsed with the change in committee in 2009 and a revised focus on local government elections.

Among the Queensland committee members interviewed, there were different views on the merit of having an automatic reference to initiate an inquiry immediately following each general election. One position was that a regular inquiry was necessary and this was best done as soon as possible after an election while issues remained fresh. It was also stated that the committee should not necessarily wait for a request from the attorney-general before an inquiry commenced—that 'an inquiry immediately after an election should be a standing order'. An alternative view was that, as the committee dealt with other issues as well as electoral matters, a regular election inquiry would take up too much time and resources. This committee member also supported the incorporation of electoral matters into constitutional and legal issues based on the broader concepts of democracy and representation.

# Senate finance and public administration standing committees[10]

The committees discussed above have an ongoing responsibility to inquire into electoral matters. Other committees receive inquiry referrals on a 'case-by-case' basis. For example, the Commonwealth Electoral and Referendum Legislation Amendment Bill 2006 was referred to the Senate Standing Committee on Finance and Public Administration in December 2006. The Bill was consequential to the major electoral reforms of the Howard Government, which had been passed earlier in 2006, and many of the amendments were considered to be 'machinery' in nature. The inquiry took just more than two months, received only three submissions (from the AEC, the Human Rights and Equal Opportunity Commission and the Department of Defence) and did not hold any public hearings. The eight-member committee delivered a unanimous 14-page report recommending that the Bill be supported in its entirety.

In contrast, earlier in 2006 the Senate Finance and Public Administration Legislation Committee considered the highly contentious major Howard Government reforms. The inquiry received 53 submissions, held a day of hearings and was completed within an intensive seven-week period. Despite numerous concerns being raised in submissions and hearings, the report essentially rubber-stamped the government legislation, making only one recommendation—that the legislation be passed without amendment. Almost half of the 92-page report consisted of dissenting reports written by the Labor and Democrats members of the committee. These two examples of committee work demonstrate the diversity that can exist in the inquiry process. The latter example indicates that where partisan interests are at stake, an inquiry will more readily split on party lines instead of seeking a common view consistent with fairness principles and accepted norms for electoral management.

# NSW Select Committee on Electoral and Political Party Funding

Political imperatives obviously play a role in how parliaments choose to inquire into electoral matters. A good example of this occurred in the NSW Parliament in mid-2007. Despite New South Wales having a dedicated electoral matters committee, the legislative council established a select committee, the

---

10  Due to a restructure of Senate committees in 2006—combining legislation and reference committees into one committee—the two committees referred to in this section have different names but are essentially the same committee.

Select Committee on Electoral and Political Party Funding (SCEPPF), to inquire into political finance and public funding issues. The political manoeuvring involved in establishing the committee, and later in determining the committee membership, is obvious from the Hansard transcripts.

The motion to establish the committee was debated on 27 June 2007, with the mover, Liberal Don Harwin, arguing that a select committee was a better option than the already established NSW JSCEM, as he envisaged 'looking over the horizon and looking at policy issues...[not] getting bogged down in the administrative minutiae of particular elections, particular donations and particular items of expenditure'.[11] Although the intention might have been genuine, the result was that by using an upper house committee the Labor government would not have a majority, as was the case on the NSW JSCEM. By winning support from other right-of-centre parties, the Liberal Party was also able to pass their motion to set up a committee ahead of another motion from the Greens, who sought to establish a similar (but joint house) inquiry.

The committee membership was determined three months later, with agreement that there would be two Labor government members, two Coalition opposition members and two crossbench members. In what was obviously further manoeuvring by the parties, however, the council had to vote to appoint two of the three crossbench members who nominated from the Shooters Party and the Christian Democratic Party (CDP), with the Greens candidate, Lee Rhiannon, losing out. As the Shooters Party and CDP are considered right-of-centre parties, this outcome could be perceived as being part of an agreement made to establish the committee. A positive aspect of the outcome, however, was that five parties were represented on the six-member committee, providing broader representation of minor parties compared with a joint house committee.

The committee carried out a nine-month inquiry, receiving 189 submissions and conducting five days of public hearings. When compared with the NSW JSCEM's 2003 and 2007 election inquiries, the SCEPPF attracted far greater public interest and media attention. It tabled an extensive 276-page report on 19 June 2008, with 47 recommendations, including a $1000 limit on the size of donations, a cap on campaign expenditure and increasing the frequency of donation disclosures to every six months (currently every four years). There was general consensus on the recommendations, with only one brief dissenting report from the two Labor members, opposing one recommendation and suggesting a minor change to one other.

The inquiry was, however, overtaken by revelations from the Independent Commission Against Corruption that Labor Party members had been involved

---

11   D. Harwin. 2007. 'Select Committee on Electoral and Political Party Funding: Establishment.' *Hansard*, 27 June. Sydney: Parliament of New South Wales, p. 1807. URL: <http://www.parliament.nsw.gov.au>

in corruption at the local government level, with political donations from developers a critical factor (the 'Wollongong scandal'). This created a major crisis for the government. In February 2008, Premier Morris Iemma announced the government's intention to reform political finance legislation. The government introduced a Bill the day before the SCEPPF tabled its report. Among other changes, the legislation introduced six-monthly donation disclosures, with a disclosure threshold of $1000. The Bill was passed the following week, progressing through both houses in less than 24 hours.

In terms of being an impetus for reform, the committee report, while substantial in its considerations and findings, was secondary to the media exposure of political finance issues and the willingness of the incumbent governing party to initiate reforms. The committee did not have a Labor majority, and the Iemma Labor Government chose to pursue a separate process of reforming electoral laws. There are, however, many issues raised by the SCEPPF inquiry that were not addressed by the government's reform Bill, and the report remains useful as a potential driver of future reforms.

The conduct of regular parliamentary inquiries also provides opportunities and forums for other organisations to make submissions based on their constituent concerns. For example, there were at least four submissions to JSCEM's 2004 federal election inquiry from organisations representing the interests of blind and vision-impaired citizens. All of these submissions advocated the use of electronic voting—an important advance when considering the secrecy of the ballot.[12] The JSCEM's report recommended an electronic voting trial at the 2007 election, which was then conducted by the AEC. The trial had limited success, with only 850 vision-impaired and blind voters choosing to vote this way, at an administrative cost of $2597 per vote. As the AEC has noted, however, consideration must be given to the value of all voters having a secret and independent vote, and it has recommended that the trial be extended at the next election.[13]

Religious groups also use the inquiry process to reaffirm their positions. A good example is contained in the submission from the Association of Australian Christadelphian Ecclesia to the 2004 federal election inquiry, which reasserts the group's conscientious objection to voting.[14] At a brief hearing in July 2005, the association expressed satisfaction that its members were able to formally express their conscientious objection to voting, in response to letters from the AEC asking to explain their failure to vote. Interestingly, one Liberal senator cited the situation of the group's members as an argument for the reintroduction

---

12  Submissions 54, 101, 135 and 138. Without electronic voting, blind and vision-impaired citizens must rely on other people to assist them to vote and therefore cannot exercise a secret ballot.
13  Submission 169.
14  Submission No. 27, at <http://www.aph.gov.au/house/ committee/em/elect04/subs/sub027.pdf>

of voluntary voting.[15] Collectively, these contributions from civil society organisations are valuable instances of democratic engagement based on the principle of equal opportunity to participate. As previously discussed, however, the value of inquiries in this respect is tempered by the influence of partisan interests on inquiry outcomes.

# The value of parliamentary committees on electoral matters

Australia's electoral institutional structure is strongly focused on parliamentary activity, both in legislating for the administrative and operational regimes in which the electoral commissions operate and in creating forums for public debate on electoral matters. The legislative focus is not surprising, given that Australian parliaments and governments use legislation to maintain a tight control on the form of electoral systems and administration of elections. In this environment, the parliamentary committee inquiry process is a critical element of the institutional structure of Australian electoral systems. In the absence of independent agencies with the powers to implement reforms, committee inquiries have become the primary forum for public debate on electoral matters. Inquiries provide a conduit through which electoral commissions and citizens can reach the electoral lawmakers. Because the submissions are made publicly available on committee web sites, a wealth of information is disseminated to interested groups, media attention is raised and the wider public becomes aware of electoral issues.

The governing party has a membership majority on all of the electoral matters committees, followed by representation from the opposition and typically one member representing minor-party interests. It is a concern, however, that the Victorian committee has only Labor and Liberal Party members, with no representation from the other three parliamentary parties. While the membership of these committees is generally representative of the composition of the respective parliaments, it does raise questions about the usefulness of the committee process and the outputs of the committees. By reflecting the make-up of the parliaments, the committees simply reinforce any disproportionality or bias that is created by election outcomes. In doing so, they create a significant incumbency advantage—primarily for the incumbent government over the opposition and minor parties, but also for parties with parliamentary representation over non-parliamentary parties (reinforcing the hierarchy of incumbency structure depicted in Chapter 1).

---

15   JSCEM [Joint Standing Committee on Electoral Matters]. 2005. *Official Committee Hansard, Joint Standing Committee on Electoral Matters, Wednesday 6 July, Brisbane*. Canberra: Commonwealth of Australia, p. 34.

Governments' dominance of these committees runs counter to the participation principle of fairness, which stresses equality of opportunity. While it is not feasible or necessarily ideal for all parties to have equal representation, an improvement on current structures consistent with the participation principle would be to have an equal number of government and non-government members on these committees. In regard to issues-specific committees, the establishment of the non-government-dominated SCEPPF in New South Wales is a good example of partisan interests at work. Although the SCEPPF membership was reflective of party numbers in that State's upper house (albeit with minor parties over-represented), the debate over membership between parties is indicative of the importance that parties place on being involved in electoral matters that directly impact on their own future prospects.

Several committee members commented in the interviews that electoral matters committees are extremely partisan and are primarily a means for furthering parties' interests rather than assessing the need for reform on the basis of fairness and equity consistent with international standards for electoral management and fair elections. It can be argued that much of the committees' work is of limited value, as members are simply pursuing a predetermined policy agenda. This is particularly evident with the Commonwealth JSCEM, given its long history of reporting and with dissenting reports a common occurrence. While there are some encouraging signs of bipartisan cooperation occurring within State-based committees, it must be remembered that all of the parliamentary oversight committees are dominated by Labor and the Coalition parties. Cooperation can be a sign of party cartelisation rather than working towards democratic values of fairness and equity.

Benefits that flow from the advocacy of representative organisations, such as the trial of electronic voting, are indicative of the value of these consultative processes. There is also clear evidence, however, that submissions (and not only those from political parties) are used to seek partisan advantage. It is disappointing that all of these contributions, irrespective of motive, are often reduced to arguments for committee members to pursue their own partisan objectives in committee reports and dissenting statements.

The experiences suggest that, on principles of fairness, a more appropriate process for inquiry into electoral issues could be the creation of a forum outside parliament that involves a broader range of political parties, electoral administrators, civil society organisations and other electoral experts, with processes and reporting not under the control of government or other parliamentary parties. Such a forum could be influential as a driver for electoral reform. Given that parliaments have the power to regulate almost every aspect of elections and electoral administration, the recommendations of such a forum would, however, ultimately be subject to the wishes of governing parties and party cartels.

With its partisan appointments, the NSW Election Funding Authority is an anomaly in the institutional structure of Australian electoral management. There appears to be no evidence of corruption or serious practical problems created by these appointments in the administration of funding, or in initiating proceedings against non-compliant candidates. With these political appointments in place, however, a perception of bias in the authority is created, and this could impact negatively in the future on the perceived independence of the NSW Electoral Commission and Commissioner. A simple solution would be to replace the partisan appointees with suitably qualified experts who have no party connections.

Despite the strong governing-party control of electoral legislation, commissions have been established in all Australian jurisdictions to administer the electoral system 'independently' of government. The next chapter examines to what degree commissions are able to exercise that independence.

# 3. The Independence of Australian Electoral Commissions

In the literature on electoral system management it is widely accepted that, to ensure free and fair elections, electoral management bodies should be independent both of the government of the day and of any political partisan connections.[1] The International Institute for Democracy and Electoral Assistance (International IDEA) argues that legitimacy is enhanced if electoral authorities are perceived to be impartial and not subject to political interference or control, the argument being that election results are more likely to be accepted by the electorate if there is a strong perception of independence, irrespective of any basic measures of independence.[2] Orr et al. identify electoral authority independence as being the single most important factor in ensuring free elections.[3]

## Models of independence

The Administration and Cost of Elections (ACE) Electoral Knowledge Network distinguishes two different dimensions of independence. First, ACE identifies 'structural' independence, in which the electoral management body is formally separated from the executive branch of government through constitutional or legislative mechanisms. Second, there is 'fearless' or 'behavioural' independence, which is a 'normative independence of decision and action' that does not allow government, political or partisan influences to alter behaviour or actions.[4] ACE goes on to point out that while the two concepts of independence are linked, structural independence does not provide any assurance that an electoral management body will act as a fearlessly independent organisation.

Different strategies can achieve such independence. In some countries, partisan balance is sought by allowing various parties to make appointments to electoral bodies. In other countries responsibility for electoral management is delegated

1   Paul Dacey. 2005. 'What Do "Impartiality", "Independence" and "Transparency" Mean?—Some Thoughts from Australia.' Paper delivered at the Improving the Quality of Election Management Conference of Commonwealth Chief Election Officers, New Delhi, India, p. 1.

2   Alan Wall et al. 2006. *Electoral Management Design: The International IDEA Handbook*, p. 71.

3   Graeme Orr, Bryan Mercurio and George Williams. 2003. 'Australian Electoral Law: A Stocktake.' *Election Law Journal* 2(3): 399.

4   ACE [Administration and Cost of Elections] Electoral Knowledge Network. 2007. *EMB Independence and the Origin of Independent Election Administrations.* URL: <http://aceproject.org/electoral-advice/archive/questions/replies/156664001>

to a non-partisan body. Both of these strategies are used by governing and opposition parties as 'structures of mutual constraint' to achieve a neutral bureaucracy.[5]

In Australia, delegation to a non-partisan body has been the typical method. The level of bipartisanship achieved in delegating control to a non-partisan public service bureaucracy has, however, been influenced by the degree of control the ruling party wishes to maintain over the electoral legislation, especially when the government has a parliamentary majority. One example of the control that governing parties can exert over electoral management is contained in Section 90B of the *Commonwealth Electoral Act 1918*. This section, which runs for 10 pages, provides parliamentarians and registered political parties with privileged access to rolls and voting information, including identifying the polling booth where individual voters lodge their vote.

Rafael López-Pintor draws on the work of Garber[6] and Harris[7] to describe four approaches to organising electoral management bodies: a *governmental* approach, with elections conducted by civil (public) servants; a *judicial* approach, in which judges are appointed to administer the election; a *multi-party* approach, where the electoral body is composed of party representatives; and an *expert* approach, in which political parties, by consensus, delegate responsibility to a group of experienced individuals with a reputation for independence.[8]

In another typology, Massicotte et al. identify three approaches to establishing electoral authorities. Their analysis focuses on who is appointed as the person responsible for making decisions about election administration.[9] In their model, they differentiate between: the appointment of multiple commissioners to represent a diversity of (usually political) views; the practice of allowing a government minister to be in charge of the electoral process; and the appointment of a single commissioner. It is the last of these that is favoured in Australia.

As previously mentioned, Australia has a long history of professional electoral management bodies that administer elections in a relatively fair and non-partisan manner. While each electoral commission is a statutory body under

---

5   Shaheen Mozaffar and Andreas Schedler. 2002. 'The Comparative Study of Electoral Governance—An Introduction.' *International Political Science Review* 23(1): 16.
6   Larry Garber. 1994. 'Election Commissions: Responsibilities and Composition.' Paper presented at the NDI-sponsored African Election Colloquium, Victoria Falls, Zimbabwe.
7   Paul Harris. 1997. 'An Electoral Administration: Who, What and Where.' Paper prepared at IDEA for the South Pacific Electoral Administrators' Conference, Fiji, October.
8   Rafael López-Pintor. 2000. *Electoral Management Bodies as Institutions of Governance*. New York: Bureau for Development Policy, United Nations Development Programme, p. 20.
9   Louis Massicotte, André Blais and Antoine Yoshinaka. 2004. *Establishing the Rules of the Game: Election Laws in Democracies*. Toronto: University of Toronto Press, p. 83.

the relevant legislation in its jurisdiction, the same legislation can also limit its ability to act independently and its capacity to provide a level playing field for participants in elections.

**Table 3.1 IDEA's Model of Independent Electoral Management Bodies**

| Aspect | Independent electoral management body |
|---|---|
| Institutional arrangement | Is institutionally independent of the executive branch of government |
| Implementation | Exercises full responsibility for implementation |
| Formal accountability | Does not report to executive branch of government but with very few exceptions is formally accountable to the legislature, judiciary or head of state |
| Powers | Has powers to develop the electoral regulatory framework independently under the law |
| Composition | Is composed of members who are outside the executive branch while in office |
| Term of office | Offers security of tenure, but not necessarily fixed term of office |
| Budget | Has and manages its own budget independently of day-to-day governmental control |

Source: Wall, Alan, Andrew Ellis, Ayman Ayoub, Carl W. Dundas, Joram Rukambe and Sara Staino. 2006. *Electoral Management Design: The International IDEA Handbook*. Stockholm: International IDEA, 9.

In research conducted for IDEA, Wall et al. identify three models of electoral authority. These models are sorted according to a range of criteria: institutional arrangements; implementation; accountability; powers; composition; security of tenure; and budget control (see Table 3.1). Briefly, the three models are: *independent* (being institutionally independent from the executive); *government* (within or under the direction of a minister and department); and *mixed* (a combination of the first two models, with a degree of institutional independence, but still within the direction and control of the government of the day).

While IDEA identifies the Australian system as an example of the independent model, there is one important criterion that the AEC and other Australian commissions do not meet—namely, having the power to independently develop the electoral regulatory framework. In Australia, this power resides with the parliament and government of the day and is critical in limiting the commissions' ability to operate independently. In this respect, Australian electoral authorities conform more to IDEA's government or mixed models. As discussed later in the chapter, it is also questionable whether Australian commissions meet the independence criterion of having the ability to manage their budgets without day-to-day government control.

The term 'independence' is often used interchangeably with 'neutrality', 'non-partisanship' and 'impartiality'; however, there are differences between the meanings of these terms. An electoral authority may be established as an independent body, but exhibit bias through partisan actions. Conversely, an authority that is not independent—for example, one that is an office entirely within a government department—might operate in a non-partisan and impartial manner due to a lack of partisan direction from the responsible minister and the neutrality of its public service bureaucracy. Paul Dacey argues that the AEC was created with the intention that it would be both independent (that is, not influenced by others and thinking for itself) and impartial (without allegiance or obligation to any political parties, candidates or other political players).[10] It cannot, however, be argued that the commission functions in a totally non-partisan manner, as it is constrained by the legislative environment in which it is required to operate.

Furthermore, it is generally agreed that electoral authorities should not only be independent and impartial, they should also not allow for any perception of dependence or partiality to occur. To this end, IDEA identifies five essential criteria for ethical electoral administration: respect for the law; non-partisanship and neutrality; transparency; accuracy; and service to voters. Under the ethical principle of non-partisanship and neutrality, it is the perception of neutrality that is seen as the critical factor in successful elections. IDEA argues that one way to maintain neutrality is for electoral administrators to refrain from expressing any view that could become a political issue in an election. When the electoral system, or a component of it, becomes an election issue, administrators can, however, be caught between the two options of remaining silent on a matter, in a way that might advantage a particular party or parties, or expressing a view that is based on the principle of electoral fairness for voters, but which might go against government policy. One commissioner expressed a preference to remain silent, as a way of both appeasing the government and not becoming a political pawn for the opposition.

A different view, at least in the context of the Australian Commonwealth system, is given by Dacey, who argues that Section 7(1) of the *Commonwealth Electoral Act 1918* places the commission at the centre of political debates on electoral matters. Through this section, the commission is required to promote public awareness, provide advice to parliament and conduct and publish research. Dacey argues that, to maintain independence, the commission should comment from the viewpoint of improving the quality of the electoral process.[11]

---

10   Paul Dacey. 2005. 'What Do "Impartiality", "Independence" and "Transparency" Mean?—Some Thoughts from Australia', pp. 2–3.
11   Paul Dacey. 2005. 'What Do "Impartiality", "Independence" and "Transparency" Mean?—Some Thoughts from Australia', p. 6.

Dacey is a long-time senior administrator in the AEC, and his view is from the perspective of electoral professionalism, in which best electoral practice is seen as taking precedence over any partisan impacts that such practices might have. For example, independent commissions may aim to maximise both the comprehensiveness and the accuracy of the electoral roll. There could, however, be considerable tension between these dual goals. Improving the accuracy of the roll might occur at the expense of its comprehensiveness and, importantly, this could have partisan impacts whereby some groups of voters, who are more inclined to support certain parties, can become disenfranchised.

In terms of independence, another aspect of electoral administration that has been debated in recent years is whether electoral commissions should be involved in policing 'truth in political advertising' legislation. Currently South Australia is the only jurisdiction with such legislation, which requires the electoral commissioner to initiate proceedings in cases of false and misleading advertising.[12] One electoral administrator explained the impact on independence this way:

> If the commissioner then takes prosecutorial activity against MPs and candidates—does he prosecute if his job comes up in two years' time, and the party has just won government, does he prosecute or not? It's the 'without fear and favour' stuff. How can you act without fear and favour if you're worried about your tenure?

An Australian Democrats proposal to replicate this power in the AEC for federal elections was opposed by the AEC on the basis that such powers would impact on the commission's independence and 'reputation for political neutrality'.[13] In its submission to a parliamentary inquiry, the AEC argued that if it had responsibility for monitoring advertising it would be accused of partisanship. As an alternative, it proposed that an 'electoral complaints authority', resourced by staff from other agencies including the AEC, be established for election campaign periods. In the same inquiry, however, the SA Commissioner stated that he 'welcomed measures that reinforce the probity of the electoral and political systems'.[14] The reluctance of the AEC to take on this role is a typical example of the tension that can exist in electoral administration—in this case, between voters being able to make an informed decision based on truthful information and having confidence that the election is being conducted by an independent and non-partisan authority.

---

12   Section 113, *Electoral Act 1985* (SA).

13   AEC [Australian Electoral Commission]. 2001. *Submission to the Senate Public Finance and Administration Inquiry into Bills Concerning Political Honesty and Accountability*. Submission no. 14. Canberra: Australian Electoral Commission, p. 2.

14   Senate Finance and Public Administration Legislation Committee. 2002. *Charter of Political Honesty Bill 2000*. Canberra: Parliament of Australia, pp. 89–90.

Based on the models of independence described above and an examination of legislation, eight factors have been identified as being pertinent to the independence of Australian commissions. These are: commissioner experience; the size of commissions; appointment processes; political affiliations; length of tenure; security of tenure; reporting mechanisms; and budget processes. The following sections analyse these factors for their impact on the fairness and independence of electoral administration.

## Commissioner experience

Commissioner experience has not typically been included as a factor in models of electoral authority independence. It is clear from the Australian experience, however, that a group of electoral professionals exists for whom electoral administration is a lifetime career. In this environment, working to professional standards rather than to political or management direction is an important component of a culture of independence. A commissioner's previous experience in electoral administration prior to appointment can impact on his or her ability to act in an independent manner. Generally Australian commissioners have each established a lengthy professional career based on the application of non-partisan principles of fair elections (see Table 3.2). Of the nine commissioners, only one, Ed Killesteyn, came into the position with no previous electoral experience. Killesteyn's professional background lies in senior public service administration, including time as a departmental deputy secretary and deputy president of the Repatriation Commission. This is the same career path followed by Killesteyn's predecessor, Ian Campbell, whose lack of electoral experience was a concern for one observer:

> I think he's misunderstood his position to a degree. That is, he's emphasised more the public servant role and the implementation of government policy due to his background, rather than his independence and guardianship of the system role, which is his as a statutory office holder.

The appointments of Campbell and Killesteyn have prompted some discussion among electoral administrators about the pros and cons of having the senior position held by a person with no previous electoral experience. While it is obviously beneficial for a commissioner to have previous electoral administration experience, good public administrators will ensure they draw on the experience they might be lacking themselves from within (and outside) their commissions. Another view, from a commissioner with a defence force background, is that electoral administration is simply logistics and 'significant event management', and is similar to organising a military operation. In the same way that you cannot be a day late going into battle, you cannot be a day late in running an election.

While commissioners' previous electoral experience can and does have an impact on the independence exhibited by commissions, it is not included in the framework analysis of the independence of electoral administration. This is due to the transient nature of this factor. It is suggested that future comparative work on electoral management bodies should take into consideration the variable of professional versus generalist appointments to determine its relevance to independence.

**Table 3.2 Electoral Experience of Current Australian Electoral Commissioners (as at 1 December 2011)**

| Jurisdiction | Commissioner | Year first appointed | Previous electoral experience | Previous electoral appointments |
|---|---|---|---|---|
| Commonwealth | Ed Killesteyn | 2008 | Nil | Nil |
| New South Wales | Colin Barry | 2004 | 16 years | Electoral Commissioner, Victoria |
| Victoria | Steve Tully | 2005 | 17 years | Electoral Commissioner, South Australia (1997–2005) |
| Queensland | David Kerslake | 2006 | 4 years | Assistant Commissioner, Industrial Elections, and Funding and Disclosure AEC (4 years) |
| Western Australia | Warwick Gately | 2006 | 3 years | Deputy Commissioner (8 months), Acting Commissioner (2 years) |
| South Australia | Kay Mousley | 2006 | 20+ years | Various—finally Director of Operations, AEC (South Australia) |
| Tasmania | Julian Type | 2011 | 25 years | Commenced with AEC, international experience with United Nations, including in Cambodia, Nepal and Afghanistan |
| Australian Capital Territory | Phillip Green | 1994 | 13 years | Australian Electoral Office (then AEC), from 1982 |
| Northern Territory | Bill Shepheard | 2005 | 26 years | WAEC (7 years), Australian Electoral Office (then AEC) (c. 17 years) NT Electoral Office (2 years) |

# The size of commissions

The number of commissioners to be appointed to commissions has not been a contentious issue in Australian electoral management. All jurisdictions operate with a single commissioner appointed in a full-time capacity as the chief executive officer of the organisation. In three jurisdictions—the Commonwealth, Tasmania and the Australian Capital Territory—two other commissioners are appointed on a permanent part-time basis, and tend to be drawn from the legal profession (a senior judge) and the senior public service (usually with expertise in statistics and demographics). In the remaining jurisdictions, additional commissioners are appointed to a separate body when there is a need to conduct a redistribution of electoral boundaries. For the purposes of this study, unless otherwise specified, a reference to a 'commissioner' refers to the commissioner appointed as the full-time chief executive officer of the organisation.

Current commissioners have differing views on the merits of having a single commissioner, as against a multi-member board commission. Some prefer autonomous decision making but there is also support for collaborative and consultative management. A preference for the latter was expressed in the following terms by a commissioner:

> A commission can stand as three people and as a body, and it's not like you've personally had any biased personal opinion. It's not just me thinking this way because of any biases. This body of three people sat down and deliberated and decided this. What my personal views are, who knows. It gives it that air of independence.

Generally, there was agreement among commissioners that the size of the commission did not have an impact on the independent conduct of commission work and that an ideal model for the size of a commission depended on each commissioner's personal preference.

# Commissioner selection and appointment processes

Clearly, the independence of an electoral management body is closely related to the method of appointment of its chief executive officer. Where the government controls appointment processes it might be difficult to sustain confidence in the impartiality of the process. Four general methods of appointment exist in Australia (see Table 3.3). In order of increasing accountability, they can be listed as follows. The first is appointment by the governor or governor-general, on the recommendation of the government of the day. This process is used in the three largest jurisdictions, the Commonwealth, New South Wales and Victoria, where the entire selection and appointment process remains within the government's control and oversight. A second type of process is used in the remaining six jurisdictions, which require consultation with other political parties represented in parliament. The third method, used in Queensland and South Australia, requires consultation with a parliamentary committee prior to the ratification of an appointment. Finally, the SA legislation also requires a resolution from both houses of parliament before the governor can appoint the electoral commissioner.

**Table 3.3 Appointment Processes for Australian Electoral Commissioners[15]**

| Jurisdiction | Appointment process (section of principal legislation) |
|---|---|
| Commonwealth | Governor-general appoints (s. 21) |
| New South Wales | Governor appoints (s. 21AA) |
| Victoria | Governor appoints (s. 12) |
| Queensland | Governor in council appoints. The position is advertised nationally and the process includes consultation with all leaders of parliamentary parties and with parliamentary committee (s. 23) |
| Western Australia | Governor appoints, on recommendation of the premier, who is required to consult with parliamentary party leaders (s. 5B) |
| South Australia | Governor appoints, on recommendation from both houses of parliament (s. 5) |
| Tasmania | Governor appoints, on recommendation of the premier, who is required to consult with parliamentary party leaders and the president of the legislative council (s. 8) |
| Australian Capital Territory | Executive appoints. Consultation with leaders of all parties and Independents required. Appointment is disallowable (s. 22) |
| Northern Territory | Administrator (equivalent to a governor) appoints, on recommendation of the chief minister, who is required to consult with parliamentary party leaders and Independents (s. 314) |

In the three jurisdictions not requiring consultation, there is a danger that appointments might be perceived as partisan. One example of this was the Howard Government's appointment of Ian Campbell as commissioner in 2005. One of Campbell's initial tasks was to advise on the significant reforms being proposed by the government at the time, and to manage their implementation once they were passed in 2006. On one particular reform—earlier closing of the roll—Campbell made comments to a parliamentary inquiry that went against the long-held AEC position and were seen to be bowing to the wishes of the government.[16]

In February 2008, the Rudd Labor Government announced a transparent and merit-based selection process for senior public servants, which involves

---

15  References to section numbers in tables in this chapter relate to each jurisdiction's primary legislation.
16  This issue is discussed more fully in Chapter 5.

public advertising and involvement by the public service commissioner. This is, however, an administrative move, and there remains no requirement for the government to consult with other parties prior to appointing an electoral commissioner.

Appointment by the government of the day, without reference to other parties, leaves such appointees open to claims of bias and partisanship. Typical was one comment that the commissioner's 'appointment allegedly had the Prime Minister's tentacles all over it'.

Such allegations have accompanied both Labor and Coalition appointments. For example, former Tasmanian Liberal MP Michael Hodgman's seat of Denison became more marginal in the 1980s due to a boundary redistribution. In a 2007 interview, Hodgman remained critical of the treatment he received from Labor-appointed Commissioner Colin Hughes, who was a member of the Redistribution Committee:

> I went along to that review expecting a fair hearing, and I walked out and they said, 'How do you think you've gone?' I said…'My appeal's going to be dismissed, absolutely…I've not had a fair hearing.' I know I was causing [Prime Minister Bob] Hawke a lot of pain and angst, and I reckon he said to [Labor Special Minister of State Mick] Young, 'Get rid of Hodgman', and Young said, 'The way to do that is change the boundaries.'

Labor perspectives on Coalition-appointed commissioners are similarly sceptical—a typical comment being that 'he was seen to be partisan, being a particularly good mate of [the minister]'.

A clear majority of comments from politicians, however, emphasised the importance of maintaining perceived and actual non-partisanship. Commissioners were seen, almost universally, as honest and incorruptible, but concerns were frequently raised that if appointments were made without consultation, the subsequent decisions of those commissioners would be open to arguments that the appointment was partisan in nature. This was particularly the case where commissioners' decisions resulted in measurable partisan advantages or detriments.

## The requirement to consult

The requirement of consultation with other parties means it is less likely that a person with perceived partisan views will be appointed; however, while there is a requirement in six jurisdictions for some form of consultation to take place, there is no requirement, except in South Australia (and to a lesser degree in the Australian Capital Territory), for the government to genuinely take the views of the other parties into account. One State minister stated that the premier was alleged to have said to the other parties that 'we're going to appoint so-and-so; you have now been consulted'.

In the case of the Australian Capital Territory, however, commissioner appointments are disallowable instruments. This means that a government without a majority in the legislative assembly may be exposed to the possibility of its appointment being rejected in a very public manner. It also means that an opposition that does have concerns about an appointment needs to decide whether such concerns warrant moving a disallowance motion. Although the ability to disallow an appointment is theoretically a safeguard mechanism that allows non-government parties a voice in the appointment process, it is a blunt instrument that is not likely to be used in practice. It would only be effective when opposition parties have the numbers in parliament and, irrespective of the outcome, moving such a motion in itself would call into question the office of commissioner. If a motion was successful, it would result in the commissioner being removed from office, damaging the public image of the office and labelling that person as partisan, without that person having a right to defend himself or herself. If a disallowance motion was unsuccessful, however, it would place the commissioner in a very difficult, or even untenable, situation. As one commissioner argued:

> The other problem with that is if you have a disallowance motion it can be lost if the government has the numbers in the house, and you get a poor lame duck electoral commissioner who says the other side don't want me. To engage them all in the first place is a much better way than people jumping up and down afterwards.

Instead of taking the negative and post-appointment approach that a disallowance motion entails, the SA process requires the positive and pre-appointment method of an affirmation resolution by both houses of parliament, following a multi-party committee process outlined below. This is the most thorough and publicly accountable consultation process of all the Australian jurisdictions. It requires the governor to appoint a commissioner based on a recommendation made by both houses of parliament. When this requirement was imposed in 2005, for the first and so far the only time, the matter was considered by the Statutory Officers Committee (SOC), a joint house parliamentary committee that was established for the purpose of appointing electoral commissioners, auditors-general and ombudsmen. The SOC is made up of six members, three from each house, with only two parties (Labor and Liberal) and an Independent represented. Although not all parties are represented on the SOC, the subsequent requirement for parliamentary ratification by way of an affirmation resolution should ensure that other parties are consulted prior to such a vote. Such consultation would not be expected to change the outcome (given the major parties' representation on the SOC); however, it could assist in alleviating any concerns that other parliamentarians might have.

After advertising nationally for the position, an interview panel, made up of an electoral commissioner from another jurisdiction and senior public servants, interviewed a short list of applicants that had been drawn up by a personnel agency. This panel provided its recommendations to the SOC, which then interviewed the recommended applicants. Based on this second round of interviews, the SOC reported to parliament its recommendation, which was agreed to by both houses without debate. In 2006, the Victorian Public Accounts and Estimates Committee recommended that the SA model be followed in Victoria, whereby future appointments would be made by a resolution of both houses of parliament, following a recommendation from an appropriate parliamentary committee.[17]

Queensland is the other jurisdiction that involves the use of a parliamentary committee in the selection process. In Queensland's process, the requirement is to consult with the relevant committee—currently the Legal Affairs, Police, Corrective Services and Emergency Services Committee, but previously the Legal, Constitutional and Administrative Review Committee (LCARC), which also had a remit to inquire into broader electoral and other matters. When this requirement was activated in 2005 for the appointment of the current commissioner, the chair (Lesley Clark, Labor) and deputy chair (Fiona Simpson, Nationals) of the LCARC both sat on the selection panel (as did the Labor Attorney-General, Linda Lavarch). Although the Act does not require committee representation on the actual selection panel, the involvement of government and opposition parliamentarians also assisted in fulfilling the additional requirement to consult with other parties. As one parliamentarian stated:

> My experience of [previously] interviewing for the information commissioner where it was just me really reinforced—where you have got the external accountability-type office holders—that you have bipartisan support in that early stage. Not just in the parliament, that's really after the event.

It was acknowledged by some interviewees that there could be a benefit in the Commonwealth's Joint Standing Committee on Electoral Matters having a role in the appointment of commissioners, either prior to or after the appointment. The dominant view, however, was that the pronounced partisan nature of the committee's membership could politicise the process and jeopardise the

---

17   Public Accounts and Estimates Committee. 2006. *Report On—A Legislative Framework for Independent Officers of Parliament*. Melbourne: Parliament of Victoria, p. 69.

independence of the commissioner's position. In contrast, Queensland's use of a parliamentary committee in appointing the commissioner appears to have been successful, although it has only been used once so far. One theme that came through strongly from committee members in response to questioning on the suitability of using committees in the selection process was the importance of personal relationships and goodwill between committee members. Such goodwill appears to be evident in the Queensland situation but is clearly lacking in the federal committee.

# Political affiliations

Another mechanism in Australian legislation that guards against partisan appointments is the inclusion of rules preventing members or previous members of political parties or parliaments from being eligible for appointment (see Table 3.4). Four jurisdictions (New South Wales, Victoria, Tasmania and the Australian Capital Territory) prevent people who have been members of a political party within the previous five years from being eligible for appointment to a commissioner's position. Queensland limits the prohibition to existing members of political parties. In addition, four jurisdictions (Western Australia, Tasmania, the Australian Capital Territory and the Northern Territory) place restrictions on current or previous members of parliament. Such requirements have generally been introduced as a result of one jurisdiction's reforms being adopted by other jurisdictions. For example, the Northern Territory's *Electoral Act 2004* was heavily influenced by the Australian Capital Territory's *Electoral Act 1992*. While such restrictions have merit in ensuring there is a check on overt partisan influence, if a partisan appointment were to be made, it is more likely to be of someone with less well-known or obvious political leanings. It is partly to counter this potentiality, and to encourage cross-party support for commissioner appointments, that recent electoral legislation often states a requirement for the government to consult with other political parties before deciding on a preferred candidate, as discussed above.

**Table 3.4 Prohibitions on Appointment of Party Members or Parliamentarians**

| Jurisdiction | Party members | Parliamentarians |
|---|---|---|
| Commonwealth | No provisions in the Act | No provisions in the Act |
| New South Wales | Members of political parties and any person who has been a member of a political party in previous five years are ineligible (s. 21AB[4]) | No provisions in the Act |
| Victoria | Members of registered political parties and any person who has been a member of a political party in previous five years are ineligible (s. 12[3]) | No provisions in the Act |
| Queensland | Members of political parties are ineligible (s. 23[4]) | No provisions in the Act |
| Western Australia | Act is silent | Any person who is or has been a member of a parliament or legislature anywhere in Australia is ineligible (s. 5B[10]) |
| South Australia | No provisions in the Act | No provisions in the Act |
| Tasmania | Members of political parties and any person who has been a member of a party in the previous five years anywhere in Australia are ineligible (s. 8[3]) | Members of parliament and any person who has been a member of parliament in the previous five years anywhere in Australia are ineligible (s. 8[3]) |
| Australian Capital Territory | Any person who is or has been a member of a political party in the previous five years is ineligible (s. 12A) | Any person who is or has been a member of a parliament or a legislature anywhere in Australia in the previous 10 years is ineligible (s. 12A) |
| Northern Territory | No provisions in the Act | MLAs ineligible for appointment (s. 327) |

# Length of tenure

The length of a commissioner's tenure can have significant impacts on his or her independence and ability to act without fear or favour. If a commissioner lacks long-term security then his or her actions could be, in a real or perceived sense, related to a desire for reappointment. The timing of a potential reappointment, irrespective of the length of appointment, can also have an impact, especially if this coincides with an election. As shown in Table 3.5, Australia's electoral commissioners generally have reasonable lengths of tenure, with eight jurisdictions providing for appointments from five to 10 years. In seven of these jurisdictions, however, this is the maximum length, with the relevant Acts allowing tenure 'up to' that term. The remaining jurisdiction, South Australia, has potentially longer security, with the appointments of commissioner (and deputy commissioner) lasting to the age of sixty-five.

**Table 3.5 Length of Tenure for Australian Electoral Commissioners**

| Jurisdiction | Length of tenure |
| --- | --- |
| Commonwealth | Up to seven years. Eligible for reappointment (s. 8) |
| New South Wales | Up to 10 years. Eligible for reappointment, for no more than one further term of up to 10 years (s. 21AB[1]) |
| Victoria | 10 years. Eligible for reappointment up to a further 10 years (s. 12) |
| Queensland | Up to seven years (s. 23[5]) |
| Western Australia | Up to nine years. Eligible for reappointment (s. 5B[4]) |
| South Australia | To age sixty-five (s. 7) |
| Tasmania | Up to seven years. Eligible for reappointment (s. 17) |
| Australian Capital Territory | Up to five years. Eligible for reappointment (s. 25) |
| Northern Territory | Up to five years. Eligible for reappointment (s. 320) |

The 'up to' provision provides governments with flexibility in determining the length of an appointment, and it has been argued by ministers that appointing for a lesser term fits with standard practice for senior public service appointments. Shorter-term appointments could, however, be associated with weak independence, if the commissioner is seeking reappointment. At the Commonwealth level, the first Commissioner, Colin Hughes, was appointed for the maximum seven years (and served just less than six before resigning). All subsequent commissioners have been appointed for only five-year terms. Similarly, in Western Australia, where terms may be up to nine years, recent appointments have been for five years. The current Commissioner, Warwick Gately, who had already served two years as acting commissioner at the time of his appointment, was appointed as commissioner for only three years, to make a total of a five-year term.

In the case of the current SA Commissioner, her appointment to the age of sixty-five is effectively a 14-year term. Her deputy commissioner was appointed at a younger age, and therefore has an effective appointment in that position of 26 years. Internationally, the only jurisdictions with a similar length of security are Ghana (to age seventy), Canada and Malaysia (to age sixty-five), India (six years or age sixty-five, whichever is earlier), and Poland (to age seventy).[18]

---

18 Alan Wall et al. 2006. *Electoral Management Design: The International IDEA Handbook*, p. 93; Louis Massicotte et al. 2004. *Establishing the Rules of the Game: Election Laws in Democracies*, pp. 85–7.

In the interviews, commissioners expressed a range of views on what they considered to be an ideal length of appointment. One argument in favour of five-year terms was that

> if you're going to shake a show up then if you haven't got everything accomplished that you want in five years, you're not going to get it. Secondly, if you were a dud, five years of coasting along, they will have a chance of replacing you.

Generally though, commissioners expressed support for a longer term. Typical of such views were these commissioners' comments.

> Having tenure in the appointment of more than five years is desirable from a perspective of long-term planning in electoral matters. I think you need to plan over two election cycles, so eight to 10 years is about a good time in my view. Otherwise you just get short-term bites at the planning and no look above the horizon.

> If you're in a job around eight years, people are getting sick of you, you're getting sick of them, and it's good for the organisation and for the commissioner to do something else.

> If you've gone through two elections, you've probably established more independence in the role, and perhaps a fairer decision can be made.

One commissioner supported appointment to the age of sixty-five, 'with the right person'. Of course, the issue is ensuring the 'right person' is appointed. A dominant view from the interviews was that commissioners should be in place for more than one election and that five-year appointments, combined with three or four-year electoral cycles, often meant that a commissioner was in the position for only one election. This could result in a reduced ability to oversee the implementation of administrative reforms based on previous experience in that jurisdiction. The timing of appointments, and whether the end of the term was close to an election, was also an issue of concern for some commissioners. Interviewees argued that if a possible reappointment coincided with the conduct of an election, this could impact on the actions of the commissioner during the election period.

## Security of tenure

Once a commissioner has been appointed, security of tenure can be enhanced or diminished by the conditions under which an appointment may be terminated. All jurisdictions provide for dismissal from office under specified circumstances, such as physical or mental incapacity, bankruptcy and misconduct. For such a dismissal to take permanent effect, however, a resolution passed by each house of parliament is required in seven of the nine jurisdictions, with the Commonwealth and Queensland the only exceptions to this requirement (see Table 3.6). In these two exceptions, a government still needs to substantiate its reasons for dismissal (under separate employment legislation). The need for a parliamentary resolution, however, provides an obviously greater safeguard against governments acting vexatiously. Some jurisdictions specify a number of sitting days within which a resolution for dismissal needs to be passed for it to take effect. Depending on the parliamentary sitting schedule, and the timing of parliament being notified, this could equate to a period of several months. Some acts do not specify a time period, but a deadline for action may be covered in other legislation, such as constitutional Acts or in parliamentary standing orders. To date, no electoral commissioners have been dismissed from office.

## Table 3.6 Dismissal Processes for Australian Electoral Commissioners

| Jurisdiction | Dismissal—reporting to parliament |
|---|---|
| Commonwealth | Governor may terminate, for specified reasons (for example, misbehaviour) (s. 25) |
| New South Wales | Governor may suspend the commissioner. A statement from the minister explaining the suspension is to be provided to parliament within seven sitting days. Commissioner may then be removed by the governor if each house of parliament passes a resolution within 21 days of statement being tabled (s. 21AB[3]) |
| Victoria | Governor may suspend the commissioner. The minister is then to notify the speaker, president and leaders of (parliamentary) political parties within two hours (s. 140). Commissioner may then be removed by resolution of both houses of parliament (s. 12[4][e]) |
| Queensland | Governor in council may terminate (s. 26) |
| Western Australia | Governor may suspend the commissioner. A statement explaining the suspension to be provided to parliament within seven sitting days. Commissioner may be removed on resolution of both houses of parliament within 30 sitting days (s. 5C) |
| South Australia | Governor may suspend the commissioner under specified circumstances. A statement explaining the suspension is to be provided to parliament within three sitting days. Commissioner may then be removed by resolution of both houses of parliament (s. 7) |
| Tasmania | Governor may suspend the commissioner under specified circumstances. A statement explaining the suspension is to be provided to parliament within seven sitting days. Commissioner may then be removed by resolution of both houses of parliament (s. 21) |
| Australian Capital Territory | Executive may suspend. Minister is to present a statement to the assembly on the next sitting day. Assembly resolution within seven sitting days required for appointment to be ended (s. 29) |
| Northern Territory | Suspension by the administrator. Minister must present statement to assembly within three sitting days. Assembly must pass a resolution for dismissal to take effect (s. 323) |

# Reporting mechanisms

The independence of electoral administrations is also influenced by the method with which they report to government and parliament. Reporting directly to parliament provides a transparent process that is accessible to all political stakeholders at the same time. Reporting only to the government can provide the political parties in government with the advantage of having earlier access to information on sensitive issues, thereby allowing the government to prepare its response prior to the public release of information. In Australia, there is a mix of reporting mechanisms for the various electoral administrations, as shown in Table 3.7. Although possibly not a major issue, delays between a government receiving a report and tabling it in parliament can lead to accusations of a closer relationship between the electoral administration and the government than is desirable. For example, the 15 sitting day period allowed in Section 17 of the *Commonwealth Electoral Act 1918* could stretch out for several months, depending on parliament's sitting schedule.

**Table 3.7 Reporting Mechanisms for Australian Electoral Administrations**

| Jurisdiction | Reporting mechanism |
|---|---|
| Commonwealth | Annual, election and financial disclosure reports to the minister, who then must table the reports in parliament within the next 15 sitting days (s. 17) |
| New South Wales | Not specified in Act. Election report sent to premier, with a request that it be tabled in parliament (from interview data) |
| Victoria | To both houses of parliament, on elections and polls (s. 8). Annually to both houses of parliament in relation to the provision of enrolment information (s. 35) |
| Queensland | Not specified in Act. Report to parliament (from interview data) |
| Western Australia | Annual report by 31 August to the responsible minister, who then presents the report to the parliament within 21 days of the auditor-general's report (ss. 62 and 64 of the *Financial Administration and Audit Act 1985*) |
| South Australia | Not specified in the Act; however, s. 8 specifies that the commissioner is responsible to the minister |
| Tasmania | Annual and other reports directly to both houses of parliament (s. 13) |
| Australian Capital Territory | Annual report to the minister responsible (attorney-general), who then presents the report to the assembly (s. 10) |
| Northern Territory | To the speaker, then tabled in the assembly within three sitting days (s. 313) |

# Budget processes

Dundas and Wall et al. identify the budgetary independence of electoral management bodies as one of the primary guarantors of electoral commission independence, pointing out that the manner in which a commission is funded can affect its independent status. Dundas argues that the need for an electoral authority to negotiate its budget can undermine its primary role as an independent agency.[19] Wall et al. conclude that the electoral administration should be provided with its own budget and should be free of day-to-day government interference in administering that budget.[20]

All Australian administrations remain reliant on governmental budget processes for their budgetary allocations. Consequently, it is possible for governments to maintain a significant degree of influence and control over the 'independent' commissions. It is important to understand the processes through which the commissions receive their financial allocations. The standard method for Australian commissions is to negotiate funds through their parent departments or with the relevant finance or treasury department, as part of the whole-of-government budgetary process. This process can diminish the commission's independence, especially when compared with the practices of some other countries, such as Canada, where the electoral body has a portion of its budget guaranteed by law.

Budgeting processes for electoral administrations are often contained within finance and public administration legislation, rather than in electoral legislation, and personal relationships between electoral officials and treasury officials can influence these processes. In order to understand budget processes, all commissioners and ministers interviewed were asked to describe how the budget process works in their respective jurisdiction. A summary of these data is provided in the following paragraphs.

## Commonwealth

The AEC undergoes the same process as all government agencies and is therefore subject to government-wide funding cuts. The AEC negotiates its budget with the Department of Finance and Administration (DoFA). Requests for funding of special programs go to the special minister of state. DoFA provides budget and policy advice (beyond just monetary matters) to the minister responsible. In 2005, the minister determined the AEC's resources following a joint finance agencies review.

---

19  Carl W. Dundas. 1994. *Dimensions of Free and Fair Elections: Frameworks, Integrity, Transparency, Attributes and Monitoring*. London: Commonwealth Secretariat, p. 40.
20  Alan Wall et al. 2006. *Electoral Management Design: The International IDEA Handbook*, p. 9.

## New South Wales

The NSW Commission undergoes the same process as all government agencies. It negotiates its budget with treasury and, if necessary, the cabinet budget committee.

## Victoria

The Victorian Commission negotiates its budget with the Department of Justice; its budget is an output within the department's budget. There appear to be no restrictions on accessing funds to conduct general elections, as the following administrator's comment attests:

> The Victorian Electoral Commissioner has a bottomless pit to draw on to run a State election, but it's accountable as to how it's spent, after the election, and that's rightly so. But there is no real impediment. The commissioner can't say 'there wasn't enough money available'.

## Queensland

The Queensland Commission negotiates its budget with treasury, for both recurring and election budgets. Appropriations for special projects require ministerial (attorney-general) support. There are no restrictions on accessing funds to conduct general elections.

## Western Australia

The WA Commission negotiates its budget with treasury and then seeks ministerial (attorney-general) support.

## South Australia

The Electoral Commission of South Australia (formerly the SA Electoral Office) experiences the same budget discipline as other agencies. It must negotiate its budget with the Attorney-General's Department and with treasury, and then seek ministerial (attorney-general) support. Special projects require cabinet approval.

## Tasmania

The Tasmanian Commission has a recurrent budget provided through the Department of Justice and is subject to government-wide funding cuts. It must negotiate its budget with the department and seek the attorney-general's support, if necessary. Budgets for general elections are 'reserved by law' and are therefore exempt from government restrictions. A commercial trust account is used for the conduct of local government and other elections.

## Australian Capital Territory

The ACT Commission negotiates its budget with the Department of Justice and Community Safety, and then seeks the attorney-general's support, before going to cabinet. Funding goes directly to the department, which then passes funds onto the commission, minus departmental expenses.

## Northern Territory

The NT Commission must seek treasury approval for its budget, based on previous recurrent and election budget costs. It is required to seek cabinet approval for additional funds.

# Budgetary independence

Around Australia, commissioners expressed a range of views about the level of ministerial or departmental control over their ongoing and election budgets. Concerns included: being part of a departmental appropriation, rather than having a separate agency budget line; being susceptible to government-wide budget cuts; the potential for a government to interfere with an upcoming election budget; and having to argue with departmental officials, rather than the minister, for funding to be maintained for specific programs within the electoral commission budget. Typical of these comments were the following commissioners' views:

> So there is a line item in the budget for electoral services, but the amount of money that's in electoral services is given to the department. They cream an amount from the top to use to fund their corporate things that they say are devoted to electoral services. You can have your budget fiddled with, and I always thought that was dangerous particularly where the CEO's responsible to the minister, and therefore there's a direct line with interfering with the election budget.

A further issue concerning whole-of-government budget cuts relates to the application of efficiency dividends, where a commission has to make savings in line with a government-wide standard. As two administrators stated:

When the government says there's a 7 per cent cut in the budget, well, they say they want your 7 per cent as well. They say you'll have to be more efficient, because you're getting less money. They're taking the dividend now, and forcing you to be more efficient.

The trouble is, this has now been in operation for maybe 15 years, maybe 18 years, so 1 per cent, 1 per cent, 1 per cent, 1 per cent. In round figure terms, we might be 20 per cent less of a budget than it would have been had it not applied. We're the same as every other agency, though.

A particular concern is where the government specifies which of a commission's programs needs to be reduced or abolished to make savings. This occurred in 1996 when the Howard Coalition Government abolished the AEC's Aboriginal and Torres Strait Islander Election Education and Information Service (ATSIEEIS) program. The impacts of this decision are discussed in Chapter 5. A further example occurred under the Rudd Labor Government in 2009. The 2009 Federal Budget stated that 'the AEC has been asked by Government to find savings measures of $6.1 million over four years including the closure of the Melbourne and Adelaide Electoral Education Centres'.[21]

Government ministers provide an alternative perspective to budget decisions, and one minister acknowledged the potential for departmental interference in a commission's budget:

[The commissioner] puts forward all of his own proposals for funding. They are brought in through the portfolio and then brought to cabinet for the budget process. I want to see all the bids from the commissioner and statutory officers, so that they're not filtered.

Can a statutory officer like the commissioner communicate fully to the minister without it being filtered through the bureaucracy? I think, 'Yes, he can.' If a minister wasn't on the ball about that, and if a department wasn't playing by the rules, things could get filtered, I guess, potentially.

The majority of commissioners expressed a reasonable level of satisfaction with the budgets they receive, but personal relationships with departmental and treasury officials were often mentioned as being very important in ensuring a smooth budgetary process. Typical of this view was a comment from one commissioner that as long as they conduct election programs cheaper than other States, treasury will be happy.

Other commissioners expressed concern that they could not necessarily implement the programs they felt were important. Instead of having

---

21    Cited in Brian Costar. 2009. 'Democracy Under Siege for the Sake of a Few Pennies.' *The Age*, 29 May.

'a bottomless pit to draw on', the situation is quite different. As one commissioner said, 'nobody has a blank cheque. No Western country gives any organisation a blank cheque.'

In 2006, the Victorian Public Accounts and Estimates Committee recommended that in the future, the Electoral Matters Committee should review the Electoral Commission's budget and report to parliament ahead of the appropriation being passed. Such a process would open the commission's budget to the scrutiny of non-government parties, and therefore could assist in maintaining the independence of the commission. This proposal, however, which models the process already in place for the Victorian Auditor-General, is yet to be adopted or implemented.

# Summary

This chapter has provided an insight into various aspects of the performance of Australia's electoral management bodies. The results of the best-practice analysis are most useful as a comparative guide between the jurisdictions assessed. This framework analysis of factors of independence is a valuable guide and can be used as a tool for jurisdictions to improve their 'true' independence—if legislators have the political will to devolve responsibilities for the administration of electoral law to professional electoral administrators.

# 4. The Franchise

By international standards, Australians enjoy a relatively broad voting franchise. All adult citizens, eighteen years old and over, are entitled to vote, with a few exceptions, such as categories relating to mental capacity, treason convictions and long-term prisoners. And of course, eligible Australians are not only entitled to vote, they are compelled to vote. The definition of mental capacity does at times raise questions over the interpretation of Section 93 of the *Commonwealth Electoral Act 1918*, which states 'by reason of being of unsound mind, is incapable of understanding the nature and significance of enrolment and voting'. While there are sound arguments to exclude those of 'unsound mind' from voting, determination of who is of 'unsound mind' is problematic, and electoral officials tend not to become involved in interpretation of the section, and rely on the medical evidence provided to them. Australia's laws on mental capacity stem from British law, and it is interesting to note that it was only in 2006 that Britain abolished its law that 'idiots' could not vote (idiocy being a permanent and congenital state), while 'lunatics' (being an acquired and transitory condition) could vote only during lucid intervals.[1]

The Australian franchise is citizen based, rather than resident based (with one significant exception, discussed below), unlike many countries that allow permanent residents, after they have lived in the country for a stipulated period, to vote. This becomes an interesting debate when compared with the right to vote for citizens living abroad. Australians living abroad, who might not be paying Australian taxes, may use their votes to influence Australian government policies and spending, while permanent, non-citizen residents who pay Australian taxes and are contributors to Australian society do not have a voice through the ballot box. This brings to mind the old phrase 'taxation without representation is tyranny'. Countries where residents may vote include Uruguay (15-year residency qualification), Malawi (seven years), Chile (five years) and New Zealand (one year). In addition, numerous countries in the European Union (EU) provide reciprocal voting rights for residents from other EU countries, though generally only for local government elections. In countries with residency qualifications where there is a significant influx of migrants, the migrants' views and policy priorities can have a significant impact on the conduct of elections. This forces political parties to consider the interests of ethnic groups, due to their voting power.

For Australian citizens living overseas, voting rights are retained if there is an intention to return to Australia within six years; however, citizens who have

---

1 Graeme Orr. 2010. *The Law of Politics: Elections, Parties and Money in Australia*. Sydney: The Federation Press, p. 59.

not applied for enrolment as overseas voters within three years of departing Australia will be disenfranchised. In 2010, more than 16 000 citizens were enrolled as eligible overseas electors. Australian voting rights for expatriate citizens are considered to be generally in the middle of the international spectrum when compared with other countries.[2] When it is time to vote in an election, eligible overseas electors and citizens temporarily away from Australia have the opportunity to attend polling stations set up at diplomatic posts, such as embassies, high commissions and consulates. For the 2010 election, more than 70 000 citizens used this service at more than 100 locations.

This chapter now concentrates on two aspects of the franchise that have attracted significant interest and discussion in recent years—that is, the right of certain non-citizen residents to vote in Australian elections, and prisoners' voting rights.

## Non-citizen residents' voting rights

In 1984 under the Hawke Labor Government, the qualification for the franchise was changed from British subjects who were Australian residents to Australian citizens. Because of the high levels of migration from Britain and other British Commonwealth countries to Australia, especially in the post–World War II period, this had the potential to disenfranchise hundreds of thousands of British subjects. So a 'grandfather' clause (Section 93 of the *Commonwealth Electoral Act 1918*) was included in the legislation to allow British subjects who were on the electoral roll prior to 1984 to remain on the roll. There are 49 countries covered by the 'British subject' clause, including the United Kingdom, Canada, New Zealand, India, Singapore, Fiji, Papua New Guinea and Sri Lanka. Interestingly, Ireland, which is not a British Commonwealth country, is included, while South Africa, which was not a member of the Commonwealth at the time of the legislation due to its apartheid policies, is not.

Although the impact of this exemption continues to dissipate over time, it remains significant, as an assessment of individual electorates indicates. In 2008, more than 162 000 electors with the British subject notation remained on the Australian electoral roll, with 13 electoral divisions where 'British subjects' made up more than 2 per cent of the roll (see Table 4.1). In general elections there are invariably several seats decided on a small margin, making the number

---

2   According to Graeme Orr, quoted in the JSCEM [Joint Standing Committee on Electoral Matters]. *Report on the Conduct of the 2007 Federal Election and Related Matters Thereto*. Canberra: Commonwealth of Australia, p. 298.

of British enrolments significant. In the past two general elections, six of the 26 results listed in the table were decided by a margin less than the number of British enrolments (in bold).

**Table 4.1 Electors with 'British Subject' Notation at 30 September 2008[3]**

| Division | British subject notation | Total enrolment | Proportion of British subjects/ total enrolment (%) | 2PP margin at 2007 election (%) | 2PP margin at 2010 election (%) |
|---|---|---|---|---|---|
| Wakefield (SA) | 3693 | 96 621 | 3.82 | 6.59 Labor | 11.95 Labor |
| Brand (WA) | 2870 | 94 849 | 3.03 | 5.62 Labor | 3.33 Labor |
| Dunkley (Vic.) | 2659 | 93 565 | 2.84 | 4.04 Coalition | **1.02 Coalition** |
| Kingston (SA) | 2784 | 98 959 | 2.81 | 4.42 Labor | 13.91 Labor |
| Canning (WA) | 2665 | 97 778 | 2.73 | 5.58 Coalition | **2.19 Coalition** |
| Flinders (Vic.) | 2595 | 96 357 | 2.69 | 8.25 Coalition | 9.11 Coalition |
| Makin (SA) | 2540 | 95 347 | 2.66 | 7.70 Labor | 12.20 Labor |
| Mayo (SA) | 2522 | 97 630 | 2.58 | 7.06 Coalition | 7.35 Coalition |
| Hasluck (WA) | 1923 | 83 412 | 2.31 | **1.26 Labor** | **0.57 Coalition** |
| Casey (Vic.) | 1959 | 90 019 | 2.18 | 5.93 Coalition | 4.18 Coalition |
| Throsby (NSW) | 1851 | 89 161 | 2.08 | 23.46 Labor | 12.11 Labor |
| La Trobe (Vic.) | 1940 | 93 304 | 2.08 | **0.51 Coalition** | **0.91 Labor** |
| McMillan (Vic.) | 1779 | 88 281 | 2.02 | 4.79 Coalition | 4.41 Coalition |

The arguments against allowing this class of voter to be enrolled are that it is discriminatory against long-term Australian residents from non-British countries and also that it is possibly racist, if not in its intent, then at least in its outcomes, as the majority of the beneficiaries are white. Another argument is put forward by Daryl Melham, a Labor MP who has chaired the Joint Standing Committee on Electoral Matters for more than 13 years. Melham argues that since the reform occurred in 1984, many more countries now allow dual citizenship, thereby removing one argument that might have discouraged British subjects from taking up Australian citizenship.[4]

The High Court has stated that permanent residents should not necessarily be regarded as part of 'the people' to whom the Australian Constitution entitles voting rights, but the current situation is discriminatory. A fairer situation would be to allow all permanent residents (including a specified qualification regarding length of residency) to be entitled to vote, irrespective of their country of origin, or limiting the voting entitlement to Australian citizens only.

---

3   From JSCEM [Joint Standing Committee on Electoral Matters]. *Report on the Conduct of the 2007 Federal Election and Matters Related Thereto*, p. 347. The final two columns are from AEC election results.
4   JSCEM [Joint Standing Committee on Electoral Matters]. *Report on the Conduct of the 2007 Federal Election and Matters Related Thereto*, pp. 348–9.

If the latter is adopted (that is, removing the British subject clause), there is a reasonable argument to retain an exemption for citizens of those countries that still do not allow dual citizenship, such as India and Singapore.

## The prisoner franchise

Supporters of prisoner enfranchisement argue that voting is a fundamental right and denial of the vote is racist, as Indigenous Australians are imprisoned at 12–15 times the non-Indigenous rate. Also, it is argued that denying a right to vote is counterproductive to the rehabilitative aspect of incarceration.[5] Detractors say that prisoners have broken the 'social contract' by committing serious crimes and therefore deserve 'civil death' by disenfranchisement.[6] While prisoners account for only a small percentage of the total potential voting population, the range of views on prisoner voting entitlements ensures that this issue becomes a 'political football' whenever reforms are suggested.[7]

There are quite divergent voting entitlements for prisoners in democracies around the world, as Massicotte et al.'s comparative study of 63 countries reveals. In 16 of the 63 countries in the study (25 per cent), all prisoners have a right to vote. This group includes Denmark, Germany, South Africa and Sweden. A further 16 countries (25 per cent), such as the Netherlands, New Zealand and Spain, allow a partial franchise, dependent on the length of sentence or the type of offence committed. In 24 of the countries studied (38 per cent), including Brazil, India and the United Kingdom, all prisoners are disenfranchised.[8]

A detailed analysis of the philosophical arguments for different countries' approaches to the prisoner franchise is outside the scope of this book. Instead, the focus is on the variation that exists within Australia and the processes undertaken to determine prisoners' entitlements at the Commonwealth, State and Territory levels. From this, an assessment is made of the motivating forces driving Australian prisoner franchise laws: the participation principle of fairness, partisan self-interest, or a mixture of both.

---

5   Graeme Orr. 2007. *Constitutionalising the Franchise and the Status Quo: The High Court on Prisoner Voting Rights.* Discussion Paper 19/07. Canberra: Democratic Audit, The Australian National University, p. 2.
6   Lisa Hill and Cornelia Koch. 2011. 'The Voting Rights of Incarcerated Australian Citizens.' *Australian Journal of Political Science* 46(2): 213–28.
7   Graeme Orr. 1998. 'Ballotless and Behind Bars: The Denial of the Franchise to Prisoners.' *Federal Law Review* 26(1): 56–82, discusses the symbolic politics of prisoner voting as a 'political football'.
8   No information was provided for the remaining seven countries. Louis Massicotte et al. 2004. *Establishing the Rules of the Game: Election Laws in Democracies,* pp. 18–25.

# Changes to Commonwealth laws

The Hawke Labor Government extended the prisoner franchise in its 1983 reforms. The franchise had remained largely unchanged since Federation, with voting rights extended only to those imprisoned for an offence with a maximum penalty of less than one year. Labor extended the franchise to those imprisoned for offences with maximum penalties of less than five years. These provisions were difficult to administer, as State controllers-general of prisons needed to determine the maximum possible penalties for offences, irrespective of prisoners' actual sentences. Subsequently, the Keating Labor Government changed the provision in 1995 so that all prisoners 'sentenced' to terms of less than five years could vote. This had the effect of further extending the franchise.

When the Coalition came to power in 1996, there was an immediate push to not only restrict the prisoner franchise, but also remove it entirely. In 1997, the Coalition-dominated JSCEM recommended that no prisoners should be entitled to enrol or vote. The Coalition's attempt to legislate for this change in 1999 was defeated in the Senate; however, the Coalition was successful in restricting the prisoner franchise in 2004, reducing the 'less than five years' provision to 'less than three years'. While the Coalition's legislation called for total prisoner disenfranchisement, Labor argued that a three-year qualification was a more suitable restriction as it coincided with a full term of the Australian Parliament. The Coalition agreed to this compromise in 2004 because it lacked the necessary numbers in the Senate to achieve its preferred outcome.

After the Coalition gained a Senate majority in 2005, it returned to its previous position of removing the franchise for all prisoners in full-time detention—a change estimated to affect approximately 20 000 prisoners.[9] While the Coalition has consistently argued against any prisoners having the right to vote, analysis of the interview data indicated some opposition to this stance within the Coalition parties. As one Liberal parliamentarian stated:

> I was a minority in my own party. The majority of my party had the John Howard/Eric Abetz line that if you were in prison, you didn't have a right to vote. I don't take that view. I think that, as the law said previously, if you're doing more than three years, you didn't have the right to vote, which is probably fair enough.

---

9   Brian Costar. 2006. Submission (no. 2) to the Senate Finance and Public Administration Committee Inquiry. Canberra: Parliament of Australia, p. 4.

> But I was dead against taking the right away from someone who was doing a short sentence. I felt that was completely unjust. They're in prison paying their debt to society. It's not as though it's a difficult matter to go and take their vote. They shouldn't have lost [the vote].

In its 2000 report, the JSCEM stated that the prisoner franchise should not be removed 'until there is sufficient and widespread public support for a change'. The government asserted that its 2006 move was supported by the Australian electorate; this is not, however, borne out by the submissions received by the Senate Finance and Public Administration Committee's inquiry into the Bill. Of the 39 submissions that addressed the prisoner franchise issue, only three expressed support for the Coalition's proposed change (from the Liberal Party, The Nationals and Festival of Light).[10] While it would be erroneous to argue that these figures are representative of the general view of the Australian electorate, it is significant that there was minimal explicit support for the change outside the Coalition parties.

There is very little information about public opinion on this issue; however, one newspaper poll in 2007 put public support for prisoners' voting rights at 62 per cent (albeit only a small, unrepresentative sample). While such an unscientific survey might be inconclusive, some of the arguments put forward by the Coalition are even more so. During one parliamentary debate on the issue, senior Liberal Senator Nick Minchin argued that the government position stood up to the 'pub test'—that is, the majority of people in a hotel bar would support the government's position—suggesting perhaps that, apart from its ideological position on the issue, the Coalition also supported the change as a populist (and partisan) measure.

Many of the submissions to the JSCEM inquiry opposing the change cited Article 25 of the International Covenant on Civil and Political Rights (ICCPR), which states that all citizens shall have the right and opportunity to vote at elections. This argument is consistent with developments in Canada and the United Kingdom in recent years. In Canada, no prisoners have been disenfranchised since the Supreme Court ruled in 2002 that disenfranchisement was in breach of the country's Charter of Rights and Freedoms. While the United Kingdom disenfranchises all prisoners, in 2004 and 2005 the European Court of Human Rights found this to be in contravention of the European Convention on Human Rights.

The ICCPR also refers to the purpose of prison being a place to rehabilitate offenders back into society. Some JSCEM submissions argued that the denial of voting rights removed the benefits of preparing prisoners for their transition

---

10   The Festival of Light was a lobby group promoting 'Christian values' and 'family values'. It is now known as Family Voice Australia.

back into society through the restoration of their responsibilities as members of the community. Furthermore, they pointed to the disproportionate impact on young males (the prison population is 93 per cent male) and Indigenous Australians.

## The 2007 High Court challenge

The Howard Government's law disenfranchising all prisoners was challenged in the High Court in 2007 by Vickie Lee Roach, an Indigenous woman who had been sentenced to prison for a total of six years on five burglary-related offences. The Roach case[11] was based on a number of arguments, but primarily that disenfranchisement of all prisoners was contrary to the constitutional requirement that parliament be 'directly chosen by the people'. In addition, it was argued that disenfranchisement denied prisoners their implied right to freedom of political expression and communication.

In September 2007, the High Court determined (by a 4–2 majority) that the blanket disenfranchisement was unconstitutional; however, it upheld the law previously in effect that prisoners serving sentences of three years or more would be disenfranchised. The reasoning of the High Court was that the blanket ban was an arbitrary disenfranchisement of a particular class of citizen, without regard to the circumstances in which those citizens became part of the prisoner class.

Justices Gummow, Kirby and Crennan's joint lead judgment refers to the 2004 legislative change that restricted the franchise to prisoners serving sentences of less than three years. They argued that such a restriction still gave regard to the seriousness of the offence as a measure of fitness to participate in the electoral process. This view was supported by Chief Justice Gleeson, who also suggested that a more restrictive disenfranchisement based on a lesser term (for example, prisoners serving terms of one year or more) would not necessarily be invalid. Gummow, Kirby and Crennan, however, appeared to be less positive towards the prospect of a more restrictive disenfranchisement, noting that the three-year sentence threshold mirrors the three-year electoral cycle that is entrenched in the Constitution.

---

11   *Roach v Electoral Commissioner* [2007] HCA 43.

# Prisoner franchise at the State and Territory levels

At the Australian sub-national level, there is a similar divergence of entitlements as occurs internationally. Three jurisdictions (Victoria, Queensland and the Northern Territory) adopt the Commonwealth standard—that is, following the High Court's 2007 Roach decision that prisoners serving terms of three years or less are entitled to vote. The Australian Capital Territory had adopted the Commonwealth standard of disenfranchisement until 2006. An aspect of the Howard Government's reforms, however, was that while prisoners were disenfranchised, they remained on the electoral roll. Section 128 of the Australian Capital Territory's *Electoral Act 1992* states that all enrolled electors are entitled to vote. The Howard reforms, perhaps unintentionally, actually extended the vote to all prisoners in the Territory. As one administrator noted:

> The ACT made it known to the Commonwealth that the ACT thought, given their human rights stance, that all prisoners should have the right to vote…I don't know who came up with the idea…which was that everyone in prison can enrol, but if you're in prison full-time you can't vote for federal elections, which gives the ACT what it wanted.

The effect of the 2007 High Court decision was to revert to the previous Commonwealth law (including the removal of prisoners from the roll). This therefore disenfranchised all prisoners for ACT elections. In response, the Stanhope Labor Government enacted its own legislation to enfranchise all prisoners. This was the first occasion on which the Australian Capital Territory administered an 'ACT only' category of enrolment separate to the Commonwealth.

Tasmania independently enfranchises prisoners serving sentences of less than three years (Section 31[2], *Electoral Act 2004*). New South Wales (Section 25, *Parliamentary Electorates and Elections Act 1912*) continues to enfranchise prisoners serving sentences of less than one year. This was also the case for Western Australia (Section 18, *Electoral Act 1907*) until it amended its Act in 2007 to completely disenfranchise all prisoners, in line with the Commonwealth change. In May 2008 the Carpenter Labor Government in Western Australia introduced new legislation to extend the franchise to prisoners serving sentences of less than three years, but the Bill lapsed on the prorogation of parliament ahead of the 2008 general election. Following a change of government in 2008, in mid-2009, the Barnett Coalition Government amended the legislation, reverting to the previous one-year sentence provision. South Australia has long-established laws enfranchising all prisoners, irrespective of the length of their sentences.

In light of the High Court decision, and particularly Justices Gummow, Kirby and Crennan's comments linking three-year sentences to the Australian Constitution's requirement for three-year electoral cycles, there could be some scope to argue that New South Wales' and Western Australia's one-year sentence threshold, alongside four-year electoral cycles, could provide conditions for a constitutional challenge. For example, the Australian Human Rights Commission does not believe that denying the vote to long-term prisoners satisfies the 'reasonableness' test at international law; however, there do not appear to be any moves in legal or human rights circles to mount such a challenge.

## Partisan impacts of prisoner voting

There is a belief, repeatedly expressed in the interviews, that allowing prisoners to vote provides a distinct advantage to the Labor Party. As one parliamentarian noted:

> Obviously that does benefit Labor. I was a scrutineer at a federal election at the remand centre and there were 14 people voting and I'm sure they all voted Labor or Green, but you're not talking a lot of people.

While results from recent federal elections do tend to suggest that this is the case, the advantage does not appear to be substantial, or beyond what could be expected in the general population. As Table 4.2 illustrates, the number of prisoners voting is small, but their votes generally favour Labor (though voting was more evenly divided at the 2010 election).

**Table 4.2 Prisoner Voting: Federal Elections 2001–10, Two-Party Preferred**

| Electorate and jurisdiction | 2001 | | 2004 | | 2007 | | 2010 | |
|---|---|---|---|---|---|---|---|---|
| | Labor | Lib/Nat | Labor | Lib/Nat | Labor | Lib/Nat | Labor | Lib/Nat |
| Fraser, ACT | 10 | 4 | 3 | 2 | 5 | 2 | - | - |
| Bass, Tas. | - | - | - | - | 3 | 1 | - | - |
| Franklin, Tas. | - | - | - | - | 3 | 3 | - | - |
| Kalgoorlie, WA | 90 | 16 | 144 | 46 | 20 | 13 | - | - |
| O'Connor, WA | 1 | 0 | 1 | 11 | 13 | 12 | 18 | 22 |
| Canning, WA | - | - | 7 | 2 | 6 | 4 | - | - |
| Durack, WA | - | - | - | - | - | - | 80 | 66 |
| Pearce, WA | - | - | - | - | - | - | 13 | 9 |
| Lingiari, NT | 77 | 10 | 90 | 9 | - | - | 89 | 98 |
| Total | 178 | 30 | 245 | 70 | 50 | 35 | 200 | 195 |

Note: These are electorates in which separate prisoner voting statistics are available.

Source: AEC election results.

Two electorates in which Labor appears to have obtained a large advantage are in the seats of Kalgoorlie and Lingiari in the 2001 and 2004 elections. These two seats have the highest proportions of Indigenous people in the country and, combined with the high imprisonment rate of Indigenous Australians, these are the likely reasons for such high Labor support in these seats. The 91 per cent support for Labor from prisoners in Lingiari in 2004 is consistent with the non-prisoner support for Labor in remote booths of Lingiari that have high Indigenous populations, such as Ti Tree Station (98.35 per cent Labor, two-party preferred), Titjikala (93.33 per cent), Kintore (86.99 per cent) and Willowra (84.19 per cent).

Analysis of interview data and parliamentary debates suggests that, although Labor might receive some electoral advantage from entitling prisoners to vote, their support for the prisoner franchise is based on genuine philosophical grounds rather than the prospect of partisan advantage. Likewise, the Liberal Party might see some small electoral advantage in denying prisoners the vote, but also tends to base its position on ideology. Comments by Liberal politicians such as Senator Minchin suggest, however, that populist positioning could also be a factor in the Liberal Party's policy. The participation principle of fairness supports the broadest possible franchise; however, Australia's mix of prisoner enfranchisement laws appears to be consistent with the diversity of laws applied internationally.

# 5. Enrolment, Turnout and Informal Voting

As the previous chapter discussed, adult Australian citizens enjoy a broad entitlement to vote at elections. That entitlement is not only a right, it is also a responsibility, due to Australia being one of only a small number of countries that enforces a compulsory voting regime. Three factors can, however, work against citizens being able to exercise this civic duty: first, getting onto the electoral roll; then getting a ballot paper (either at a polling booth or through the mail); and finally, making a formal vote.

## Closing the electoral roll

Ease of enrolment is an important element of access and equity for voters in the electoral process. Early closure of electoral rolls has the potential to impact in a negative way on such access, particularly for people who are in the process of moving location or are living in a remote area, and for young people wanting to enrol for the first time. Australia does not have fixed-date elections at the federal level. The prime minister is able to call an election, within a specified time frame, without notice. The writs for the election are issued shortly thereafter. In February 1983, Prime Minister Malcolm Fraser called an election for which the rolls closed 'almost immediately' after the announcement. The combination of an election being called with almost no warning and the sudden closure of the rolls meant that many citizens who would normally be eligible to vote were disenfranchised. As a result of this, the JSCER recommended that the rolls remain open for at least seven days following the formal announcement of an election. This seven-day period was duly brought into legislation in late 1983. During the seven days, citizens were able to newly enrol or update their enrolment if they had moved address or changed their name.

As a result of the Howard Coalition Government's 2006 legislation, however, the electoral rolls closed for new enrolments at 8 pm on the day that writs were issued, and three business days after the issuing of the writs for enrolment changes. The Howard Government's stated justification for this change was that it would enhance the integrity of the roll by preventing people from making fraudulent enrolments after an election is called. The government argued that by closing the roll earlier, the AEC would have additional time to verify new and updated enrolments. The government majority on the JSCEM recommended this change, with one of its arguments being that significant numbers of voters delayed updating their enrolment although legally required, waiting for the calling of an election to be prompted into action. Labor members of the committee argued otherwise, stating that the proposed change would reintroduce the problems that had occurred with the sudden close of rolls in 1983, when many potential voters were turned away at polling booths because they had been deleted from the roll or were enrolled at the wrong address.

A number of academics and human rights activists also mounted campaigns against this reform. For example, former Australian Electoral Commissioner Colin Hughes and Melbourne academic Brian Costar were vocal in opposing the change. Criticising the JSCEM arguments that the change would prevent fraud and ensure proper scrutiny of enrolments, Hughes and Costar argued that there was minimal evidence of fraud, and that the Australian National Audit Office had reviewed the roll and found it to have 'high integrity'. They also noted that the AEC had confirmed that all enrolments were equally scrutinised, irrespective of timing.[1] The Democratic Audit of Australia, based at The Australian National University, also promoted debate on the reform.[2]

At the 2004 election, during the seven-day period following the issuing of the writs, the AEC processed 78 816 new enrolments and 345 159 updated enrolments.[3] A further 150 000 people applied after the seven-day period, but prior to the election, and therefore were prevented from being placed on the roll, or having their enrolment amended, in time for the election.[4] The Howard Government provided the AEC with additional funding for a public awareness campaign to alert people to the earlier cut-off date. As a result, for the 2007 election, there was a combined total of 279 469 new enrolments and enrolment updates between the calling of the election and the close of the roll[5]—a reduction of 34 per cent from the 2004 figures.

The close of rolls for the 2010 general election was complicated by two court decisions that were handed down following the official close-of-rolls date. On 6 August (just two weeks prior to the election), the High Court ruled (the Rowe decision) in a 4–3 decision that the provisions for the earlier close of rolls was unconstitutional.[6] This required those people who had applied to be enrolled following the issuing of the writs, but within seven days of the issuing of writs (the pre–2006 period allowed), to be added to the roll. In addition, just eight

1   Colin Hughes and Brian Costar. 2005. 'Fiddling the Ballot Books.' *The Age*, 3 November.
2   For example, see Marian Sawer. 2006. *Damaging Democracy? Early Closure of Electoral Rolls*. Canberra: Democratic Audit of Australia, The Australian National University.
3   AEC [Australian Electoral Commission]. 2004. 'Over 13 Million Australians Have the Right to Vote in the 2004 Federal Election.' Media Release, 10 September. Canberra: Australian Electoral Commission.
4   Ian Campbell. 2006. 'Senate Finance and Public Administration Legislation Committee Hearing.' 7 March, *Hansard*. Canberra: Parliament of Australia, pp. 1–26.
5   AEC [Australian Electoral Commission]. 2008. *Submission to the Inquiry by the Joint Standing Committee on Electoral Matters into the 2007 Federal Election*. Canberra: Parliament of Australia.
6   *Rowe v Electoral Commissioner* [2010] HCA 46.

days before the election, and after pre-poll voting had commenced, the Federal Court ruled that electronically completed enrolment forms were acceptable, requiring further changes to the roll (the Getup! decision).[7] To accommodate these rulings, supplementary rolls were created, with more than 57 000 electors being added to the roll for the election.

Despite the confusion that had been created, and the administrative difficulties the AEC had in creating new rolls in the midst of an election period, these court decisions highlight the importance of having an independent arbitrator overseeing legislative reforms that are often driven by political self-interest. The Howard Government change to an earlier close of rolls is viewed as favouring the Coalition electorally, with groups more likely not to be enrolled, or correctly enrolled, at the calling of an election being the young, itinerant and Indigenous—all groups seen as more likely to vote Labor. The Australian Election Study figures from 2004 show that only 43 per cent of young people (under twenty-five years, the age cohort with the lowest proportion of eligible citizens enrolled) supported the Liberal and Nationals parties, while 49 per cent supported the left-wing parties (Labor, 32 per cent; Greens, 17 per cent).[8] A State Labor MP succinctly stated the argument to the author:

> It is a travesty of our democratic system that the Commonwealth committee pushed these changes through. It is nothing more than a deliberate attempt by a Liberal conservative government to disenfranchise further all of those people who may be Labor voters.

Over time, the AEC has adopted varying positions on the close-of-rolls issue. In a submission to the JSCEM in 2000, it noted that neither it nor the JSCEM had uncovered any organised or widespread attempt to defraud the roll through false enrolments in the previous 15 years. The AEC went on to state that the proposed early closure of the rolls would not improve the accuracy of the rolls for an election, and in fact the rolls would be less accurate, as electors would not have enough time to correct their enrolments or to apply for new enrolments. The AEC also stated that the change would have a negative impact on the franchise, that it would delay election results due to an anticipated rise in declaration voting, that it would have a particularly negative impact on young people seeking to vote for the first time, and that it would cause public confusion due to different systems operating at the State and Territory levels.

During questioning before the committee in 2005, the AEC reasserted the above position. At a hearing in March 2006, however, the newly appointed AEC Commissioner, Ian Campbell, stated that the earlier closure of the roll would

---

7   *Getup Ltd v Electoral Commissioner* [2010] FCA 869.
8   Clive Bean. 2005. 'Young People's Voting Patterns.' Paper prepared for the Youth Electoral Study Workshop, Old Parliament House, Canberra, June.

not create any difficulties and would actually 'make our life easier'.[9] Under new leadership, the AEC's focus appeared to have switched from accuracy at election time to ongoing accuracy between elections; however, the current Commissioner, Ed Killesteyn, appears to be more circumspect with his comments on this issue.

In 2010, the Rudd Labor Government had tried to reintroduce the seven-day period between the issuing of the writs and the closing of the rolls, but was blocked by the Coalition's opposition. Following the court decisions and the 2010 election, the Gillard Labor Government reintroduced legislation in November 2010. This was passed in May 2011, with the support of the Greens senators and Independent Senators Steve Fielding and Nick Xenophon. During the parliamentary debate, the Coalition continued to oppose the seven-day period, using arguments from the dissenting High Court judges, and in one case arguing that, in reference to the AEC's advertising campaign, 100 000 people being left off the roll in 2007 was actually a positive outcome:

> In 2004 168,394 people missed the deadline of seven days after the writs were issued. Yet in 2007, when the deadline fell at 8 pm on the day the writs were issued, only 100,370 people missed the deadline.[10]

## Automatic enrolment

There is growing concern as to the accuracy and completeness of electoral rolls in Australia. Although enrolment is compulsory for eligible Australians, an estimated 1.1–1.4 million people are not enrolled.[11] In the Howard Government's 2006 reforms, more stringent 'proof of identity' requirements were introduced (arguably to prevent fraudulent enrolments) for people wishing to enrol or to change their enrolment. The new identification rules made it more difficult for the AEC to enrol people, even when the commission was aware of an enrolled person's new address (for example, when the commission receives updates of motor vehicle registrations and rental agreements). Under current Commonwealth rules, the AEC may send an enrolment form to a person's new address, but the person has to fill out, sign and return the form to the AEC before becoming enrolled. The AEC and State commissions operate 'joint roll' agreements, where information is shared to make enrolment easier for voters, but differing rules between jurisdictions can create confusion.

---

9    Ian Campbell. 2006. 'Senate Finance and Public Administration Legislation Committee Hearing.' 7 March, *Hansard*.
10    Senator Mitch Fifield, *Senate Hansard*, 11 May 2011.
11    Australian National Audit Office. 2010. *The Australian Electoral Commission's Preparation for and Conduct of the 2007 Federal General Election*. Report 28/10. Canberra: Commonwealth of Australia.

An alternative to the current system is 'automatic enrolment' (also known as 'direct enrolment' or 'smart enrolment'), which takes advantage of modern technologies and database sharing, and is extensively used in many modern democracies, especially in Europe (see ACE Encyclopaedia). Under automatic enrolment a commission automatically enrols citizens when they turn eighteen years of age, and updates a person's enrolment once it is notified by government agencies that a person has changed address. The person is then informed that they are enrolled and is asked whether they have any objection to this. This changes the emphasis, requiring the person to take action to un-enrol, rather than to enrol.

Automatic enrolment would address, in particular, the relatively low enrolment of young people who tend to be highly mobile and either drop off the roll or never get on it. This, in turn, would give young people greater political voice. As with all attempts to achieve a more comprehensive roll, however, this might be seen as having partisan effects. Young people are less likely to vote for the conservative parties and more likely to vote for Labor or the Greens. In 2009, the NSW Parliament passed legislation for automatic enrolment, which was in place ahead of that State's 2011 election. The Victorian Parliament passed similar legislation in 2010. Nearly 60 per cent of Australia's voters live in these two states, and to avoid major disruption from having separate rolls for federal and State elections, it makes sense for the Federal Government to adopt automatic enrolment.

During debates on the close of rolls and automatic enrolment issues, reference is often made to the integrity of the roll, with Coalition politicians arguing that sufficient time is needed to verify new enrolees to prevent fraudulent enrolment. The Coalition has also argued for the introduction of 'proof of identity' requirements on the same 'integrity' grounds. Another integrity issue, however, is the integrity of the election result, which requires the largest possible participation of eligible voters in an election. While the two sides of politics in Australia's inherently two-party system see a partisan advantage in regulating enrolment, it will continue to be difficult for international best practice to be adopted in Australia.

# Voter turnout

The level of voter turnout in democratic elections is an indicator of the health of a democracy. An election is the primary interaction between citizens and government, and a decline in turnout levels can undermine the legitimacy of a democratic system.[12] With compulsory enrolment and voting in place for all Australian jurisdictions, it could be expected that voter turnout would not be a significant issue. An assessment of turnout at the 75 general elections that have been conducted in Australia from 1983 to 2011 demonstrates this is the case, except in the Northern Territory. As Table 5.1 shows, turnout at NT elections is consistently more than 10 per cent lower than all other jurisdictions, which regularly have a voter turnout of more than 90 per cent. It is also important to note that turnout figures compare the number of people who actually voted with the number of people enrolled, and not with the number *eligible* to be enrolled, which will be a larger figure, thereby reducing the turnout rate. With otherwise consistently high rates under compulsory regimes, a drop of a few per cent can be a cause for concern. The figures therefore indicate that there is a serious issue to be addressed in the Northern Territory.

### Table 5.1 Turnout Rates, Australian Elections, 1983–2011

| Jurisdiction | Turnout (%) 1983 ⟶ 2011 | Average turnout (%) |
|---|---|---|
| Common-wealth | 94.6 - 94.2 - 93.8 - 95.3 - 95.8 - 95.8 - 95.0 - 94.9 - 94.3- 94.8 -93.2 | 94.7 |
| New South Wales | 92.5 - 93.6 - 93.6 - 93.8 - 93.1 - 91.9 - 92.6 - 92.6 | 93.0 |
| Victoria | 93.2 - 92.4 - 95.1 - 94.1 - 93.2 - 93.2 - 92.7 - 93.0 | 93.4 |
| Queensland | 91.7 - 91.3 - 91.2 - 91.5 - 91.4 - 92.9 - 92.6 - 91.4 - 90.5 - 90.9 | 91.5 |
| Western Australia | 89.0 - 91.4 - 90.7 - 93.5 - 90.0 - 90.6 - 89.8 - 86.5 | 90.2 |
| South Australia | 93.5 - 94.4 - 93.6 - 91.8 - 93.6 - 92.3 - 92.8 | 93.1 |
| Tasmania | 94.2 - 93.1 - 95.6 - 96.0 - 95.0 - 93.7 - 95.0 - 93.9 | 94.6 |
| Australian Capital Territory | 88.8 - 90.3 - 89.5 - 92.6 - 90.9 - 92.8 - 90.4 | 90.8 |
| Northern Territory | 81.6 - 71.2 - 81.6 - 80.7 - 79.0 - 80.6 - 80.1 - 75.7 | 78.9 |

Sources: Various electoral commission reports and web sites.

12   Andrew Ellis, Maria Gratschew, Jon H. Pammett and Erin Thiessen. 2006. *Engaging the Electorate: Initiatives to Promote Voter Turnout from Around the World—Including Voter Turnout Data from National Elections Worldwide 1945–2006*. Stockholm: International IDEA, p. 12.

# Indigenous enrolment and turnout

A comparison between NT Assembly election turnout and voting in the Northern Territory at federal elections (Table 5.2) shows that turnout is consistently lower at assembly elections. There has, however, also been a notable drop in federal election turnout figures in the Northern Territory during the 2000s (average 84.9 per cent), compared with the 1990s (average 89.4 per cent). The Northern Territory has the highest proportion of Indigenous people in Australia (31.6 per cent)—significantly higher than the second-highest ranking jurisdiction, Western Australia (3.8 per cent).[13] One possibility for the drop in turnout at federal elections in the Northern Territory could be the abolition of the Aboriginal and Torres Strait Islander Election Education and Information Service (ATSIEEIS).[14]

**Table 5.2 Northern Territory Voter Turnout, 1983–2010 (per cent)**

| Year | Federal House of Representatives | NT Assembly |
|------|----------------------------------|-------------|
| 1983 | 81.4 | 81.6 |
| 1984 | 85.5 | - |
| 1987 | 79.9 | 71.2 |
| 1990 | 89.4 | 81.6 |
| 1993 | 88.8 | - |
| 1994 | - | 80.7 |
| 1996 | 89.1 | - |
| 1997 | - | 79.0 |
| 1998 | 90.3 | - |
| 2001 | 86.1 | 80.6 |
| 2004 | 84.3 | - |
| 2005 | - | 80.1 |
| 2007 | 86.5 | - |
| 2008 | - | 75.7 |
| 2010 | 82.7 | - |

Sources: AEC; Northern Territory Electoral Commission; Australian Government and Politics Database.

---

13 Australian Bureau of Statistics. 2007. '4705.0—Population Distribution, Aboriginal and Torres Strait Islander Australians, 2006.' Canberra: Australian Bureau of Statistics <http://www.abs.gov.au>

14 Although the ATSIEEIS was abolished in 1996, it can be argued that the positive impact of its programs remained for the 1998 election.

The ATSIEEIS program was concentrated in the federal electorate of Lingiari, which takes in all areas of the Northern Territory outside Darwin. Lingiari, established when the Northern Territory was split into two seats for the 2001 federal election, has the highest concentration of Indigenous voters in the country (43.5 per cent). This is more than double the next highest concentration—18.2 per cent in Kalgoorlie, Western Australia.[15] Since Lingiari's creation, it has recorded turnout figures of 80.6 per cent (2001), 77.7 per cent (2004), 81.3 per cent (2007) and 75.9 per cent (2010). Lingiari's are the lowest turnout rates in Australia.

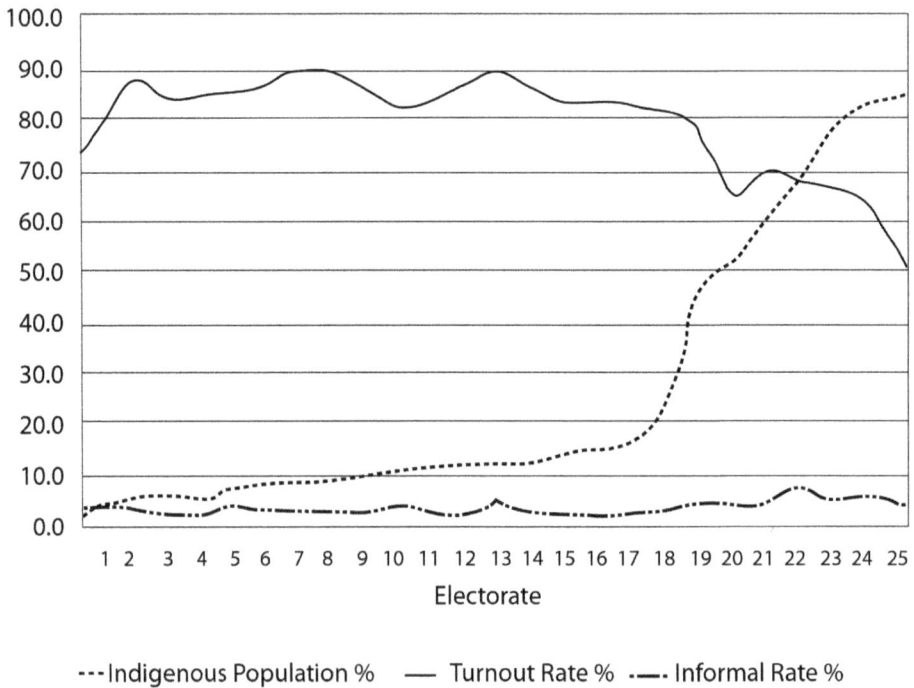

··· Indigenous Population %      —— Turnout Rate %   ·—· Informal Rate %

**Figure 5.1 Turnout at the 2005 NT Assembly General Election**

Note: See Appendix B for electorate data.

An analysis of elector turnout at NT elections presents a similar story, and, with its smaller electorates (about 4000–5000 enrolled), provides a more nuanced understanding of the issue. Figure 5.1 shows the correlation between Indigenous population and voter turnout at the 2005 general election. The six electorates with the lowest Indigenous populations (average 6.6 per cent Indigenous)[16] have an average turnout of 84.2 per cent, while turnout for the six highest Indigenous

---

15    Paul Nelson. 2007. *Electoral Division Rankings: Census 2006 First Release*. Research Paper 12 2007–08. Canberra: Parliamentary Library, Parliament of Australia, p. 33.
16    Port Darwin, Wanguri, Nelson, Nightcliff, Fannie Bay and Casuarina.

population electorates (average 70.7 per cent Indigenous)[17] averages only 64.4 per cent. The lowest voter turnout was in the Stuart electorate, with an 84.3 per cent Indigenous population and only 59.3 per cent turnout. Generally, voter turnout at by-elections tends to be lower than that for general elections, and at a by-election for the seat of Stuart in 2006, turnout was down to 53.9 per cent.

It is an added concern in the context of the legitimacy of election results if low turnout figures are compounded by high levels of informal voting, resulting in a significant gap between the level of formal votes and the number of people eligible to vote. It can be anticipated that there would be a correlation between literacy levels in remote Indigenous populations and the number of informal votes, and there is a trend over time towards higher informality in high-Indigenous electorates. The average informality rate at the 2005 general election for the six low-Indigenous electorates was 3.3 per cent, compared with an average 5.3 per cent for the six high-Indigenous electorates. Another factor in high-Indigenous areas could be the number of candidates contesting seats. Results from the assembly seat of Stuart emphasise this. In 2005, when only two candidates stood, the informal rate was 4.6 per cent. The following year six candidates contested the Stuart by-election, and the informality rate increased to 13.6 per cent.

# Abolition of ATSIEEIS

The abolition of the ATSIEEIS in 1996 is a good example of a government impacting directly on the ostensibly independent operations of an electoral management body, and potentially providing partisan advantages to the governing parties. The ATSIEEIS was a unit of the AEC that had been established in 1979 to target remote and urban Indigenous communities, with an ongoing focus on encouraging enrolment. In the nearly two decades for which it operated, the unit was seen as instrumental in improving the rates of Indigenous enrolment and voting, especially in remote areas. The value of ATSIEEIS was explained by one commissioner:

> They used to rip these poor Indigenous people off the roll, send out an objection letter, wouldn't matter if you couldn't read the bloody thing, you're off the roll. In the early '80s they were ripping them off the roll. It was a shocker. Then ATSIEEIS came along and started rectifying a lot of the stuff to quite a meaningful extent, but then when ATSIEEIS stopped, the capacity to send people out with non-voters' notices also stopped.

---

17   Stuart, Arnhem, Arafura, MacDonnell, Barkly and Nhulunbuy.

It is argued that since the abolition of the unit, enrolment rates for Indigenous people have dropped markedly.[18] This is seen as a distinct advantage for the Coalition, due to the high level of support for Labor in remote Indigenous communities. As one administrator stated:

> The issues are: we've got a high Indigenous rate, we've got a lot of people living in remote areas, it's a very young population, we've got a highly mobile population—so the more people you get on the roll, the more people you educate to participate in a meaningful way in elections. [It] would tend to advantage the ALP. That's not the reason we do it.

The Howard Government's move to abolish this unit was the first time that the AEC had been given an explicit instruction about how it may spend its budget. This instruction therefore raises the issue of whether such an intervention is a challenge to the AEC's independence. The impact of removing the ATSIEEIS program is summarised by two electoral commissioners as follows:

> Taking away ATSIEEIS's program in '97 had a significant impact on the delivery of education services and enrolment potential. In 10 years, you can actually see how it's affecting the roll.

> The best example of political interference in funding of electoral authorities is the fate of [ATSIEEIS]. It was a separate line item in the budget and they said, 'No, we're not giving you that any more, and you're not allowed to spend any other part of your budget on it. If you do, we'll take it off you.' I think that's entirely inappropriate and it should never have happened.

It was confirmed in interviews that if the AEC wished to reinstate a program such as the ATSIEEIS, it would not do so independently, but instead would make a request to the government to fund what is considered by the AEC as a politically sensitive program. As one administrator said:

> If there's sensitivity about it then you go through the minister's office... given that it was a program that was abolished by government then, yeah [it was politically sensitive]. No matter how independent you are, everybody is dependent upon somebody for money.

The AEC's dependence on government approval to undertake a program that could improve the accuracy and comprehensiveness of electoral rolls diminishes the independence of the electoral administration. That such a program was

---

18   Warren Snowdon. 2004. 'Senate Victory Used to Silence Voters.' Media Release, 20 December.

considered politically sensitive indicates that decisions might not be made in the interests of best electoral practice, but in response to the political leanings of the government.

Following the 2007 federal change to a Labor government, the AEC received $13 million in the 2009 Budget to establish the Indigenous Electoral Participation Program. The program has four objectives: electoral education, increased enrolment levels, increased election turnout, and reduced informal voting. This is a well-intentioned response to the declining participation rates shown above, but also will have electoral benefits for Labor. If an independent body could make budgetary decisions (as the AEC would have done if it had the power) then perceptions of partisanship would be removed.

# Administrative response to Indigenous enrolment and turnout

As discussed above, the manner in which Indigenous voter enrolment and turnout are dealt with by administrators and legislators provides a good insight into the drivers of reform—that is, whether reforms are driven by the interests of governing parties or are based on accepted norms for good electoral management. Interviews in jurisdictions with high proportions of Indigenous people consistently identified Indigenous enrolment and turnout as major and ongoing issues. This is especially so in remote areas with low accessibility, which are among those most likely to have high proportions of Indigenous people. A 2003 JSCEM report noted that the AEC, the Aboriginal and Torres Strait Islander Commission and the Labor Party had all expressed concerns about the under-enrolment of Indigenous people. The Labor submission to the inquiry estimated that Indigenous enrolment was only 54 per cent of those eligible, compared with 95 per cent of non-Indigenous Australians.[19] JSCEM stated in its 2003 report that it would pursue this issue, but the committee's report into the 2004 election did not refer to it.

A number of reasons have been suggested to explain low Indigenous turnout. Kate Alport and Lisa Hill cite antipathy, largely brought about by a lack of efficacy in terms of the relevance and impact of votes in determining election outcomes. They argue that the lack of enforcement of compulsory voting in remote areas is another key factor.[20] It is important to note that seats with

---

19   The ALP estimated 140 000 enrolled out of a possible 260 000 Indigenous people. Australian Labor Party. 2002. *Joint Standing Committee on Electoral Matters Inquiry into the 2001 Federal Election: Submission by the Australian Labor Party*. Submission no. 153. Canberra: Parliament of Australia.
20   Kate Alport and Lisa Hill. 2008. 'Voting Attitudes and Behaviour Among Aboriginal Peoples: Reports from 29 Anangu Women.' Refereed paper delivered at the Australian Political Studies Association Conference, Brisbane, 6–9 July, p. 3.

high Indigenous populations tend to be safe Labor seats. For example, the six high-Indigenous NT seats referred to earlier are held by Labor with margins of 62–76 per cent of the two-party preferred vote. There is therefore no electoral advantage for Country Liberal Party governments to encourage greater levels of Indigenous enrolment and participation, and in fact there is a disadvantage. One electoral administrator expressed a view on this issue:

> I said here's where we think we should be going with mobile polling places, what do you think? Well, the conservative side of politics don't like that idea, but they're not going to come out and say 'we don't want to see these people voting'.

Aspects of the Howard Government's 2006 reforms—especially the earlier close of rolls and the need for proof-of-identity for enrolment and provisional voting—were seen as additional barriers to higher levels of participation among Indigenous people. As Alport and Hill point out, '[m]any Aboriginal people do not carry a wallet, therefore there is nowhere to keep any cards and they are easily lost'.[21] Furthermore, because these are such safe seats, there is little incentive for Labor governments to take action to encourage participation.

Low voter turnout can also be a reflection of protest against government authority and can further explain low participation for this social group. This view was supported by one interviewee:

> You would have to work out how much of it was the abolition of the [ATSIEEIS] program and people going around, and how much was a general disillusionment with a particular section of the community with the government of the day. And certainly in the first six to eight years of [the Howard] government there's been quite a bit of tension between the Indigenous community and the government.

## NT Assembly elections: time frame

As shown in Table 5.2, voter turnout for NT Assembly elections is consistently and significantly lower than that for federal elections in the Northern Territory. A reason for this difference appears to be the short election campaign period between the calling of an assembly election and polling day. The Territory's *Electoral Act 2004* (Section 28, amended in 2009) requires that polling day must be 19 days after the issuing of the writ. This is the shortest timetable in operation in Australia and, as a result, all procedural aspects of NT elections

---

21   Alport and Hill go on to suggest, however, that photo identity cards could be useful to encourage enrolment and turnout, as a form of civic engagement.

need to meet tight deadlines. For example, rolls close two days after election writs are issued, nominations close a further two days later, and postal and mobile voting commences three days after that.

In addition to the short timetable for campaigns, until 2009 elections could be called at any time after the first three years of an assembly first sitting, enabling the chief minister to call an election with little warning. Together, these two factors would make it logistically difficult to conduct an election in any jurisdiction, but this is especially so in the Northern Territory, which has a large geographic area of dispersed settlement. The previous 18-day time frame was more than a week shorter than other Australian jurisdictions without fixed election dates. As one administrator noted in an interview, 'the ALP in opposition were very critical of the cramped timetable…certainly a government of any colour prefers to have control'.

The Minter Ellison report commissioned by the Labor government in 2003 was opposed to this short election period and recommended extending the timetable to 33 days. In addition, the NT Electoral Commissioner recommended that either fixed-date elections be introduced or the election time frame be lengthened by at least seven days.[22] It is evident that the short election campaign period can impact on voter turnout. Problems include accessing people in remote areas for enrolment, especially when they might have only one chance to vote at a mobile polling booth less than two weeks later, and having enough time for postal voters to receive and return their completed ballot papers. In some instances, election dates are known well in advance based on comments from the government. The 2008 general election, however, held on 9 August was considered to be a 'snap' election, with the announcement made only 19 days earlier. Turnout at the election was 75.65 per cent—the lowest for more than 20 years.

In 2009, the NT Government amended the *Electoral Act*, introducing fixed dates for future elections; however, the government extended the election period by only a day, from 18 to 19 days, to fit in with a timeline based on a five-day working week. The government's argument for not extending the period further was that with the introduction of fixed-date elections, people will have more warning. It does not, however, address the logistical issues of printing and distributing ballot papers, issuing postal voting papers, and voters not knowing the full field of candidates until, in some cases, a couple of days prior to voting.

---

22  Northern Territory Electoral Commission. 2007. *2005 Legislative Assembly General Election Report: Part 1 of 2*. Darwin: Northern Territory Electoral Commission.

# Informal voting

Any level of informal voting diminishes the legitimacy of election results and alienates voters through disaffection. The pattern and extent of informal voting provide insight into the health of an electoral system on a number of levels. Informal voting can be either deliberate (when voters choose not to make their vote count, for example, to make a protest) or accidental (as when voters inadvertently make a numbering mistake). Both deliberate and accidental informal voting are concerns for electoral administrators, the former because it signifies citizens' disconnection and disillusionment with the democratic system, and the latter because it indicates that voters do not understand the voting method, or that the process is too confusing or burdensome. Accidental informal voters are disenfranchised because the system has failed to provide an adequately simple method of voting.

In their study of informal voting in the 1987 and 1990 elections, McAllister et al. note that among established liberal democracies, Australia has one of the highest rates of informal voting.[23] Their study identified Australia's social structure as being a key determinant of informal voting. In particular, ethnicity is a significant indicator of informal voting levels, with a lack of English language proficiency increasing the likelihood of informal voting. In recent years, the AEC has published a number of reports assessing informal voting rates. The reports on the 2001 and 2004 elections[24] support McAllister et al.'s argument that proficiency in English is a significant determinant of informal voting. In addition, Gina Dario identifies two other important factors that influence levels of informal voting: the use of optional preferential voting at the State level (for New South Wales and Queensland) and the number of candidates contesting an election. These factors are discussed in relation to federal, State and Territory elections.

# Informal voting at federal elections

The high levels of informal voting in Senate elections were identified as a concern by the JSCER, which published the results of two informal voting surveys in its first report in 1983. These surveys—of the Senate elections in 1977 (Australia wide) and 1983 (14 selected divisions)—showed that more than 50 per cent of all informal Senate votes were a result of incorrect numbering caused by

---

23   Ian McAllister, Toni Makkai and Chris Patterson. 1992. *Informal Voting in the 1987 and 1990 Australian Federal Elections*. Canberra: Australian Government Publishing Service.
24   Rod Medew. 2003. *Informal Vote Survey, House of Representatives, 2001 Election*. Research Report no. 1. Canberra: Australian Electoral Commission; Gina Dario. 2005. *Analysis of Informal Voting During the 2004 House of Representatives Election*. Research Report no. 7. Canberra: Australian Electoral Commission.

either a break in the sequence or duplicating numbers. A further 25 per cent of informal votes resulted from voters not numbering all the squares. The Hawke Government's introduction of above-the-line Senate voting, which was used by more than 85 per cent of voters at the 1984 election, was instrumental in lowering the rate of informal voting for the Senate (see Table 5.3).

**Table 5.3 Senate and House of Representatives Informal Voting Rates (per cent)**

|        | 1980 | 1983 | 1984 | 1987 | 1990 | 1993 | 1996 | 1998 | 2001 | 2004 | 2007 | 2010 |
|--------|------|------|------|------|------|------|------|------|------|------|------|------|
| Senate | 9.7  | 9.9  | 4.7  | 4.0  | 3.4  | 2.6  | 3.5  | 3.2  | 3.9  | 3.8  | 2.6  | 3.7  |
| HoR    | 2.4  | 2.1  | 6.3  | 4.9  | 3.2  | 3.0  | 3.2  | 3.8  | 4.8  | 5.2  | 4.0  | 5.6  |

The relaxation of the requirement to number all boxes for those voting below the line was another intervention that further lowered the informal rate. From 1984, Senate ballot papers were formal if they clearly identified a sequence of preferences against at least 90 per cent of the candidates listed. For example, where there are 50 candidates on the ballot paper, numbering the ballot paper from 1 to at least 45 constitutes a formal vote.

While the 1983 reforms were successful in lowering the Senate informal rate, informal rates for the House of Representatives increased markedly following the same reforms. The AEC identified in its 1988 report that first preferences were clearly indicated in more than 62 per cent of all informal House of Representatives votes cast in the 1987 election. A relaxation of the rules to allow these votes to be added to the count would have reduced the informal rate from 4.9 per cent to 1.9 per cent.

**Table 5.4 Informal Voting Rates: 2004 House of Representatives Election**

| No. of candidates | No. ofseats | Highest rate (%) | Lowest rate (%) | Average rate (%) |
|-------------------|-------------|------------------|-----------------|------------------|
| 4                 | 3           | 5.53             | 3.61            | 4.31             |
| 5                 | 18          | 9.11             | 2.87            | 4.44             |
| 6                 | 29          | 9.24             | 2.76            | 4.68             |
| 7                 | 39          | 9.10             | 2.77            | 4.89             |
| 8                 | 30          | 11.71            | 3.40            | 5.64             |
| 9                 | 18          | 8.43             | 4.22            | 5.70             |
| 10                | 6           | 7.45             | 4.49            | 5.81             |
| 11                | 5           | 8.53             | 5.89            | 6.64             |
| 12                | 1           | 7.41             | 7.41            | 7.41             |
| 13                | 0           | -                | -               | -                |
| 14                | 1           | 11.83            | 11.83           | 11.83            |
| Total             | 150         | 11.83            | 2.76            | 5.19             |

As previously mentioned, the number of candidates contesting an election is a determinant of informal voting. The 2004 election figures show a positive correlation between candidate numbers and informal votes, with a steady increase in the informal rate as the number of candidates increases (Table 5.4). An examination of the highest and lowest informal rates for each category (of number of candidates) highlights the influence of other factors, such as ethnicity. For example, the high rate of 11.71 per cent of informal votes with eight candidates contesting occurred in the seat of Reid, an inner metropolitan electorate in Sydney. Reid has the highest proportion of people born overseas of all Australian electorates (49.5 per cent), and the second-highest proportion of people from non–English-speaking countries (35.5 per cent).[25] This relationship is further illustrated in Table 5.5, which presents electorates with the highest informal rates per candidate by location and ethnicity.

**Table 5.5 2004 House of Representatives High Informal Rates: Ethnicity**

| No. of candidates | Highest informal rate (%) | Electorate | NESC ranking |
|---|---|---|---|
| 4 | 5.53 | Throsby | 62 |
| 5 | 9.11 | Fowler | 8 |
| 6 | 9.24 | Prospect | 12 |
| 7 | 9.10 | Watson | 1 |
| 8 | 11.71 | Reid | 2 |
| 9 | 8.43 | Kingsford Smith | 25 |
| 10 | 7.45 | Lindsay | 65 |
| 11 | 8.53 | Parramatta | 16 |
| 12 | 7.41 | Dobell | 124 |
| 13 | - | - | - |
| 14 | 11.83 | Greenway | 48 |

Note: NESC = born in a non–English-speaking country. Ranking is of 150 electorates; 1 indicates the highest proportion of NESC.

Of the 10 seats with the highest rates of informal voting per number of candidates, more than two-thirds (seven) are ranked in the top third of electorates for numbers of people born in non–English-speaking countries. It is also significant that all of these 10 electorates are in New South Wales, where an optional preferential voting system is used at State-level elections. In an assessment of informal votes in New South Wales, Dario found that 35.65 per cent were made informal by the voter numbering '1' only, with a further 10.71 per cent of voters having incorrectly used a tick or cross. In all, 46.36 per cent or more than 116 000 voters in the State attempted to vote correctly but

---

25   Paul Nelson. 2007. *Electoral Division Rankings: Census 2006 First Release.*

were accidentally disenfranchised.[26] All of these votes would be formal under State election voting rules. It is important to note that the informal rate at the 2003 NSW Legislative Assembly election was 2.6 per cent—less than half of the 6.1 per cent the State recorded at the 2004 Federal House of Representatives election in New South Wales. This disparity is further evidence that confusion about different voting rules and making voting unduly burdensome contribute to informal voting.

**Table 5.6 2010 House of Representatives: 10 Highest Informal Rates**

| Informal rate (%) | Electorate | Number '1' only (% of total informal) | Ticks and crosses (% of total informal) | No. of candidates | NESC ranking |
|---|---|---|---|---|---|
| 14.06 | Blaxland | 29.6 | 12.0 | 8 | 3 |
| 12.83 | Fowler | 36.8 | 20.9 | 4 | 8 |
| 12.80 | Watson | 38.6 | 16.7 | 4 | 1 |
| 11.16 | Chifley | 31.4 | 14.5 | 7 | 18 |
| 10.84 | McMahon[a] | 34.1 | 22.5 | 4 | 12 |
| 10.35 | Werriwa | 33.5 | 18.8 | 3 | 26 |
| 10.27 | Greenway | 23.9 | 8.6 | 11 | 48 |
| 9.82 | Barton | 42.8 | 16.6 | 3 | 7 |
| 8.80 | Reid | 39.7 | 14.1 | 5 | 2 |
| 8.65 | Parramatta | 31.5 | 14.8 | 7 | 16 |

[a] formerly Prospect

Note: NESC = born in a non–English-speaking country. Ranking is of 150 electorates; 1 indicates the highest proportion of NESC.

Analysis of informal voting at the 2010 election reaffirms the influence of ethnicity and having a different voting system at the State level. Of the 150 House of Representatives seats, the 10 highest levels of informal voting were in contiguous electorates in western metropolitan Sydney, New South Wales (see Table 5.6). All of these seats also ranked in the top third of voters from non–English-speaking countries. The number of candidates contesting appears to have less influence in the 2010 election, with half of these seats having only three or four candidates. In analysis conducted by the AEC, it is shown that more than half of informal voters in these seats had shown a clear first

---

26 Gina Dario. 2005. *Analysis of Informal Voting During the 2004 House of Representatives Election*, pp. 15–16.

preference on their ballot paper, by marking a '1' only, or using a tick or cross.[27] This equates to nearly 48 000 voters being accidentally disenfranchised in these 10 electorates.

Proposals to introduce optional preferential voting have lacked support at the federal level. Parliamentarians have raised concerns about the potential impacts of relaxing the rules to allow '1 only' votes or votes using ticks and crosses. Concerns are largely based on the difficulty in discouraging voters from intentionally voting this way. The JSCEM report on the 1990 election highlighted this difficulty, with the committee stating that a change to the rules would encourage optional preferential voting, as well as 'Langer'-style voting.[28] The concern that a change to optional preferential voting would become a de facto first-past-the-post voting system has been confirmed by the experience of Queensland elections since optional preferential voting was introduced in that State.

In Queensland, a significant unforeseen impact of the reform to optional preferential voting is the change in how political parties run their campaigns. Prior to the 2001 election, the major parties advocated filling out all preferences. From 2001, however, parties have increasingly advised voters to 'just vote one', with all major parties now advocating this option on their how-to-vote material. As a result, approximately two-thirds of voters—63.03 per cent—used the '1 only' option at the 2006 election. This is confirming that the system is turning into a de facto first-past-the-post system, where seats are determined by a minority of votes and voters are not appropriately informed of their options. Consequently, while the reform is an improvement on fairness in regard to ease of voting, voters' ability to make an informed choice is diminished due to the limited information provided in parties' how-to-vote material.

## Informal voting at State and Territory levels

Analysis of informal voting at State and Territory elections provides an insight into the impacts of the voting systems in use. Using data for the lower house (or single house in unicameral systems) from the past three elections (Table 5.7), it is evident that the optional preferential voting system in place in New South Wales and Queensland consistently produces lower rates of voting informality.

---

27   AEC [Australian Electoral Commission]. 2011. *Analysis of Informal Voting: House of Representatives, 2010 Federal Election*. Research Report no. 12, 29 March. Canberra: Australian Electoral Commission, p. 30.

28   JSCEM [Joint Standing Committee on Electoral Matters]. 1991. *1990 Federal Election: Report from the Joint Standing Committee on Electoral Matters*. Canberra: Australian Government Publishing Service, pp. 41–2. Langer-style voting was promoted by Albert Langer so that voters could avoid directing preferences to one major party over the other by duplicating a number in their preferences—for example, by numbering the ballot paper 1, 2, 3, 4, 5, 5.

## Table 5.7 State and Territory Informal Rates: Lower/Single Houses

| Jurisdiction | Voting system | Informal voting rate (%) 1996 → 2007 | | | Average informal rate (%) | System average (%) |
|---|---|---|---|---|---|---|
| New South Wales | OPV | 2.51 | 2.62 | 2.77 | 2.63 | 2.37 |
| Queensland | OPV | 2.27 | 1.99 | 2.08 | 2.11 | |
| Victoria | FPV | 3.02 | 3.42 | 4.56 | 3.67 | 4.26 |
| Western Australia | FPV | 4.39 | 4.54 | 5.24 | 4.72 | |
| Northern Territory | FPV | 5.17 | 4.27 | 3.75 | 4.40 | |
| South Australia | FPV-Ticket | 4.04 | 3.12 | 3.60 | 3.59 | 3.59 |
| Tasmania | Hare-Clark | 3.91 | 4.87 | 4.49 | 4.42 | 4.04 |
| Australian Capital Territory | Hare-Cark | 4.32 | 3.97 | 2.68 | 3.66 | |

Notes: OPV = optional preferential voting; FPV = full preferential voting; FPV-Ticket = a '1 only' vote is formal, with full preferences distributed according to a ticket lodged by the candidate.

South Australia is the only Australian jurisdiction that uses ticket voting as an option for single-member electorates. Where voters make a '1 only' vote, preferences flow according to a ticket lodged by the candidate of their first (and only) choice. This could partially explain why South Australia's informal rate is lower than the other jurisdictions with full preferential voting. Ticket voting, however, makes up less than 5 per cent of all votes in SA Assembly elections, so its effect on informal voting cannot be substantial. The two jurisdictions operating under the Hare-Clark system of proportional representation, with no ticket voting, also record relatively high levels of informality. At the federal level, the average House of Representatives informal rate over the same period is 4.2 per cent—in line with other jurisdictions with full preferential voting.

## Table 5.8 Informal Voting: Queensland State Elections

| 1983 | 1986 | 1989 | 1992 | 1995 | 1998 | 2001 | 2004 | 2006 | 2009 |
|---|---|---|---|---|---|---|---|---|---|
| 1.47 | 2.17 | 3.00 | 2.25 | 1.75 | 1.45 | 2.27 | 1.99 | 2.08 | 1.94 |

Sources: Electoral Commission of Queensland; Australian Government and Politics Database.

The introduction of optional preferential voting in Queensland for the 1992 election appears to have had little impact on the rate of informal voting, which has already been at a low level since the 1980s (see Table 5.8). Optional preferential voting is usually expected to reduce rates of informal voting (as discussed above in the Victorian case study). There are two reasons this has not occurred in Queensland. First, the rate of informal voting was already low prior to the change; second, voters fill out only one ballot paper on election day, removing the confusion experienced by voters in bicameral jurisdictions.

Another interesting aspect of the State and Territory figures is the decreased rate of informal voting when electronic ballots are used in the Australian Capital Territory, which has been partly a result of the introduction and increasing use of electronic voting. The use of electronic voting can have significant democratic benefits, including increased accessibility for people with a disability and voters living in remote areas. It also enables more rapid and accurate counting of votes. Electronic voting was introduced as a trial for the 2001 ACT general election. The almost accidental initiation of the reform process that occurred for the introduction of electronic voting provides insight into the importance of personal relationships in achieving reforms, especially when there are no apparent partisan advantages to the reform. The Australian Capital Territory's Electoral Commissioner described the process as follows:

> Electronic voting and counting was a huge coup…The main reason we succeeded was that after the 1998 election we had to do a recount in Molonglo, when we had three or four votes difference between two candidates and we did a full recount, and actually worked out we got it wrong the first time around. I was wanting to do something that was more accurate and Kate Carnell got in as chief minister at that election.

> At the declaration of the poll, we started talking about electronic voting and counting. I said I would love to do electronic voting and counting but it's going to cost a bomb. I can't imagine you would be prepared to pay that. She said, 'Yes, we would—do it.'

**Table 5.9 Use of Electronic Voting and Informality Rates in the Australian Capital Territory**

| Election | Paper votes | Informal rate (%) | Electronic votes | Informal rate (%) |
|----------|-------------|-------------------|------------------|-------------------|
| 2001 | 182 162 | 4.3 | 16 559 | 0.6 |
| 2004 | 181 580 | 2.9 | 28 169 | 1.1 |
| 2008 | 176 199 | 4.1 | 43 820 | 2.6 |

Sources: ACT Electoral Commission, 2002, 2005, 2009.

At the 2004 election, 13.4 per cent of all votes were lodged electronically—an increase from 8.3 per cent at the 2001 election. The 2008 election saw a further increase in electronic votes to 19.9 per cent of all votes. While the electronic voting system allows voters to make an informal vote, accidental informal voting is almost entirely eliminated, as the system issues a warning to the voter that their vote will be informal if they continue. The impact of electronic voting can be seen in the reduced level of informal voting in the past three elections compared with votes cast by paper ballots (Table 5.9).

The reduction of informal voting has democratic implications for voters: with unintentional informal voting being virtually eliminated, fewer voters are accidentally disenfranchised. It has been suggested by Elections ACT that the particularly low level of informal electronic voting in 2001 (0.6 per cent) was due to electronic voters in 2001 being a self-selecting sample of voters who opted to use the new system, who were possibly more committed to lodging a formal vote than other voters. In 2004, electronic voting was the more common form of voting at booths where this was possible; the informal rate in the 2004 election therefore more accurately reflects the impact of electronic voting on the general population. The level of informal electronic voting at the 2008 election was significantly higher than in previous elections. Part of the reason was that about one-quarter of the informal votes (295 of 1152) were due to barcodes being discarded by electors prior to their votes being lodged. This could be intentional informal voting or, more likely, a problem with inadequate voter education.

## Reducing the level of informal voting

It can be seen from the examples in this chapter that there are several mechanisms available to reduce the relatively high levels of informal voting in many Australian jurisdictions. While shifting from a bicameral parliament to a unicameral system simply to reduce the informal rate by a couple of per cent would understandably be viewed as an extreme measure, easier solutions are readily available to legislators.

First, a move from full to optional preferential voting would not only reduce the informal rate, but also quash the argument that voters should not be compelled to number all boxes when they are also compelled to vote. Positions on optional preferential voting tend to be based on political pragmatism. In brief, although Labor governments introduced optional preferential voting in New South Wales and Queensland, the party currently supports full preferential voting because it means they receive the majority of preferences from Greens voters, ahead of the Coalition. Under an optional system, many of these votes would likely be exhausted prior to reaching the Labor candidate. Interestingly, the Coalition also supports full preferential voting as it allows Liberal and Nationals candidates to support each other in contests against Labor candidates. Some Coalition members, however, are now supporting optional preferential voting as a means of limiting the preference flow from the Greens to Labor.

JSCEM's report on the 2010 federal election provides interesting political arguments for reducing informal voting. While the Labor members were opposed to optional preferential voting, they did support a saving provision (which currently exists in SA state elections) where '1 only' votes would be directed in a way determined by the '1' candidate/party. This is incorrectly called a saving provision, which implies an accidental mistake made by the voter filling out the ballot paper. It actually enables the candidate/party to capture first-preference votes and direct them to other candidates in a way that might go against a voter's wishes. The Coalition committee members were strongly opposed to this recommendation.

A simpler and more effective solution would be to have a genuine saving provision that captures '1 only' votes, with those votes exhausted once the candidate is eliminated. To prevent elections becoming pseudo first-past-the-post contests, candidates and parties could be prohibited from advocating '1 only' voting in their campaigning material. This would be a fairer outcome, as it would not be subverting informal voters' preferences to candidates/parties.

The use of electronic voting in the Australian Capital Territory has clearly shown its value in reducing the rate of informal voting. While electoral commissioners around Australia have shown genuine interest in implementing similar systems, their difficulty, as with many innovations, is in getting legislative reforms to allow this to be used. The ACT jurisdiction has an ideal geographic and demographic profile to implement electronic voting, with a small, well-educated population situated in the northern half of the Territory. Ideally, the computer hardware could be used for trials in other jurisdictions, as a step towards more widespread implementation.

# 6. Registration of Political Parties

Political parties play a critical role in healthy democracies. One of their main functions is to provide an organised way of developing policy that represents societal cleavages. In addition, parties cultivate a democracy's future leaders, they give a sense of order and stability to parliamentary organisation and debate, they bring together disparate groups and individuals into processes of democracy, they recruit political activists, and they provide defined choices in election campaigns.[1] In modern democracies, it would be hard to imagine an organised and stable political environment without some form of political party structure.

While there might be a tendency for parties to naturally form to embrace new or existing social views, the institutional design of electoral systems allows for a form of 'political engineering' to occur—either encouraging the formation of new parties (typically where a democracy's party system is weak) or creating barriers to the continuation of existing parties or the formation of new parties. Barriers are typically erected in multi-party democracies where an excess of parties has created confusion for voters at elections or where there might be instability in government or parliament. Barriers can also be used as an anticompetitive measure in democracies where established parties seek to thwart potential new participants (or to deter non-genuine competition). A healthy democracy would normally provide a balance between encouragement and restriction in its party regulation regime.

Organised political parties and other political bodies have existed in Australia for more than 100 years, but it is only in the past 30 years that significant reforms have occurred to recognise parties in a formalised sense for electoral purposes. These purposes include ballot paper design, funding and disclosure requirements, and the distribution of voter preferences. In addition to influencing the capacity for citizens to coalesce into political groupings, such reforms impact on the ability of candidates to compete on a fair and equal basis. The favoured status given to registered political parties—for example, in accessing public funding and identification on ballot papers—also impacts on the ability of political organisations to deliver messages to voters during election campaigns. Such messages are essential to enable voters to make an informed choice.

---

1   Benjamin Reilly, Per Nordlund and Edward Newman. 2008. *Political Parties in Conflict-Prone Societies: Encouraging Inclusive Politics and Democratic Development*. Policy Brief no. 2. Tokyo: United Nations University.

# Registration criteria

The formal registration of political parties in Australia commenced in New South Wales in 1981, and has generally been viewed as a necessary corollary to other reforms such as public funding, party identification on ballot papers and above-the-line ticket voting. All jurisdictions impose conditions concerning the name of a party. Consistent across all jurisdictions are requirements that

- party names are to have a maximum of six words
- obscene names are prohibited.
- In addition, in every jurisdiction, party names are not to
- resemble the name of another, unrelated party
- be likely to cause confusion with another party
- contain the word 'independent' or 'independent party'.

Commonly, the following information is a condition of application for registration

- the name of a person to be the party's registered officer (in Western Australia, the party secretary)
- an abbreviated form of the party name, for ballot paper purposes
- a copy of the party's constitution (except Tasmania).

In Queensland, the constitutions of registered parties must include rules stipulating that preselection ballots are to be based on 'principles of free and democratic elections'. In addition, four jurisdictions require a fee for registration: $500 for the Commonwealth, Victoria and the Northern Territory; and $2000 for New South Wales.

All Australian jurisdictions also require a minimum membership size before a party may be registered. The minimum number of members differs widely, especially when compared with the total number of people enrolled in the jurisdiction. As Table 6.1 illustrates, the variation currently extends by a multiple of approximately 47, from the Commonwealth's one member per 28 174 enrolled to the Northern Territory's one member per 599 enrolled. Apart from these two outlier jurisdictions, however, the remaining seven jurisdictions are reasonably consistent, with a ratio of about 2400–7200 enrolled per party member. The capacity of citizens to form into political groupings is evident from Table 6.1. The Commonwealth, with a relatively low threshold, has the highest number of parties; conversely, the Northern Territory has the lowest number of parties contesting elections.

## Table 6.1 Party Membership Requirements for Registration

| Jurisdiction | Minimum required members | Enrolled at most recent election (year) | Enrolled/ required members | Parties contesting most recent election* |
|---|---|---|---|---|
| Commonwealth | 500 | 14 086 869 (2010) | 28 174 | 23 |
| New South Wales | 750 | 4 635 810 (2011) | 6181 | 14 |
| Victoria | 500 | 3 582 232 (2010) | 7164 | 10 |
| Queensland | 500 | 2 660 940 (2009) | 5322 | 6 |
| Western Australia | 500 | 1 330 399 (2008) | 2661 | 10 |
| South Australia | 150 | 1 093 316 (2010) | 7289 | 15 |
| Tasmania | 100 | 357 315 (2010) | 3573 | 4 |
| Australian Capital Territory | 100 | 243 471 (2008) | 2435 | 8 |
| Northern Territory | 200 | 119 814 (2008) | 599 | 3 |

* Separate divisions of a party (for example, Liberal NSW, Victoria; Labor, Country Labor, and so on) or cooperative alliances (for example, Australian Greens, Greens NSW) are counted as one party.

Sources: Electoral Commission election data.

The Commonwealth has a relatively low party membership requirement, given the size of the Australian electorate. Understandably, there have been suggestions that the threshold should be increased, possibly to 1000 members.[2] Based on the 'members to electors' ratio, and given the number of parties contesting recent elections, this suggestion appears to be reasonable. It is not unusual, however, for parties to have a distinct geographical base. Indeed, for Commonwealth registration, the major parties register separate parties based on State and Territory divisions.

A 500-member requirement assists the formation of parties based on local or regional issues, an example being the Save the ADI Site Party (SAS) in the 2001 and 2004 elections. SAS was registered in October 2001 to campaign for the retention of government-owned bushland in Sydney's western suburbs. The land had previously been used by Australian Defence Industries (ADI) and the government was proposing to sell it for residential development. In 2001, SAS fielded candidates in four House of Representatives seats, achieving a substantial vote of 3.29 per cent (in Chifley). In the 2004 election, SAS contested three lower house seats (receiving a strong vote of 2.67 per cent in Lindsay) and stood two candidates for the Senate. Once the ADI bushland was sold to developers, SAS's reason for existence was eliminated, and the party was voluntarily deregistered

2  JSCEM [Joint Standing Committee on Electoral Matters]. 2005. *The 2004 Federal Election: Report of the Inquiry into the Conduct of the 2004 Federal Election and Matters Related Thereto*, p. 91.

in August 2005. An increased threshold for registration would limit local-issue groups having a democratic voice via mobilisation as a political party in this way.

# Parliamentary representative alternative for party registration

As an alternative to meeting the membership requirement to register a party, four jurisdictions allow that a party may be registered if it has a parliamentary representative. South Australia adopts a relaxed approach with its parliamentary representative rule, requiring only that the representative be a member of a parliament or assembly of any of Australia's nine jurisdictions (*Electoral Act 1985*, s. 36). The other three jurisdictions—the Commonwealth, Queensland and Western Australia—specify the parliamentary representative must be a member of that jurisdiction's parliament.

In the case of Western Australia's amending legislation in 2000, the Electoral Commissioner, Ken Evans, recommended that Queensland's registration procedure be followed.[3] This procedure included a provision that parties with current parliamentary registration did not have to satisfy the 500-member rule. As a preventative measure to preclude independent members of parliament from subsequently setting up their own separate party, the WA legislation (*Electoral Act 1907*, s. 62I) specifies that the 'parliamentary representative' rule applies only to pre-existing parties that had a parliamentary representative on 14 June 2000, when the legislation was introduced to parliament. At the time, there were five independent parliamentarians, of whom four were originally elected as either Labor or Liberal party representatives, and this provision was considered to be a measure with those members specifically in mind. The provision also allowed at least one party, the Australian Democrats, to contest the general election six months later as a registered party at a time when it would not have satisfied the 500-member rule.

The Commonwealth, Queensland and SA Acts do not contain any provisions to prevent a member of parliament from establishing his or her own party after being elected either as an Independent or as a representative of another party. At the Commonwealth level, this loophole was used by Senator Meg Lees to establish the Australian Progressive Alliance party after she resigned from the Australian Democrats in 2002.

---

3 Norman Moore MLC. 2000. *Electoral Amendment Bill 2000—2nd Reading Speech*. Parliamentary Debates, *Hansard*, vol. 363. Perth: Parliament of Western Australia, pp. 8530–1.

Where the legislation provides two separate ways to qualify for party registration—by either membership level or parliamentary representation—there is a question of fairness based on equal opportunity. The membership-level criterion requires identified membership support within the community, while the parliamentary representation criterion is based on having sufficient voter support for an individual to be elected. When a party is registered because it has an existing parliamentary representative, there is no requirement to demonstrate any minimum level of party membership support. It could be argued that having a representative elected demonstrates that such parties have a significant level of electoral or community support; however, this argument does not hold where the representative was elected as a member of another party and later resigned (as in Meg Lees' case).

The lack of equity in the registration of parties is compounded in the three jurisdictions that allow parliamentarians to form new parties after they have been elected. In those cases, the representative does not have to show that there is any level of support for the party, in terms of either membership or public support. The Northern Territory's Minter Ellison report did not recommend a parliamentary representative criterion due to the inequitable effects of such a provision:

> It is arguable that a political party that only has one member does not fall within the meaning of 'political party', which is usually taken to denote a collection of people sharing some common political principles or goals.[4]

## SA registration regime

South Australia has difficulties with its party registration regime, which was introduced as part of the State's 1985 electoral reforms. Parties are able to lodge a voting ticket for the direction of preferences for both legislative council and house of assembly elections. This provides an incentive, as has occurred in New South Wales, for multiple parties to register and to then trade preferences for the 'harvesting' of votes. This incentive also appears to have driven the growth in registered parties in South Australia since 1985.

---

4   Minter Ellison Consulting. 2003. *Independent Review of the Northern Territory Electoral System: Final Report and Recommendations*. Canberra: Minter Ellison Consulting, p. 85.

## Table 6.2 South Australia: Registered Parties

| Election | Registered parties | Parties standing candidates | |
|---|---|---|---|
| | | Council | Assembly |
| 1985 | 5 | 5 | 4 |
| 1989 | 10 | 7 | 7 |
| 1993 | 14 | 10 | 9 |
| 1997 | 24 | 12 | 8 |
| 2002 | 30 | 19 | 10 |
| 2006 | 28 | 10 | 8 |
| 2010 | 34 | 15 | 13 |

Sources: State Electoral Office. 2007. *Election Report: South Australian Election: 18 March 2006*. Adelaide: State Electoral Office; House of Assembly. 1986. *General Elections 1985*. Adelaide: Government Printer.

As Table 6.2 illustrates, a larger number of parties compete in council elections, where preference flows are especially important due to the proportional representation voting system. The incentive of directing preferences was described well by one legislator:

> Once again, the rules are written for one regime, but someone gets smart about it, and I think what happened [is] a large number of parties were registered when someone was going for an upper house seat.

> Someone twigged that if they could set up enough parties, there'd be enough people who would vote for each named party that by the time those preferences flowed on—because someone with a bit of political nous figured out that I might pick up about 1 per cent if I called a party this, and half a per cent for this, and I might actually get over the line simply because of the preferences of those particular groups.

In South Australia, the legislation also enables a person to be counted as a member of more than one party, for the purpose of meeting the registration requirement. This provision underpins the groupings of parties that occur. The Australian Labor Party (which has also registered the New Labor Party and Country Labor Party) and the Nationals Party (and its Young Nationals Party) probably have a sufficiently high membership to have distinct members for each party. The most extreme overuse of this provision, however, is the Over-Taxed Motorists, Drinkers, Smokers Association, which registered five other parties (four of which were registered on the same day): the Smokers Rights Association, the Over-Taxed Smokers Association, the Over-Taxed Drinkers Association, the Over-Taxed Motorists Association and the Over-Taxed Pokies Party. Despite repeated calls by the Electoral Commission for reform, the ability to use the same individuals to register multiple parties remains unchanged. As one administrator explained:

From time to time electoral commissioners have made recommendations—1997 election, 2002 election, and now the 2006 election. There was a recommendation made that the same voters should not be used in reaching the membership thresholds of more than one party, and that's perfectly sensible.

Similarly, the commission has called for a restriction on the use of frivolous party names—again, without success.[5] This recommendation appears to be directed at parties such as the Stormy Summers Reform Party and Albert Bensimon's No Hoo Haa Party.

Three other jurisdictions—Queensland, Tasmania and the Australian Capital Territory—also allow the same members to be used to register more than one party. In these jurisdictions, however, the incentive to use multiple parties to direct preference flows is absent. In Queensland (six parties at the past election), the system of single-member electorates and optional preferential voting removes this incentive, while in Tasmania (four parties) and the Australian Capital Territory (10 parties, including two 'Independent' groupings) the Hare-Clark voting system precludes ticket voting. It is therefore more likely in these jurisdictions, compared with South Australia, that electoral outcomes will more accurately reflect voters' wishes.

## Determining the Northern Territory's party registration regime

Prior to reforms in 2004, political parties were not recognised in the Northern Territory's *Electoral Act*. Reasons for this included the lack of a public funding scheme and the fact that party names were not shown on ballot papers prior to the 2005 election (candidates' photographs were shown; see Figure 6.1).

The 2003 Minter Ellison review of the electoral system recommended that, as with all other Australian jurisdictions, ballot papers should show party affiliations, and therefore a party registration regime should also be introduced. The review considered the question of a reasonable membership level, drawing on examples in other Australian jurisdictions. In its report, the review team recommended that the threshold be 20 members, noting that they had received evidence that a higher threshold requirement of 50 members could prevent

---

5   State Electoral Office. 2007. *Election Report: South Australian Election: 18 March 2006*, p. 61.

some of the larger parties from registering.[6] While the figure of 20 members might appear to be very low, this was at a time when there were only about 112 000 registered voters in the Territory.

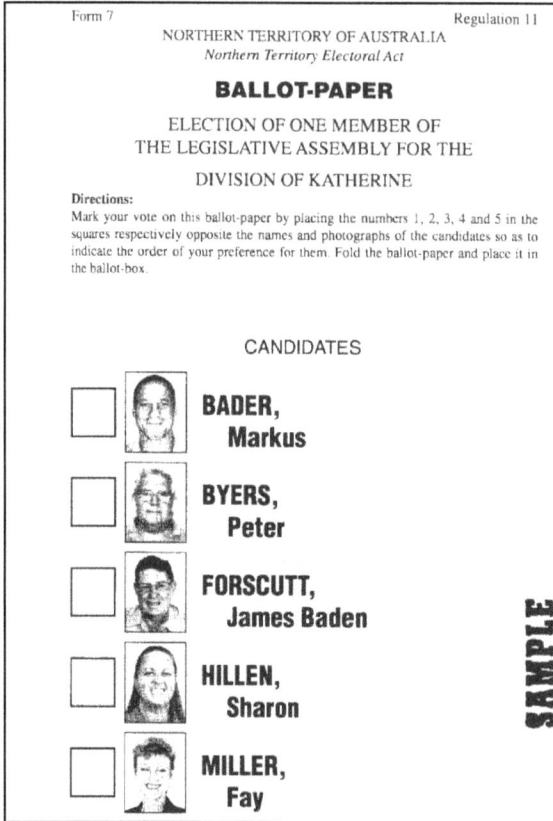

**Figure 6.1 NT Ballot Paper (from Katherine by-election, 2003)**

When the government introduced its legislation in November 2003, it stipulated a 50-member registration requirement. The day before debate on the legislation commenced in February 2004, the government lodged an amendment, changing the figure to 200 members—a tenfold increase on the original number recommended by Minter Ellison. The only explanation that the government gave for increasing the proposed threshold was the need to protect access to the electoral roll, which was available to registered parties but not to other parties or candidates (except by viewing at electoral offices). The late change resulted in party registration being the most hotly debated issue of the new electoral framework, as the following Hansard extracts attest:

---

6   Minter Ellison Consulting. 2003. *Independent Review of the Northern Territory Electoral System: Final Report and Recommendations*, p. 85.

[N]ow the Labor Party has come to power, the power has seduced so that, by the utilisation of this mechanism with 200 required to formulate an official party, it basically takes it out of the reach of community groups and puts it largely into only the domain of more established parties such as the ALP or CLP. (Terry Mills, CLP)

This is a deliberate attempt to obliterate opposition by the Labor government. (John Elferink, CLP)

[T]his has been brought in to kill off political opposition. I just think this is a crying shame…This is anti-democratic…supporting this bill means that I will sign the death warrant for any small party that wants to start in the Northern Territory…This is putting politics ahead of principle. (Gerry Wood, Independent)

The high threshold required to register parties in the Northern Territory is reflected by the low number of registered parties, with only three—the Country Liberal Party (CLP), Labor and the Greens—contesting the 2005 and 2008 elections. It can be argued that this registration scheme restricts citizens from being able to organise into political groups to access the political process; however, statistics from the NT elections held prior to the party registration legislation being passed in 2004 do not support this (see Table 6.3). Before party registration, an average of 3.8 parties contested each general election from 1983—similar to the three parties contesting the two most recent elections. The number of candidates ranged from 63 to 85 during the earlier period, compared with 80 and 66 in 2005 and 2008 respectively. To date, the legislation has not resulted in any significant difference in terms of electoral competition by parties and candidates.[7]

**Table 6.3 Candidates and Parties Contesting NT Elections**

| Election | Seats | Candidates | Parties |
|---|---|---|---|
| 1983 | 25 | 66 | 3 |
| 1987 | 25 | 85 | 3 |
| 1990 | 25 | 80 | 4 |
| 1994 | 25 | 63 | 3 |
| 1997 | 25 | 66 | 4 |
| 2001 | 25 | 86 | 6 |
| 2005 | 25 | 80 | 3 |
| 2008 | 25 | 66 | 3 |

7  It is also interesting to note that two candidates were elected unopposed at the 2008 election (in the seats of Arnhem and MacDonnell)—a rarity in modern Australian elections.

With no evidence to the contrary—apart from Chief Minister Claire Martin's claim regarding access to the electoral roll—it would appear that Labor's move in 2003–04 to ignore the review's 20-member recommendation and increase the threshold first to 50 members and then to 200 members was purely a manoeuvre to damage its major opponent: the CLP. This is borne out by the CLP's strong criticism during debate on the legislation, and is supported by the comments of one electoral official:

> It's a bit subjective. There was some suggestion that even the CLP was struggling to get 200. If they were governing for 27 years, and they've only been out of power for a few years, you'd have to say if that was the case, you should probably err on the side of not being too demanding.

While the Territory's reform process appears to have been quite comprehensive and broadly consultative, it was restricted due to the powers that the Commonwealth retains over certain aspects of the Territory's electoral system. Electoral issues beyond the scope of the Minter Ellison review included the manner of representation—the Commonwealth's *Northern Territory (Self-Government) Act 1978* stipulates that there are to be single-member electorates, each having no greater than a 20 per cent variance (higher or lower) from the average enrolment. In addition, it is not possible for the Territory to specify the extent of the franchise (Section 14 of the Commonwealth Act) or extend the period between elections (Section 17). In 2003, the Territory's Solicitor-General was unable to give a definitive position on whether the Territory could legislate for fixed-date elections.[8] Fixed-date elections were introduced, however, in an amendment to the *Electoral Act* in 2009. There also appears to have been a desire for the Minter Ellison review to satisfy the Labor government. As one review team participant noted:

> [The government] ended up adopting pretty much everything that was recommended, but the consultant team from Minter Ellison was very keen to put up proposals that would be smiled upon, so whenever we met anything that was likely to be contentious, we said: 'Here are the options; you choose.'

In the Northern Territory, the primary catalyst for electoral reform in the past 25 years was the 2001 change of government. Once Labor achieved government, it immediately set about reforming the system (and particularly the administration), which was viewed as being too close to the former Country Liberal Party. A year after the reform process was completed, Labor won the 2005 election with an increased majority. Whether the reforms serve to entrench Labor in power is

---

8   Minter Ellison Consulting. 2003. *Independent Review of the Northern Territory Electoral System: Final Report and Recommendations*, p. 45.

hard to determine. As the reforms were largely administrative, it is doubtful that there is any significant partisan advantage, except for the party registration regime, which is contrary to the participation principle of fairness.

# Too many parties: the 1999 NSW Legislative Council election

The March 1999 NSW Legislative Council election produced one of the largest ballot papers ever used in Australia (and possibly the world), with 81 groupings (including 78 parties) comprising 264 candidates. The 'tablecloth' ballot paper measured 102 cm by 72 cm. Its size created major logistical issues for the election, requiring the construction of wider voting booths and the use of larger planes for transporting papers. The election also produced some intriguing results, including the election of an Outdoor Recreation Party candidate, Malcolm Jones, who polled 0.19 per cent of the primary vote (a quota being 4.5 per cent). Jones was elected with the support of preferences from 21 other parties, including eight that had received a higher primary vote than the Outdoor Recreation Party.[9] The problems associated with the 1999 legislative council election represented the culmination of a series of earlier reforms and provided the impetus for further reforms.

From the mid-1980s, reforms were introduced by both Coalition and Labor governments, initially by Liberal Premiers Nick Greiner and John Fahey, and later by Labor Premier Bob Carr. Some Coalition reforms also required approval by referendum, with successful referenda being held in conjunction with the 1991 and 1995 elections. Reforms affected many aspects of elections, including: the number of members to be elected and the length of terms; ballot paper design, including the use of above-the-line ticket voting (single vote and preferential) and group voting tickets; and party registration requirements.

Table 6.4 presents a summary of legislative council election results from 1984 to 2011, and highlights several issues relevant to democratic principles of equity and access. As the table shows, the increase in parties and candidates at the 1999 election is obvious; however, significant increases in both are apparent prior to this (in 1995). The success of A Better Future For Our Children candidate, Alan Corbett, in being elected in 1995 on a low 1.28 per cent primary vote and a favourable flow of preferences (requiring 4.5 per cent to achieve a quota) obviously encouraged the formation of many parties for the 1999 election. The electoral laws in place at the time facilitated the formation of new parties.

---

9   Antony Green. 2003. *Prospects for the 2003 Legislative Council Election.* Background Paper no. 3/03, NSW Parliamentary Library Research Service. Sydney: Parliament of New South Wales, p. 27.

Although one of the party registration criteria was a requirement for 200 members, a person could be a member of more than one party for registration purposes and it appears that several parties used petition lists to meet their 200-member requirement.[10]

**Table 6.4 NSW Legislative Council Election Results, 1984–2011**

| Year | Groups/parties[1] | Candidates | Informal vote (%) | Gallagher's Least Squares Index[2] |
|------|------|------|------|------|
| 1984 | 8 | 43 | 6.66 | 3.77 |
| 1988 | 13 | 56 | 8.08 | 4.84 |
| 1991 | 12 | 54 | 5.67 | 4.68 |
| 1995 | 28 | 99 | 6.11 | 9.47 |
| 1999 | 81 | 264 | 7.17 | 8.69 |
| 2003 | 16 | 284 | 5.34 | 4.88 |
| 2007 | 20 | 333 | 6.11 | 5.47 |
| 2011 | 16 | 311 | 8.00 | 5.78 |

[1] Includes 'Independent' groupings and 'Ungrouped' column.

[2] The smaller the index figure, the more proportional is the result. Data in Appendix C.

The Carr Labor Government responded quickly to the negative publicity received by the tablecloth ballot paper. The *Parliamentary Electorates and Elections Amendment Act 1999* was passed in November 1999, driven by a desire to avoid the complexities and difficulties of the 1999 election. The Act's amendments were targeted at ballot design and party registration, to reduce the number of parties contesting council elections. The main amendments were

- abolishing group ticket voting (removing the ability for parties to direct preferences)
- allowing voters to record preferences above the line
- increasing the membership requirement for party registration from 200 to 750
- removing the opportunity to register a party based on having a member of parliament (rather than having a minimum number of members)
- removing the capacity for a person's membership to be used to meet the membership requirement of more than one party
- requiring a $2000 registration application fee
- parties to be registered one year ahead of an election for party identification on ballot papers
- increasing the powers of the electoral commissioner to investigate whether party membership is genuine.

10   Antony Green. 2003. *Prospects for the 2003 Legislative Council Election*, p. 8.

The impacts of these reforms can be clearly seen in Table 6.4. There was a significant reduction in the number of parties contesting the 2003 election (16, down from 81); however, there was an increase in the number of candidates (284, up from 264). This was due to the combined effect of removing ticket voting, introducing optional preferential voting above the line, and the pre-existing requirement for a voter to indicate preferences from one to 15 in order for a vote to be counted as formal. That is, parties needed to field at least 15 candidates for a vote that is recorded as a '1' or a tick for the party to be counted.

The final two columns of Table 6.4 provide evidence of other impacts that the system, and its reforms, has had. In regard to informal voting, it can be argued that reforms have had little impact, as the rate has remained consistently high throughout the study period. Reforms have, however, included the introduction of above-the-line ticket voting (from the 1988 election), being able to use a tick to record a formal vote (from 1995) and optional preferential voting (from 2003)— all innovations that would be expected to lower the informal rate. One of the reasons these interventions have not reduced the informal vote is that the size of the ballot paper, especially since the 1995 election, has been intimidating and confusing to voters. This might be especially so as voters are confronted with a vastly different (and smaller) ballot paper for legislative assembly elections, and have to deal with different above-the-line rules for federal Senate elections. In addition, the changes that have occurred throughout the period have potentially made it difficult for voters to become familiar with any one format, or for voter education programs to make a long-term impact.

Using Gallagher's Least Squares Index (LSI), the impact of the reforms is evident for the 1995 and 1999 elections, with disproportionality in these polls at its worst out of the seven elections during the study period. Proportionality improved at the 2003, 2007 and 2011 elections, but remains at a level higher than pre 1995. This could, however, be due to the general increase in legitimate minor parties in more recent times. Another factor is the methodology in calculating the index, which accentuates the impact of very small parties being grouped together.[11]

In terms of fairness, the ultimate results of these reforms are positive for candidates and parties, with competition now more genuine. In addition, representation now more closely reflects voters' choices, with an average proportionality index value of 5.38 for the three most recent elections, compared with an average of 9.08 for the 1995 and 1999 elections. While it might now be easier to make an informed choice, the continuing high level of informal voting remains a serious concern.

---

11   For these calculations, all parties receiving less than 1 per cent were grouped together under 'Independents and Others'.

# Party registration: achieving a balance

A well-constructed party registration regime could assist the conduct of fair elections by organising election candidates into clearly identifiable groupings, providing genuine competition and allowing voters to make informed choices. If the regime does not strike the right balance, it could unfairly restrict competition or allow excessive competition, as seen in the 1999 NSW election. Generally, however, when asked about their party registration procedures, electoral administrators were satisfied with existing provisions, particularly in regard to membership requirements. Responses included the following commissioners' comments:

> If they've got any worthwhile support, they can register quite easily. The reality is that after an election or two, if they don't get many votes, they fade away. But it's not that there's a problem—it's difficult enough so that you're not going to get nutty parties too often.

> If you're serious about contesting then you should have...people who are prepared to say I support you publicly. I think if you can't find... members, how are you going to win seats?

An argument supported by several administrators is that systems with single-member electorates create a disincentive for registration, as small parties do not see a great opportunity to win seats. This was particularly the case in Queensland and the Northern Territory, the two jurisdictions without any form of proportional representation. These jurisdictions had only seven (Queensland) and three (Northern Territory) parties contesting their most recent elections. This is consistent with research conducted by Duverger, Rae and others, who have argued that majoritarian systems support two-party systems.[12]

The 2004 NT parliamentary debate on party registration raised a further issue in relation to the benefits of registration: access to the electoral roll. It is common for members of parliament and registered parties to receive details of the electoral roll in electronic form. The main reasons cited for this are the need to promote their policies and to converse with the public. Access to the roll in this form is, however, denied to potential Independent candidates prior to an election being called, and this puts those candidates at a disadvantage, as they are not able to compete on an equal basis with party-nominated candidates.

---

12    Maurice Duverger. 1951. *Political Parties: Their Organization and Activity in the Modern State*. New York: Wiley; Douglas Rae. 1967. *The Political Consequences of Electoral Laws*. Clinton, Mass.: Colonial Press.

# Deregistration of the Liberals for Forests

The ability of a government to use legislation to structure electoral competition is evident in the case of the Liberals for Forests party. One component of the 2006 Howard Government's reform package was deregistration of all parties that did not have existing or past parliamentary representation. This resulted in the deregistration of 19 parties in December 2006. It is believed that the key motivation for this aspect of legislation was to prevent the Liberals for Forests party from continuing to use 'liberal' in its name. The legislation was based on a recommendation by the JSCEM in its 2004 election inquiry report. The JSCEM recommendation reflected previous Liberal Party concerns about the use of 'liberal' and the Richmond electorate result in 2004.

The Liberals for Forests was originally registered in 2001, following an Administrative Appeals Tribunal of Australia (AATA) ruling against the AEC's decision not to register the party (which was in part based on objections from the Liberal Party). In support of its decision, the AATA referred to words such as 'liberal', 'labour', 'progressive', 'national', 'socialist' and 'democrat' as being generic and therefore not owned by one particular entity.[13] The Liberals for Forests had registered its name in the lower case, to identify its ideological position as 'small-"l" liberals' and to differentiate itself from the Liberal Party. The Howard Government legislated[14] to prevent the use of names that could be confused with existing parties, but could not apply this condition to parties already registered. A solution was to deregister all parties without parliamentary representation, requiring a reapplication under the new law. Of the 19 parties deregistered, eight have re-registered.[15] Possible reasons other parties have not re-registered include an inability to meet the 500-member test or a lack of ongoing activity.

While the Liberal Party has been successful in removing registration of the Liberals for Forests at the federal level, it has not had the same success at the State level. In Western Australia, Liberals for Forests was registered as a party from July 2001, and stood candidates in the 2005 state election. The process of deregistering the party at the Commonwealth level, however, raises two main concerns. First, it is through legislation that

---

13 See paragraph 40, *Woollard and Australian Electoral Commission and Liberal Party of Australia (WA Division) Inc* [2001] AATA 166.

14 *Electoral and Referendum Amendment (Enrolment Integrity and Other Measures) Act 2004*, Amending Section 129 of the *Commonwealth Electoral Act 1918*.

15 As of December 2008, the parties that had re-registered were the Christian Democratic Party (Fred Nile Group), Citizens Electoral Council of Australia, Non-Custodial Parents Party, One Nation Western Australia, Queensland Greens, Socialist Alliance, The Australian Shooters Party and The Fishing Party.

governing parties have enormous power to limit electoral competition. This reflects the importance of the institutional structure of Australian electoral administration—a key theme in this thesis.

Second, the AATA has raised the important question of whether existing parties should be able to control the use of names that are based on ideology or history, such as those mentioned above. The possibility of voter confusion is, however, a real concern. The AATA made its position clear: 'It is unlikely that any elector, seeing the two names on a ballot paper, will draw the conclusion that "liberals for forests" is a political party related to the Liberal Party of Australia.'[16] The only other debate on the issue has occurred in the highly partisan JSCEM inquiry. There does not appear to be any systematic assessment of whether voters are confused by subtle variations in names.

This analysis of party registration regimes has shown that partisan interests have heavily influenced the development of party law. Some reforms have been initiated by governing parties for the purpose of eliminating opponents, such as the Coalition's actions in deregistering the Liberals for Forests and Labor's high threshold for registration in the Northern Territory. Other developments in this area have resulted from party cartelisation, as in Western Australia's 2000 reform. It can be seen from the examples discussed that the participation principle of fairness, under which citizens should have equal opportunities to form political parties, is diminished by the partisan behaviour of governing parties.

---

16  Administrative Appeals Tribunal of Australia. 2001. *Woollard and Australian Electoral Commission and Liberal Party of Australia (WA Division) Inc* [2001] AATA 166 (6 March 2001).

# 7. Political Finance

It is not surprising that money is one of the most critical factors in election campaigns. Access to money has become even more important in Australia in recent decades with the increasing role of electronic advertising, which consumes a significant share of the major parties' campaign expenditure. Therefore, the ways in which parties may receive and spend money have been the subject of significant public debate. The Coalition and Labor are keenly divided on some aspects of regulation—for example, donation disclosures; however, they act as a cartel in areas where there is joint benefit, such as public funding.

By international standards, Australia is relatively unregulated in the ways political parties and candidates may raise and spend money. Australian jurisdictions have few limitations on who money may be received from, how much may be raised or how much may be spent on election campaigns. In addition to having virtually no limits on the amount that may be raised through private donations, most Australian jurisdictions also provide public funding of parties and candidates, based on their vote at elections.

Many democracies place limits on the influence of private money in electoral contests. In IDEA's 2003 survey of 111 countries, a majority had donation disclosure regimes, while a significant number (32 countries) placed caps on contributions to parties.[1] Partially to compensate for these restrictions, and to limit the influence of private money, there are currently 112 countries (of 196) that provide direct public funding to political parties.[2] It is unusual to allow unrestricted levels of private funding while also providing substantial amounts of public funding.

This chapter concentrates on three aspects of political finance in Australian electoral law, which have been the focus of debate and legislative reforms in recent years. First, the origins of public funding and its subsequent growth are examined. Second, the setting of a threshold for disclosures of private donations provides a good example of the major parties legislating for self-interest (and possibly with some ideological basis). Finally, the tax deductibility of donations raises questions of fairness and equity.

This is therefore not an attempt to cover all matters relating to political finance, but instead to explain some of the history of current political finance law and how regulation of political money is decided by those who stand to benefit. For

---

1   Reginald Austin and Maja Tjernström, eds. 2003. *Funding of Political Parties and Election Campaigns.* Stockholm: International IDEA.
2   ACE Electoral Knowledge Network, <http://aceproject.org>

more comprehensive discussions on the role of money in Australian politics, the writings of Joo-Cheong Tham, Graeme Orr and Sally Young provide useful insight.

# Public funding

The importance of public funding for the fairness of political financing regimes is suggested by the Australian Democratic Audit assessment question 'is there fair access for [candidates and parties] to the media and other means of communication with the voters'. With a few exceptions, the public funding of parties' and candidates' participation and campaigning in elections is a relatively recent democratic initiative, occurring in Australia since the early 1980s.

The arguments for public funding put forward by American political scientist Michael Johnston are that some level of funding encourages electoral competition and strengthens parties both organisationally and for campaigning purposes.[3] Sally Young and Joo-Cheong Tham contend that public funding can provide a way to introduce accountability measures, such as financial reporting and disclosure.[4] Some parties, particularly those in government, are able to attract substantial private funding. Public funding provides a mechanism to cover basic administration and campaign costs for all parties, based on criteria such as registration, meeting reporting deadlines, voting support and party membership. Johnston goes on to argue that while partial public funding is beneficial for the health of a democracy, full public funding can be counterproductive, introducing disincentives for citizen mobilisation and the possibility of corruption.[5]

The introduction of public funding at the Commonwealth level in 1983 changed the nature of electoral competition by providing a guaranteed source of income for parties and candidates who achieve at least 4 per cent of the formal vote. When introduced ahead of the 1984 election, funding was based on the reimbursement of election campaign expenditure, with the rate of funding (per vote) based on the cost of a postage stamp for each of the three years between elections, and indexed to the rate of inflation. This amount (originally 90 cents) was then divided, with two-thirds for House of Representatives votes and one-third for Senate votes. Parties and candidates had to submit expenditure receipts

---

3   Michael Johnston. 2005. *Political Parties and Democracy in Theoretical and Practical Perspectives: Political Finance Policy, Parties, and Democratic Development*. Washington, DC: National Democratic Institute for International Affairs, p. 9.

4   Sally Young and Joo-Cheong Tham. 2006. *Political Finance in Australia: A Skewed and Secret System*. Canberra: Democratic Audit of Australia, The Australian National University, p. 37.

5   Michael Johnston. 2005. *Political Parties and Democracy in Theoretical and Practical Perspectives: Political Finance Policy, Parties, and Democratic Development*, p. 15.

for reimbursement from their public funding entitlement. The application of different rates for the House and the Senate was explained by arguing that MPs experienced greater constituency demands than Senators; however, it potentially disadvantaged those parties that targeted Senate elections and thereby gained greater numbers of Senate votes than House votes.

In its first report in 1983, the JSCER stated that the Labor Party and the Australian Democrats were supportive of a public funding system. Labor's support was based on the argument that elections should be decided on the quality of policies rather than the ability to raise campaign funds. Labor went on to argue that public funding would 'narrow the differential in the financial resources available to the various competing parties'. The Liberal and National parties were initially opposed to public funding, citing the lack of public support and that public funding would entrench incumbent parties and disadvantage potential new entrants.

In 1995, two major changes occurred to the public funding regime, following recommendations by the JSCEM. The *Commonwealth Electoral Amendment Act 1995* removed the need to prove expenditure, thereby changing the nature of funding from a reimbursement to an entitlement. This change broke the direct connection between funding and election campaign costs. Second, the funding rate was substantially increased. There was a 50 per cent increase for House of Representatives votes, from $1.01 to $1.50, and, in a move to equalise funding between House and Senate votes, public funding for Senate votes was trebled from 50.4 cents to $1.50. The rationale put forward during the parliamentary debate for the Senate increase was based on the JSCEM recommendation that House and Senate votes should receive the same level of funding, because 'as much effort is required to gain a Senate vote as a House of Representatives vote'.[6] While the JSCEM had recommended equal funding, it left unanswered the question of whether funding levels should be increased or simply redistributed equally between the two houses.

The Hansard records show that both the Labor and the Liberal parties strongly supported the changes. In his second reading speech, the Labor Minister for Administrative Services, Frank Walker, referred to JSCEM's rationale for equalising House and Senate payments, but made no reference to the fact that the rate was being substantially increased, and did not provide a supporting argument for the increase. In a similar vein, Liberal MP Peter Slipper simply stated: 'The rate will be increased to $1.50 per vote and will be indexed. The Coalition will not be opposing this.' Apart from Labor and the Coalition, the

---

6   JSCEM [Joint Standing Committee on Electoral Matters]. 1994. *Financial Reporting by Political Parties: Interim Report from the Joint Standing Committee on Electoral Matters on the Inquiry into the Conduct of the 1993 Election and Matters Related Thereto*. Canberra: Parliament of Australia, p. 9.

Australian Democrats were the most significant beneficiaries of the increase. Their spokeswoman, Senator Meg Lees, made no reference to the increase in her second reading speech.

In contrast, the Greens received far less public funding during this period and were more vocal in their opposition to the increase. Greens spokeswoman Senator Christabel Chamarette stated that:

> The amendments to the bill were not recommended by the joint committee…they were part of a private deal which appeared to be engineered by the Federal Secretary of the ALP and agreed to in letters to the Minister for Administrative Services from the Liberals, the Nationals and the Democrats…Everybody is going to have at least a doubling of their funding.[7]

As a result, the cost of public funding has substantially increased since the 1996 federal election, as Table 7.1 shows. Due to the funding rate being linked to the consumer price index (CPI), the rate has increased from $1.50 per vote in 1995 to its current (January to June 2012) rate of $2.42. In recent elections, public funding has accounted for about one-third of the total cost of conducting federal elections.

**Table 7.1 Public Funding Payments ($ million)**

| 1984 | 1987 | 1990 | 1993 | 1996 | 1998 | 2001 | 2004 | 2007 | 2010 |
|------|------|------|------|------|------|------|------|------|------|
| 7.81 | 10.30 | 12.88 | 14.90 | 32.15 | 33.92 | 38.56 | 41.93 | 49.00 | 53.16 |

Sources: JSCEM; AEC.

At the State and Territory levels, three jurisdictions—South Australia, Tasmania and the Northern Territory—do not have public funding. The other jurisdictions also use the 4 per cent threshold for funding, with rates of approximately $1.50 to $1.70 per vote. Funding is provided as either full or partial reimbursement of electoral expenditure, whereas for federal elections, funding is provided automatically, irrespective of expenditure.

In 2005, the JSCEM acknowledged the ability for candidates to profit from the public funding scheme. The committee's concerns were raised after Pauline Hanson received nearly $200 000 in public funding as a Senate candidate at the 2004 federal election, despite spending only $35 000 on campaign expenses. Labor claimed this was 'blatant profiteering for personal benefit'.[8] The committee

7  Senator Christabel Chamarette. 1995. 'Commonwealth Electoral Amendment Bill 1995—Second Reading Speech.' *Hansard*, 11 May. Canberra: Parliament of Australia.
8  JSCEM [Joint Standing Committee on Electoral Matters]. 2005. *The 2004 Federal Election: Report of the Inquiry into the Conduct of the 2004 Federal Election and Matters Related Thereto*, pp. 325–6.

did not recommend changes at the time, but in 2011 recommended reverting to a reimbursement-based scheme.[9] The Gillard Labor Government currently (March 2012) has legislation before the Senate to return to a reimbursement of expenditure requirement.[10]

New South Wales has the most progressive funding scheme, with funds also provided for the administration of registered parties ($80 000 per elected member, up to a maximum of $2 million). For registered parties without elected members, funds are available for policy development, based on 25 cents per vote received at the most recent election, up to a maximum $5000, paid annually. This scheme is in line with the recent electoral funding reforms in that State, which include caps on electoral campaign expenditure and political donations, as well as prohibiting political donations from specific sources: property developers and the gambling, liquor and tobacco industries. The need for such prohibitions highlights the influence that donations can wield and leaves open the question as to what influence legitimate donations might have.

By their nature, public funding schemes ensure that the major vote winners at an election are the major funding recipients. Currently, the major parties— Labor, Liberal and The Nationals—can be relatively assured of a certain amount of public funding, as can the Greens (and previously the Democrats), to a lesser extent. For other parties, particularly new parties, it is not easy to predict whether the 4 per cent threshold in votes, which is required to receive any public funding, will be achieved. It is difficult therefore for such parties to budget for an election campaign. Table 7.2 shows the level of funding received by selected parties and candidates over the past four federal elections.

It can be seen from the table that for most parties, public funding provides a relatively reliable income stream. For parties that experience greater fluctuations from election to election, such as was the case for the Democrats, a drop in voter support can have serious financial implications in planning an election campaign. In the Democrats' case, their vote dropped for the House of Representatives from 5.41 per cent (2001) to 1.24 per cent (2004), and then to 0.72 per cent (2007). For the Senate, the Democrats' vote decreased from 7.25 per cent (2001) to 2.09 per cent (2004), and then to 1.29 per cent (2007). The amount received by parties or candidates without parliamentary representation is quite small, as can be expected. This might indicate that the public funding scheme is simply supporting existing parties, rather than new entrants. The growth of the Greens, One Nation and Family First since 1983 is, however, a counterargument to this proposition. The numbers of parties and candidates receiving public funding

---

9    Recommendation 15, in JSCEM [Joint Standing Committee on Electoral Matters]. 2011. *Report on the Funding of Political Parties and Political Campaigns*. Canberra: Commonwealth of Australia, p. 128.
10    Commonwealth Electoral Amendment (Political Donations and Other Measures) Bill 2010.

since 1993, shown in Table 7.3, suggest that there is no significant trend in the number of parties receiving support, but further analysis would be required to assess other factors in the number of parties receiving public funding.

**Table 7.2 Public Funding Payments: Selected Parties and Candidates ($ million)**

| Party/candidate | 2001 | 2004 | 2007 | 2010 |
|---|---|---|---|---|
| Labor | 14.917 | 16.710 | 22.030 | 21.226 |
| Liberal | 14.492 | 17.956 | 18.134 | 21.098* |
| Nationals | 2.845 | 2.967 | 3.240 | 2.486 |
| Democrats | 2.412 | 0.008 | 0.000 | 0.000 |
| Greens | 1.594 | 3.317 | 4.371 | 7.213 |
| Family First | - | 0.158 | 0.141 | 0.407 |
| Country Liberal Party | 0.139 | 0.159 | 0.169 | 0.179 |
| Pauline Hanson's One Nation | 1.170 | 0.056 | - | - |
| Pauline's United Australia | - | - | 0.213 | - |
| Peter Andren MP | 0.073 | 0.079 | - | - |
| Bob Katter MP | 0.064 | 0.064 | 0.068 | 0.088 |
| Tony Windsor MP | 0.064 | 0.090 | 0.111 | 0.130 |
| Nick Xenophon | - | - | 0.312 | - |
| Other | 0.789 | 0.418 | 0.435 | 0.336 |
| Total | 38.559 | 41.926 | 49.003 | 53.163 |

* Includes Liberal National Party of Queensland.

**Table 7.3 Number of Parties and Independents Receiving Public Funding, 1993–2010**

| | 1993 | 1996 | 1998 | 2001 | 2004 | 2007 | 2010 |
|---|---|---|---|---|---|---|---|
| Parties | 11 | 8 | 12 | 13 | 10 | 7 | 10 |
| Independents | 17 | 12 | 16 | 21 | 15 | 15 | 17 |

Although the public funding rate was originally calculated on a three-year funding cycle, by-elections held between general elections also attract funding. The cost of this additional funding is currently about $150 000 per by-election (depending on the size of the electorate and results). The by-elections held in the seats of Mayo and Lyne in September 2008 had a combined cost of almost $299 000 in public funding. In December 2009, two more by-elections (Bradfield and Higgins) cost $260 000. The substantial cost raises the question of whether public funding should be provided for by-elections, especially where by-elections are caused by the voluntary resignation of an MP, as was the case in these four examples, and especially as the original premise of public funding was based on postal expenses over a three-year electoral cycle.

In sum, public funding has produced mixed results in terms of fair access to communicate with voters. While the major parties are the significant beneficiaries of the regime, smaller parties have been able to compete and grow, with public funding an important component of their financial support. For the purpose of political parties playing an important role in informed public debate, the NSW reforms that provide funding for parties' core administrative functions and policy development are refreshing. The primary driver of public funding, however, both in its implementation and in most subsequent amendments, is partisan self-interest. As one Labor politician commented to the author, 'both the Liberal Party and the Labor Party could see that they were going to pick up an enormous amount of taxpayers' money for nothing'.

## Donation disclosure thresholds

As Ewing and Ghaleigh point out, the concerns of ensuring that political parties are adequately funded and that individuals' rights to privacy in making donations are protected need to be balanced by the democratic state's interest in having a political system free of corruption and with voters being able to make informed decisions.[11] These informed decisions include knowing the causes and interests that a candidate is likely to represent in parliament. With these reasons in mind, there is a strong argument for establishing and maintaining an effective disclosure regime.

Public funding schemes provide an opportunity to introduce accountability and transparency regimes. This is regarded as part of the social contract; if parties and candidates are to receive public money for campaigning purposes, they need to disclose to the public the amounts and sources of private money donated towards the same purpose. In 1983, the Hawke Labor Government introduced donation disclosure legislation, requiring donors and political parties to disclose donations above a specified amount. The threshold for disclosure was originally set at $1000, and increased to $1500 in 1991. The Howard Coalition Government's 2006 legislation increased the disclosure threshold from $1500 to $10 000, and introduced annual indexation based on the CPI.[12] Due to inflation, the threshold currently (to June 2012) sits at $11 900. From the time the Coalition obtained a majority on the JSCEM in 1996, the committee recommended increases to the threshold—of $5000 in 1996 and to $10 000 following the 2004 election. In its submission to JSCEM in 2005, the Liberal Party noted that it would not be realistic to expect that amounts below $10 000 could create an undue influence

---

11    Keith Ewing and Navraj Singh Ghaleigh. 2006. 'Donations to Political Parties in the United Kingdom.' Paper prepared for the Political Finance and Government Advertising Workshop, The Australian National University, Canberra, 25 February, p. 9.
12    Days after the legislation was passed by parliament, the threshold had already increased to $10 300.

on government. The government argued that it is not in the public interest for donations below this amount to be disclosed. The Labor Party strongly opposed the increase to the threshold.

With the change to a Labor government in 2007, and changed JSCEM membership, the committee supported the Rudd Government's legislation to revert to a $1000 fixed threshold for disclosure. Without sufficient numbers in the Senate, the amendment was not successful; however, with a Labor/Greens majority in the Senate from July 2011, it is now expected to pass. This will bring the Commonwealth in line with most Australian jurisdictions, which have thresholds of $1000–2100.

Individual but related entities (such as members of a family or directors of a company) are currently treated separately under the disclosure laws, as are State and Territory divisions of the same party. For example, a husband and wife could separately donate $10 000 to each of the nine State, Territory and federal divisions of a party—a total of $180 000—without any of the donations being disclosed. Although the ability to donate separately was already in the Act, the increased threshold makes this option more attractive to major donors. Countries such as Canada have managed to place stringent caps on total party donations, so the provision for separate donations appears to be a deliberate legislative loophole that advantages Australian parties with a federal administrative structure.[13]

Miskin and Baker highlight the impact that the increased threshold could have in monetary terms. In the 2004–05 financial year (an election year), $33.1 million in donations to the major parties was disclosed under the old $1500 threshold. That figure would have dropped to $25.2 million under the new regime.[14] That is, an additional $8.1 million would be removed from public accountability, assuming that donating patterns remain the same. It can be expected, however, that political parties have adapted their fundraising and donation strategies, and donors who previously donated up to the old cap are now encouraged to donate up to the new threshold. The combination of the increased threshold and allowing foreign and corporate donations is also a cause for concern, as are the timing of disclosure and the absence of caps on donations or campaign expenditure. These are all areas where Australia falls far behind the practices of countries such as the United Kingdom and Canada. In terms of fairness, the

---

13    The Gillard Government is proposing in the Commonwealth Electoral Amendment (Political Donations and Other Measures) Bill 2010 to remove the loophole that allows splitting donations between party divisions, but family splitting will continue to be allowed.

14    Sarah Miskin and Greg Baker. 2006. *Political Finance Disclosure Under Current and Proposed Thresholds.* Research Note 27 2005–06. Canberra: Parliamentary Library, Parliament of Australia.

current threshold results in a greater proportion of donations being hidden from voters, which is contrary to the principle of being able to make an informed choice.

The timeline for reporting and disclosing donations is such that donations to registered parties made in 2006–07 for the 2007 federal election were not disclosed until 2 February 2009. The long period between donation and disclosure is a serious concern in terms of accountability and transparency, as media and public interest generally will have moved on from these issues. One of the underlying arguments in favour of a disclosure regime is to allow voters to make an informed choice at the time of an election. If information is provided only retrospectively then voters remain in the dark about what possible influences are affecting a party's policy platform. Typically, the major parties argue in JSCEM inquiries that more up-to-date disclosure of donations would add an unreasonable administrative burden on parties; however, in these modern times of electronic transactions and Internet access, if a party has the ability to bank a donation, it has the ability to provide that donation information to the public at the same time.

While the Labor and Liberal parties use ideological arguments to put their positions on disclosure thresholds, their real motivations are pragmatic. It is well known that the Labor Party's major donors are trade unions, and therefore there is little to be lost in disclosing such donations (which often would be disclosed under the higher thresholds anyway). The Liberal Party, however, relies heavily on donations from the business sector, and a lower threshold could frighten off these donors, who might not want to be exposed as Liberal supporters, especially when they might need to deal with Labor governments at either the federal or the State level.

# Tax deductibility of political donations

Provisions exist in several countries, including the United Kingdom, the United States, Canada, Italy and Australia, to provide tax benefits for making political donations and contributions. Such schemes typically provide tax credits or treat the contributions as a tax-deductible expense. The reasoning behind this is to encourage political participation and broaden parties' support bases. It is also viewed as a form of public funding of political parties.

In Australia, tax deductibility for party contributions was introduced in 1991. Prior to 2006, political donations were tax deductible to a maximum of $100 per year, and for individuals only. In 2006, the Howard Government increased this limit to $1500 per year, and extended it to businesses. The government's argument for this increase was that it would encourage participation in the democratic process, by providing tax relief. In its report on the 2004 election, the Coalition-controlled JSCEM recommended that the limit be increased to $2000, arguing that it would encourage small to medium donations, but the only submissions cited by the report as being in support of such an increase were from the Liberal and National parties. Labor was opposed to the proposal.

A counterargument to the JSCEM's recommendation for higher levels of tax deductibility is that the ability of people to participate in political discourse should not be related to their capacity to pay. An increase to $1500 skews political influence to the wealthier in society, as not only do higher-earning individuals have greater capacity to make donations, they also receive a proportionately higher (taxpayer-funded) subsidy. Based on the tax scales in place at the time of the reform (2006–07 rates), an individual earning $20 000 per year who made a $1500 party donation would receive a $190 tax rebate. Another individual who made the same donation, but was earning $100 000 per year, would receive a $600 rebate—an additional $410 benefit.[15]

In early 2008, the Rudd Labor Government introduced legislation to remove tax deductibility for all political donations and contributions. This was a result of Labor's policy platform of finding budget cuts in government expenditure. A JSCEM inquiry into the amending legislation was highly political, with Coalition members referring to the unrelated Wollongong Council donations scandal as a reason for not supporting the reform. Without the numbers in the Senate, Labor was unable to pass the legislation. Like many proposed reforms in the political finance area, however, the 2011 change in Senate numbers is expected to provide the opportunity for the reform to take place.

While the Labor government is seeking to remove tax deductibility for all donations and contributions, there remain good arguments for retaining a tax incentive for small-scale political activity, such as party membership fees.

---

15   Norm Kelly. 2006. 'The Howard Government's Electoral Reforms—A Blight on Democratic Principles.' Paper delivered at the Australasian Political Studies Association Conference, Newcastle, p. 12.

# 8. One Vote, One Value

It is important to consider the values placed on electors' votes. These can range from voting equality to massive malapportionment or vote weighting. When discussions on malapportioned systems occur, the term 'gerrymander' (or 'Bjelkemander', after a former Queensland premier) is often mistakenly used. A gerrymander occurs when a dominant political party is able to dictate the drawing of electoral boundaries in a way that maximises the benefits for that party, even when all electorates have an equal number of enrolments. Typically, this would result in the non-governing party having large majorities in a minority of seats, while the dominant party holds smaller majorities, but in a greater number of seats. This maximises the value of the dominant party's votes, while non-governing parties have excess votes 'wasted' in safe seats.

Systems of malapportionment, however, establish electorates of different enrolment size according to the creation of zones, where areas receive a greater or lesser voting weight, or power, according to their location. In these systems it is usually the rural areas that receive additional voting power, with countries such as Australia, Norway, New Zealand, Canada and South Africa having used such weighting. According to William Mackenzie, typical arguments used to support malapportionment include the need to recognise the wealth of the farming estate for a nation's economic prosperity and that the rural areas represent a nation's patriotic values and virtues.[1]

In considering malapportioned systems, it is pertinent to assess the 'fairness' of the system. As described above in relation to gerrymanders, voting parity can be corrupted through the drawing of electorate boundaries to unfairly advantage or disadvantage a certain party. In a malapportioned system, however, inequality of voting power does not necessarily translate to being an unfair system. Fairness can still occur if the parties' overall number of seats is proportionate to their level of voting support, or at least in relative terms due to the magnification effect that occurs for the two major parties in single-member seats. The geographic concentration of different parties' voting support in different areas might balance out in an overall sense, thereby achieving a fair result. Despite this, it is usually possible to identify particular parties that are unfairly affected by malapportioned systems.

Early examples of Australian electoral systems were generally a continuation of the British precedent of differentiating between rural and urban areas in terms of voting value, with there being a traditional bias, or vote weighting, in favour of rural and remote areas. These were designed, and have been successful, in

---

1   William James Millar Mackenzie. 1967. *Free Elections*. London: George Allen & Unwin, pp. 110–11.

working in favour of the conservative or non-Labor parties. A malapportioned system, however, can be subject to demographic change. For example, a rural constituency close to a metropolitan centre might experience rapidly changing demographics due to the spread of urbanisation, and thus shift the political balance of the electorate.

Australian electoral systems have generally moved away from malapportionment to systems based on the principle of one vote, one value. In all cases, Labor governments have initiated these reforms. A tolerance of plus or minus 10 per cent variation from the average electorate enrolment is considered to be the uniform minimum standard for the principle of one vote, one value. Arguments are regularly put forward, however, for more generous tolerances to be allowed so that special interests can be accommodated, particularly in the case of remote areas and Indigenous communities.[2] For example, the Northern Territory, with a significant Indigenous population living in remote areas, has adopted an electoral system based on vote parity, but allowing a plus or minus 20 per cent tolerance from the average enrolment.

Despite the relative merits of such arguments, this study adopts the definition of one vote, one value having a tolerance of up to and including plus or minus 10 per cent. It should also be noted that while 'structural' malapportionment can occur as explained above, it is also possible for vote weighting, or 'incidental' malapportionment, to occur in a system of one vote, one value, through the application of allowable tolerances and electoral laws. For example, while Australia's House of Representatives is elected using a one vote, one value system, the value of a Northern Territorian's vote is more than double that of a voter living in the Australian Capital Territory. There are only two Australian houses of parliament that use an electoral system where all voters are provided with an equivalent vote value. These are the NSW and SA legislative councils, where members are elected by proportional representation in a state-wide electorate.

## One vote, one value at the federal level

The primary law for Australia's federal electoral system is the Australian Constitution, which sets out the requirements for the form of representation for the two houses of the Federal Parliament. The Constitution also empowers the parliament to pass legislation amending the original representational and electoral requirements (for example, the number of senators, Section 7; qualification of electors, Section 30; conduct of House of Representatives

---

2   Senate Legal and Constitutional References Committee. 2004. *State Elections (One Vote, One Value) Bill 2001 [2002]*. Senate Legal and Constitutional References Committee. Canberra: Parliament of Australia.

elections, Section 31). The primary piece of legislation relating to electoral matters is the *Commonwealth Electoral Act 1918*. In the federal electoral system, while one vote, one value exists for the Senate and House of Representatives within each State and Territory, a wide disparity in the value of votes may occur between different States and Territories.

# The Senate

At the time of Federation, the smaller colonies were concerned that their interests would be swamped by the more populous larger colonies. As a way of protecting their interests, the Australian Constitution (Section 7) dictates that an equal number of senators is to be elected from each State, irrespective of the size of the State's population. This currently results in malapportionment of up to 12.9:1, with the quota (based on enrolled voters) to elect a senator from New South Wales at the 2010 election being 658 685 votes, compared with only 51 230 votes to elect a Tasmanian senator. Table 8.1 shows the disparity in representation that occurs due to the constitutional and legislative requirements for Senate elections.

**Table 8.1 Enrolments per Elected Senator (based on the 2010 half-Senate election)**

| State/Territory | Total enrolled | Average enrolled per elected senator | Difference from national average (%) | Quota[1] |
|---|---|---|---|---|
| New South Wales | 4 610 795 | 768 466 | 118.2 | 658 685 |
| Victoria | 3 561 873 | 593 646 | 68.6 | 508 839 |
| Queensland | 2 719 360 | 453 227 | 28.7 | 388 480 |
| Western Australia | 1 362 534 | 227 089 | −35.5 | 194 648 |
| South Australia | 1 104 698 | 184 116 | −47.7 | 157 814 |
| Tasmania | 358 609 | 59 768 | −83.0 | 51 230 |
| Australian Capital Territory | 247 941 | 123 971 | −64.8 | 82 647 |
| Northern Territory | 121 059 | 60 530 | −82.8 | 40 353 |
| Australia—Total | 14 086 869 | 352 172 | - | - |

[1] Quota = total enrolled ÷ (number of senators to be elected + 1).

Additionally, the Federal Parliament has the ability to influence the level of malapportionment through its constitutional powers to pass legislation that determines the manner and form of Australia's electoral system. For example, the parliament's law-making power under Section 122 of the Constitution allowed the parliament to legislate in 1973 for two senators to be elected for each of the Australian Capital Territory and the Northern Territory (*Senate*

*[Representation of the Territories] Act 1973*). Section 40 of the *Commonwealth Electoral Act 1918* ties increases in the number of senators for the Territories to population growth, through a correlation with the Territories' entitlement of House of Representatives seats. The result is malapportionment of 16.3:1 when comparing the NT quota (40 353 votes) with the NSW quota. Using the Gini and Dauer-Kelsay indices, Figure 8.1 depicts the high levels of malapportionment that exist in the Senate, based on the 2004 election when 40 senators were elected.

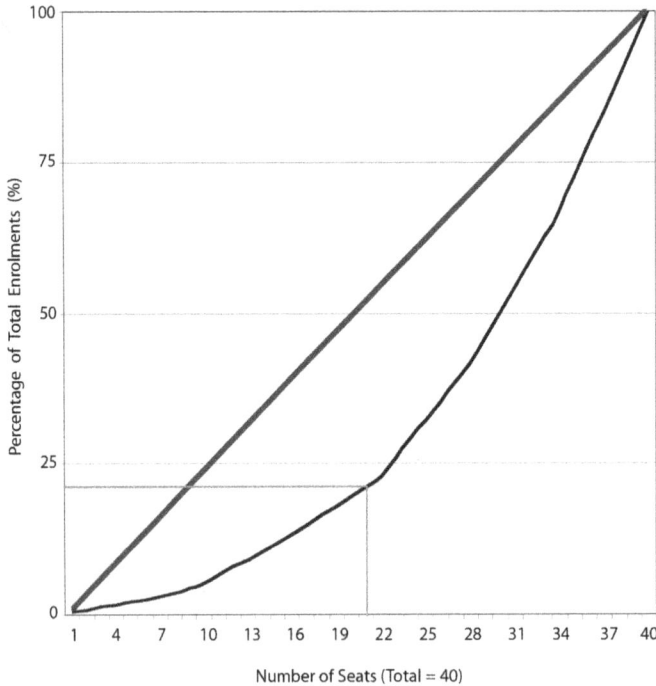

**Figure 8.1 Australian Senate: 2004 Half-Senate Election**

## The House of Representatives

While the electoral system for the House of Representatives is also primarily based on one vote, one value, the Australian Constitution enables two significant ways for vote weighting to occur. First, Section 24 of the Constitution requires electorates (districts) to be evenly divided within a State, and Section 29 stipulates that a 'division shall not be formed out of parts of different States'. This has led to wide disparities in enrolment for jurisdictions with smaller populations, particularly within the Australian Capital Territory and the Northern Territory, when compared with other jurisdictions. At the 2010 election, for example, the two NT seats had less than half the enrolment, with an average 60 530 enrolment, of the two ACT seats, which averaged 123 971 enrolments. Table 8.2 shows the disparities that exist.

**Table 8.2 Enrolment Numbers for House of Representatives Electorates, by State/Territory (2010 election figures)**

| State/ Territory | No. of Seats | Average enrolled per electorate | Deviation from Australian average (%) | Lowest enrolment | Highest enrolment | Deviation from State/ Territory average (%) |
|---|---|---|---|---|---|---|
| New South Wales | 48 | 96 058 | 2.3 | 90 059 | 101 464 | −6.2/5.6 |
| Victoria | 37 | 96 267 | 2.5 | 86 275 | 117 023 | −10.4/21.6 |
| Queensland | 30 | 90 645 | −3.5 | 82 558 | 98 224 | −8.9/8.4 |
| Western Australia | 15 | 90 836 | −3.3 | 85 782 | 93 892 | −5.6/3.4 |
| South Australia | 11 | 100 427 | 6.9 | 96 263 | 104 888 | −4.1/4.4 |
| Tasmania | 5 | 71 722 | −23.6 | 71 090 | 72 865 | −0.9/1.6 |
| Australian Capital Territory | 2 | 123 971 | 32.0 | 123 444 | 124 215 | −0.4/0.2 |
| Northern Territory | 2 | 60 530 | −35.5 | 59 879 | 61 126 | −1.1/1.0 |
| Australia | 150 | 93 912 | - | 59 879 | 124 215 | −36.2/32.3[1] |

[1] Deviation from national average.

The second aspect of the Constitution that creates vote weighting for the House of Representatives is the Section 24 requirement that 'five members at least shall be chosen in each Original State'. Western Australia and Tasmania were beneficiaries of this condition from Federation in 1901. In 1933, Western Australia's population had grown sufficiently to no longer require this safeguard, however, Tasmania has continued to benefit, as the State would otherwise be entitled to only three seats based on its current population. At the 2010 election, Tasmania's electorates had an average enrolment of 71 722, compared with an average of 94 678 for the other States and Territories.

Disparity also exists between the more highly populated states, due in part to redistributions taking place at different times for each State/Territory. Part IV of the *Commonwealth Electoral Act 1918* prescribes the manner in which redistributions are to be conducted, providing for a projected tolerance of plus or minus 3.5 per cent of a State or Territory's average electorate enrolment (Sections 63A and 66). The timing of when redistributions are calculated can significantly influence the degree of deviation that occurs. As Table 8.2 shows, actual deviations might be substantially outside the plus or minus 3.5 per cent range.

The Federal Parliament is also able to override decisions of the AEC, as occurred with the passing of the *Commonwealth Electoral Amendment (Representation in the House of Representatives) Act 2004*. This legislation set aside the Electoral Commissioner's determination in 2003, based on population figures, that the Northern Territory's representation in the House of Representatives be reduced from two seats to one seat. Irrespective of the merits of such legislative changes, the impact on vote weighting can be quite pronounced, as presented in Table 8.2. In the case of the Northern Territory, the Federal Parliament's decision doubled the weight, or value, of each Northern Territorian's vote.

Figure 8.2 illustrates small levels of malapportionment for the House of Representatives (using 2004 election figures), especially when compared with the Senate (Figure 8.1). A comparison of the two graphs also highlights the impact that malapportionment has on the Dauer-Kelsay Index. The large deviations that exist for Tasmania and the Northern Territory, as outlined above, can be seen to have only a minor impact on the Lorenz Curve, as these special conditions affect only seven of the 150 House of Representatives seats.

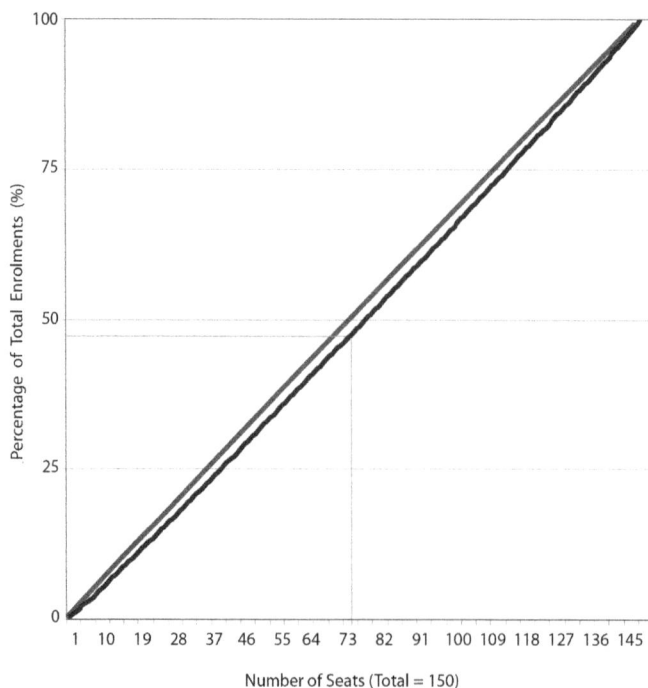

**Figure 8.2 Australian House of Representatives: 2004 Election**

# Recent reform attempts at the federal level

There have been a number of attempts in recent decades to entrench the principle of one vote, one value into Australia's electoral system. At the 1963 federal election, size disparity within States for House of Representatives seats was as high as 3.1:1 (Victoria, seats of Bruce and Scullin) and 2.5:1 (New South Wales, seats of Mitchell and West Sydney). By the 1966 election, this disparity had increased to 3.8:1 and 3.4:1 respectively. In 1968, Senator Lionel Murphy QC, the Leader of the Labor Opposition in the Senate, introduced two Bills with the purpose of altering the Constitution to require one vote, one value for the States and the Commonwealth. Following Murphy's second reading speech, the Bills failed to be progressed by the Coalition government.[3]

In 1974, the Senate voted against Prime Minister Gough Whitlam's Constitution Alteration (Democratic Elections) Bill 1974, which sought to amend the Constitution to 'ensure that the members of the House of Representatives and of the parliaments of the states are chosen directly and democratically by the people'.[4] With the Governor-General's approval (as provided for in Section 128 of the Constitution; see Appendix A), the proposal was, however, put forward in a constitutional referendum on 18 May 1974. The proposal received no support from the Opposition and was defeated, with only 47.2 per cent of voters, and with only one State, New South Wales, in support.

The High Court heard a case in 1975 relating to the alleged disparity in size of House of Representatives seats (the McKinlay case).[5] In its decision, the High Court ruled that while 'something approaching numerical equality' was important, the Australian Constitution does not require this to occur. In its ruling, the High Court stated that Section 24 of the Constitution does not provide a 'guarantee of equality in the voting value or weight of each vote cast in an election for the House of Representatives'.

The Bob Hawke Labor Government was successful in passing legislation in 1983—the *Commonwealth Electoral Legislation Amendment Act 1983*—which amended the *Commonwealth Electoral Act 1918*, by setting three criteria for the redistribution of seats. These criteria are that redistributions must occur: at least every seven years; if more than one-third of the seats in a State deviates from

---

3   Gough Whitlam. 2003. 'One Vote One Value.' The Whitlam Institute web site, URL: <http://www.whitlam.org/collection/2000/ 20000406_onevoteonevalue/index.html>

4   Parliament of Australia. 2004. 'Referendum Results 1974.' Parliamentary Handbook of the Commonwealth of Australia. Parliament of Australia web site, URL: <http://www.aph.gov.au/library/handbook/referendums/r1974.htm>

5   High Court of Australia. 1975. Attorney-General (Cwlth); *Ex rel. McKinlay v The Commonwealth; South Australia v The Commonwealth; Lawlor v The Commonwealth* [1975] HCA 53; (1975) 135 CLR 1 (1 December 1975).

the average enrolment by more than 10 per cent; or when a State's entitlement to its number of seats changes (Section 59). These changes moved the Australian electoral system to one vote, one value, but as it was only a legislative change, there was no constitutional guarantee.

Senator Michael Macklin (Queensland, Australian Democrats) introduced Bills in 1984, 1985 and 1987 for a constitutional amendment to enshrine the principle of one vote, one value. They were designed to improve on the 1974 Whitlam model, which had based equality on the population of each electorate, rather than on the number of eligible people enrolled to vote. In his 1987 Bill, Senator Macklin sought a requirement for equality in electorate enrolments 'as nearly as practicable', but with a tolerance of plus 10 per cent, and with no lower limit. The Bill was referred to the JSCEM, which reported in April 1988, finding that 'equity in voting power is a necessary first step in achieving a fair electoral system'. The committee recommended that electoral enrolments should be within 10 per cent of the average enrolment and that the issue be put to a referendum. Five months later, in September 1988, a referendum was held to amend the Australian Constitution to 'ensure that democratic electoral arrangements would be guaranteed for Commonwealth, State and Territory elections'. This referendum was defeated, largely due to the Coalition parties campaigning against the proposal, on the basis that States should maintain control over their own electoral matters.[6] It has also been argued that the Liberal Party was simply bowing to pressure from the National Party—traditional supporters of bias to rural electorates.

# The WA case

Western Australia has had a historically high level of malapportionment favouring rural and north-west seats. For example, in 1917 the average enrolment in metropolitan seats was 6108, compared with 2642 for rural seats and 958 for seats in the north-west of the State.[7] In one particular case, the effects of malapportionment reached 65:1 in the late 1920s with the extremes of the seat of Canning, with 17 347 voters, and the seat of Menzies, with only 265 voters.[8] Reforms in 1929 (amendments to the *Electoral Districts Act 1922*) and 1947

---

6    James Jupp and Marian Sawer. 2001. 'Political Parties, Partisanship and Electoral Governance.' In *Elections: Full, Free & Fair*, ed. M. Sawer. Sydney: The Federation Press, p. 219.

7    N. F. Byrne. 1959. 'A Historical Survey of the Western Australian Electoral System, 1917–1956.' Master of Arts thesis. Perth: University of Western Australia.

8    George Cash MLC. 2001. 'Electoral Amendment Bill 2001—Second Reading Speech.' *Hansard*, 18 September 2001. Perth: Parliament of Western Australia, pp. 3806–24.

(*Electoral Distribution Act 1947*) resulted in a lessening of malapportionment, but non-metropolitan areas generally remained favoured by about 2:1 for the legislative assembly and 3:1 for the legislative council.[9]

In the 1980s, the Burke Labor Government proposed electoral reforms including the introduction of State-wide proportional representation for the legislative council. At the time, the council had dual-member electorates, with each vacancy elected every second election on a rotational basis. The Burke Government also proposed voting equality for the legislative assembly. In order to obtain National Party support for the legislation, which eventually passed in 1987, the Labor Party was forced to retain a level of zonation for the legislative council, with proportional representation based on three metropolitan and three non-metropolitan regions, and abandon attempts to reform the assembly.

While the council's combined metropolitan regions now had representative parity with the country regions (17 members each), the population disparity meant that a significant level of malapportionment (2.8:1) was retained in favour of the non-metropolitan regions, and the National Party's interests.[10] In addition, malapportionment remained for assembly elections. Table 8.3 depicts the level of malapportionment that has existed for the WA Legislative Assembly over the past century, using the David-Eisenberg (most extreme example of malapportionment), Dauer-Kelsay (smallest percentage of enrolments to produce a majority) and Gini (zero being absolute voting parity) indices. The significant reduction in malapportionment of the assembly as a result of the 2005 reforms (discussed later in this chapter) can be seen with the increase in the Dauer-Kelsay Index—from 38.14 in 2005 to 47.70 at the 2008 election.

**Table 8.3 Malapportionment in the Legislative Assembly, Western Australia**

| Year | David-Eisenberg Index | Dauer-Kelsay Index | Gini Coefficient[a] |
|------|----------------------|--------------------|--------------------|
| 1894 | 77.46 | 18.37 | 0.514 |
| 1904 | 17.37 | 29.36 | 0.337 |
| 1914 | 8.95 | 29.71 | 0.326 |
| 1924 | 23.89 | 25.26 | 0.402 |
| 1936 | 17.04 | 32.94 | 0.282 |
| 1947 | 30.37 | 28.64 | 0.351 |
| 1956 | 9.70 | 34.50 | 0.239 |
| 1965 | 7.21 | 33.07 | 0.250 |
| 1974 | 9.64 | 31.90 | 0.244 |

9 Another good account of the history of malapportionment in Western Australia can be found in Harry Phillips and Kirsten Robinson. 2006. *The Quest for 'One Vote One Value' in Western Australia's Political History*. Perth: Western Australian Electoral Commission.

10 Harry Phillips. 1991. 'The Modern Parliament, 1965–1989.' In *The House on the Hill: A History of the Parliament of Western Australia 1832–1990*, ed. Black. Perth: Parliament of Western Australia.

| Year | David-Eisenberg Index | Dauer-Kelsay Index | Gini Coefficient[a] |
|------|----------------------|--------------------|---------------------|
| 1983 | 5.79 | 36.06 | 0.194 |
| 1996 | 2.78 | 38.52 | - |
| 2001 | 4.01 | 37.80 | - |
| 2005 | 2.45 | 38.14 | - |
| 2008 | 2.34 | 47.70 | - |

[a] Gini coefficients not available for 1996, 2001, 2005 and 2008 elections.

Sources: Colin Hughes. 1977. *A Handbook of Australian Government and Politics 1965–1974*. Canberra: Australian National University Press; Colin Hughes. 1986. *Handbook of Australian Government and Politics 1975–1984*. Canberra: Australian National University Press; author's own calculations.

# The Gallop Government reforms

Following Labor's victory at the 2001 election, and the subsequent changeover of council members in May 2001, for the first time in its history, the WA Parliament had a non-conservative majority in both houses.[11] Therefore, Labor finally had the opportunity to legislate for significant electoral reform. With the election of a Labor president and the support of the five Greens council members, Labor could secure a 17–16 majority on the floor of the council.

Within a month of Labor winning the 2001 election, Labor's Electoral Affairs Minister, Jim McGinty, approached the Greens to seek their position on the government's proposed electoral reforms. Labor's proposal was for one vote, one value to be adopted for both the assembly and the council, with an allowable 10 per cent tolerance for assembly seats. For the legislative council, Labor was open to the idea of either amalgamating existing regions into a single state-wide electorate or retaining regionalism, but with revised boundaries drawn using voting equality principles. As explained by a Greens interviewee:

> They [Labor] were very keen on a straightforward model for the assembly and they seemed to be more flexible about the upper house, but basically they wanted the upper house to be on a one vote, one value system. Either you went to a model where there was one State-wide seat on one vote, one value principles, or there was a radical realignment of the regions in order to remove vote weighting.

It was also acknowledged at this time that the government would require an absolute majority of 18 votes to pass its proposed electoral reforms. This was

---

11    The legislative council's 34 members were made up of 13 Labor, five Greens, 12 Liberal, one Nationals and three One Nation. The Greens effectively held the 'balance of power'.

due to the 'entrenchment' provision (Section 13) of the *Electoral Distribution Act 1947*, which requires an absolute majority of both houses for amendments to that Act to be made. In June 2001 it was announced that Labor was planning to amend legislation, if the Greens members were supportive, to allow the president to have a deliberative vote—a change that required only a simple majority to pass the council. This would then allow the government to make the electoral reforms it was planning, using an absolute majority of council members, assuming that it could win the Greens' support.

The Greens MLCs adopted a consensus approach in determining their position, which allowed for Dee Margetts' (Greens' Agricultural Region MLC) opposition to a blanket application of the one vote, one value principle. This was achieved by making concessions to allow for a special provision for remote (that is, geographically large) electorates. In July 2001, the Greens agreed to a model that would bring about voting equality for the assembly, with the exception of the special consideration for remote electorates (similar to the Queensland model). For the council, however, the Greens' model retained the existing level of malapportionment between metropolitan and non-metropolitan council regions—another concession to Margetts. The Greens' model also included an increase of council members from 34 to 36, based on three metropolitan and three non-metropolitan regions, each with six members.

The community debate on the merits of voting equality that ensued as a result of the Gallop Government's push for electoral reform was largely influenced by the public arguments put forward by the political parties and the consequent media commentary. Similar to most parliamentary political environments, however, here, negotiations and strategies that are not necessarily obvious to outside observers were being played out, particularly between Labor and the Greens.

It was generally agreed during parliamentary debates that Labor's proposed reforms would result in a shift of eight legislative assembly seats from country regions into the metropolitan area. In the non-metropolitan regions, the Greens' requirement of a consideration for geographically large electorates meant that the Mining and Pastoral Region would lose only two assembly seats, rather than the three seats it would lose under a system based strictly on voting equality. A probable impact of this provision would result in Labor being able to retain a seat at the expense of a Coalition seat in the other non-metropolitan regions. Labor acknowledged that this special exemption from one vote, one value would be to its own advantage, but argued that the exemption was included in the legislation due to the Greens' insistence, 'based on an argument more for remoteness and biodiversity type…[Labor] didn't go in seeking that'.

Overall, the eight seats to be shifted from non-metropolitan regions to metropolitan regions were primarily Coalition seats, with an estimation that only one or two non-metropolitan Labor seats would be lost in the proposed change. The most severe negative impact would be to the National Party, with an anticipated loss of three seats, primarily as a result of its concentrated voting support in the Agricultural Region and lack of support in metropolitan regions.

On balance, the Greens' council model appeared to disadvantage themselves, especially when the party's primary vote is taken into account. The Greens have never achieved a quota with their primary vote and thus have always had a reliance on preferences to win seats. This was particularly the case in the Agricultural and Mining and Pastoral regions in 2001, where the Greens' primary vote was little more than one-quarter of a quota. It is anticipated that preference arrangements will remain a significant factor in the Greens' prospects at future elections. In determining a model, the Greens sought a balanced position that neither seriously advantaged nor disadvantaged the party, and it appears they were successful in achieving that objective. The following comments illustrate the Greens' views on the model:

> The electorate suicide model...when we were going through the process of devising that, I got advice that the six-by-six model was roughly neutral. There were academic people that made contact with me to suggest that it was actually a very bad model for the Greens...I'm not so altruistic as to want to advocate a position that was suicidal for the Greens but nor did we want to come up with a position that was blatantly self-interested. We actually wanted to come up with a position that we could sit comfortably with ethically.

In drafting its legislation, the Labor government reluctantly accepted maintenance of malapportionment for the legislative council, including the Greens' 'six by six' model, and adopted the special provision for remote areas. The government did not, however, include the increase in council numbers, which the Greens made clear was necessary if they were to support the reforms. This meant that the Greens were forced to initiate amendments to increase the number of members from 34 to 36, and take the force of public and media criticism for imposing the costs of two additional members of parliament. Simultaneously, the government was able to state opposition to the imposition of the added costs, and claim they were being forced into supporting the change in order to have their electoral reforms passed. This stance enabled the Labor government to deflect public and media criticism of the Greens' 'six by six' model, despite having privately agreed to it, albeit reluctantly. The Greens erred strategically, allowing themselves to be exposed to public criticism by not requiring that Labor include the entire Greens model in its legislation. The Greens' perspective was that 'the Labor Party brought this in cold, and let us take the heat, as it were'. The Labor perspective was:

Our proposal was not to have that exception; the Greens insisted on that exception as a condition of their support. The Bill made no impact on malapportionment in the upper house. The original Bill was structured knowing that the Greens would amend it this way in the upper house as their requirement, but it was our clear understanding that that's what they'd do and we'd cop it. The Bill was structured such as to allow the Green amendment in the upper house to do that. We understood that we would accept an amendment along those lines.

Labor was also aware they would face heavy criticism, particularly from the opposition and rural interest groups, by reducing representation in country areas. This was exacerbated by the adoption of an exemption from one vote, one value that could be construed as manipulation of the system to their own advantage. Labor was, however, able to ensure that during the parliamentary debates on the Bills, the Greens would be blamed for the proposed change in legislative council numbers, regardless of maintaining the malapportionment that Labor's opponents were supporting. As a result, media commentary centred negatively on the Greens' role, with headlines such as 'Greens Threat to Vote Reform', 'Vote Reform Comes at a Cost', and 'Reform Move Simplistic, Selfish and Undemocratic'.[12] Public awareness of the Greens' 'balance of power' role was, however, clearly increased by the media debate, subsequently allowing the party to more effectively publicise its position on other legislation.

On 1 August 2001, Labor's Minister for Electoral Affairs (and Attorney-General), Jim McGinty, introduced his party's electoral reform legislation, the Electoral Distribution Repeal Bill 2001 (the Repeal Bill) and the Electoral Amendment Bill 2001 (the Amendment Bill), into the legislative assembly. The primary purpose of the Repeal Bill was to repeal the *Electoral Distribution Act 1947*, which provided the basis for the system of vote weighting for non-metropolitan regions and electorates. The Amendment Bill primarily sought to apply the principle of one vote, one value to assembly elections. This was to be done by transferring the relevant sections of the (to be) repealed *Electoral Distribution Act 1947* into an amended *Electoral Act 1907*, with the major modification being that the division of enrolments into electorates would be on a State-wide basis. For electorates of less than 100 000 sq km, projected enrolments were to be within a plus or minus 10 per cent tolerance from the State average district enrolment. Electorates with an area of 100 000 sq km or more would be weighted by adding an 'additional large district number'—0.5 per cent of the electorate's area in square kilometres ('notional' enrolments)—to the number of actual enrolments, and with a broader tolerance of projected enrolments (notional and actual) to be allowed, within plus 10 per cent or minus 20 per cent of the State average district enrolment.

---

12   *West Australian*, 19 September 2001; 30 November 2001; 14 December 2001.

McGinty stated that the legislation did not represent absolute principles of one vote, one value—referring to the special provisions for large electorates and the lack of reform of the legislative council—because it reflected a compromise position that took into account the Greens' requirements. Importantly, in the context of the ensuing debate, by repealing the *Electoral Distribution Act 1947*, Labor also expected to be able to avoid the Act's Section 13 provision requiring amendments to that Act to be passed by an absolute majority. The Bills were passed unamended by the assembly in August–September 2001.

Although it was stated that there was a unanimous decision within the Liberal Party Caucus to oppose Labor's Bills,[13] indications are that a significant number of Liberal members were supportive of one vote, one value and would cross the floor and vote with the government if not bound by party discipline. As one interviewee described it:

> If they were given a free vote on the issue, there were a number of Liberals who would cross the floor and I suspect the majority of their members in the upper house would be in that position to cross the floor and vote with the Labor Party, but it was introduced in such a way that it polarised views from the outset. Almost half of the parliamentary Liberal Party were in favour of the change.

The Liberal Party has historically required National Party support to form government, so it is important for the Liberal Party to retain a reasonable working relationship with its Coalition partner. Some members of the Liberal Party, however, would appreciate not having to accommodate the Nationals, and see electoral reform as a way to achieve this, provided there is no overall loss of conservative seats. As one interviewee stated:

> There is a strain of opinion within the Liberal Party that sees one of the great advantages of ending malapportionment is ending the existence of the National Party, who they see as a major nuisance and that if eight seats go to the city, the Liberal Party may only get four out of the eight, but the National Party will get none, and that's seen as a distinct advantage.

The National Party is the only party clearly advantaged by the malapportionment existing in the WA system. Thus, it is not surprising that the party has fought vehemently against the introduction of voting equality. The combination of geographically concentrated voting support, and the effect of malapportionment providing a greater number of rural electorates in comparison with an equally apportioned system, has allowed the Nationals to remain a significant political

---

13  Dan Barron-Sullivan MLA. 2001. 'Electoral Amendment Bill 2001—Second Reading Speech.' *Hansard*, 22 August 2001. Perth: Parliament of Western Australia, pp. 2731–40.

party in WA State politics. An indication of the Nationals' motives is evident in its strategy to amend the legislation in two ways. First, the party considered an amendment to return the legislative council to single-member electorates, with 15 metropolitan electorates and 15 non-metropolitan electorates. This amendment would have had the effect of removing proportional representation, and probably eliminating the Greens from the parliament, but leaving the Nationals able to win two or three seats in their agricultural heartland. The second proposal was to broaden zonation for assembly electorates, with metropolitan, regional and remote zones. Under this proposal, weighting would be allowed for regional and remote electorates. Although not ultimately moved in parliament, these proposals give an indication of the National Party's preferred electoral system.

The legislative council referred both Bills to the Standing Committee on Legislation. The standing committee's membership for the inquiry was three Labor, two Liberal, a Green and a One Nation member. The committee's report included 31 recommendations, but apart from recommending that the existing weighting in favour of non-metropolitan council regions be maintained, the committee was unable to agree on any other issues relating specifically to electoral reform. This was not surprising, given the positions of the different parties. Of particular importance though was Recommendation 5, supported by the Liberal, Greens and One Nation members, which recommended that the council take action to obtain a Supreme Court ruling on the legality of the Bills being presented for Royal Assent in the event that they were passed without an absolute majority. This indicated that there would be a willingness for the council to pursue clarification from the Supreme Court on the 'absolute majority' question.

The possibility of amending Section 14 of the *Constitution Acts Amendment Act 1899* to give the president a deliberative vote was raised at the time of the standing committee inquiry in 2001. The Greens came to a view that an existing right to a deliberative vote existed, and encouraged the president to vote. Following the tabling of the standing committee report, the Clerk of the Parliaments, Laurie Marquet, informed the president that in the event that the Repeal Bill was passed by the council without an absolute majority, he intended to seek a declaratory statement from the Supreme Court as to whether he could present the Bill for Royal Assent. The major contention in this aspect of the debate was whether the repeal of the *Electoral Distribution Act 1947* actually constituted an 'amendment' of the Act, which would therefore require it to be passed with an absolute majority, as per Section 13 of the Act. The president informed the council of the clerk's position on 28 November 2001. The Bills were subsequently passed by the council in December 2001, with simple, but not absolute, majorities.

Within less than five months, the Labor government had been able to pass its electoral reform legislation, with the support of the five Greens members in the legislative council. Despite a standing committee inquiry, and lengthy and heated debates in both houses, the legislation passed without any major changes to the original model that had been agreed to between the government and the Greens prior to the legislation being introduced. Before the legislation could become law through receiving Royal Assent, however, the question of whether the Repeal Bill was bound by the 'absolute majority' provision of the *Electoral Distribution Act 1947* was still to be answered by the WA Supreme Court. Following the passing of the legislation, Marquet sought a declaratory statement from the Supreme Court on the validity of the Bills. Although the clerk's action in seeking a declaratory statement from the Supreme Court was taken with the support of the council, it was viewed by the government as thwarting its agenda. Labor only supported the Supreme Court action under sufferance, knowing that the Bills would be defeated if a declaratory statement was not sought. The following Labor comment illustrates this:

> The Greens said there was some doubt about the legality of the Bills and it all looked a bit shonky...they were not willing to pass the Bill at the third reading unless we can assure them that they're legally in order. They were not satisfied with respect to [the] Solicitor-General's opinions and basically without this device it looked as though the Greens would defeat it at [the] third reading. This was concurred under much sufferance by the government...because at least it effected the passage of the Bills and we had some chance in the courts.

The five-member full bench of the Supreme Court heard the case in April 2002. The government put forward three main arguments in support of the legislation, being that: repealing an Act is not the same as amending it, and therefore Section 13 of the *Electoral Distribution Act 1947* did not apply; it is not competent for a parliament to bind a future parliament in the way that Section 13 of the *Electoral Distribution Act 1947* does; and Section 13 of the *Electoral Distribution Act 1947* had been repealed implicitly by Section 2(3) of the *Acts Amendment (Constitution) Act 1978*.[14] In a four-to-one decision, the court stated that an absolute majority was required to pass the legislation in the council.[15] In summary, the ruling stated that: parliament intended that the word 'amend' encompassed a repeal of the Act; parliament is able to enact a manner and form provision that requires a particular majority to amend or repeal legislation; and the legislation was captured by Section 73(1) of the *Constitution Act 1899*, irrespective of the later subsections of Section 73.

---

14  Section 2(3) of the *Acts Amendment (Constitution) Act 1978* added new subsections to Section 73 of the *Constitution Act 1899*, stipulating specific actions that required an absolute majority.

15  *Marquet v the Attorney-General of Western Australia* [2002], Supreme Court of Western Australia, 2002.

This meant that the Bills could not be presented for Royal Assent and represented an emphatic win for the opponents of the government's electoral reforms. It also shifted attention to the issue of amending Section 14 of the *Constitution Acts Amendment Act 1899* to give the president a deliberative vote in the legislative council. If the Greens were to support such a change, the government could achieve the absolute majority that was required, as ruled by the Supreme Court. A month after the Supreme Court decision, Premier Geoff Gallop announced that the government would appeal the decision to the High Court, stating that the government's legal advice was that an appeal 'should succeed'. A week after the premier's announcement, the High Court action became even more critical when the Greens stated that they would not support legislation giving the president a deliberative vote, arguing that their legal advice had stated that Section 73 of the *Constitution Act 1899* already provided the president with a deliberative vote on constitutional matters, and that further legislation to provide a deliberative vote would affect the impartiality of the president's position.[16] The interests of political parties became further apparent with the appeal attracting legal intervention from the Labor governments of Queensland and New South Wales, and the federal Attorney-General.

The Supreme Court decision confirmed that the Labor government would need an absolute majority to pass its electoral reforms. The Greens' preferred position was for legislation to be amended to clarify the president's voting rights, but, in doing so, the Greens felt that the implications of such a change needed investigating (such as the increased likelihood of deadlocked votes, and therefore the need for a casting vote). Additionally, the Greens believed that broader issues of reforming the WA Constitution should be addressed at the same time. Following the Supreme Court decision, Labor was unwilling to have the president exercise a deliberative vote, as it believed that such an action would inevitably be subject to a legal challenge, and that the Supreme Court may look upon the government unfavourably given the previous history of the legislation.

Following the Supreme Court decision, the government was left with three choices: accept the decision and not pursue the reforms any further; challenge the decision in the High Court; or pursue changes to the legislation that would win the support of an absolute majority. While the first option was not seriously considered given the importance Labor placed on the reforms, the government used its High Court appeal as a bargaining point in attempting to win Liberal support, arguing that the Liberal Party risked 'losing everything'.

> We offered to cut a deal...the Libs would have extracted a high price for their cooperation. Whether we could have paid that in the end

---

16   Ben Harvey. 2002. 'Greens Sink Votes Bid.' *West Australian*, 18 November 2002.

is a different matter. The price was the destruction of proportional representation, reintroduction of a staggered term…it destroys minor representation.

The reintroduction of staggered terms would mean that members of the legislative council would be elected for two terms (eight years), with only half of the council seats up for election at each general election. This would effectively double the quota required for election; however, before the High Court made its decision, the WA Electoral Distribution Commissioners published their decision on the redistribution of electoral boundaries, which was seen to favour the Liberal Party.[17] Following this, the issue of a compromise was not pursued further, prior to the High Court decision. As observed by one interviewee: 'People like Dan [Sullivan, Liberal Deputy Leader], the man who had a very nice 62 per cent Leschenault seat, decided they had no interest in overturning this draft redistribution.'

The High Court delivered its decision in November 2003,[18] upholding the Supreme Court decision, and therefore ruling the electoral reform legislation invalid, by a five-to-one majority. The decision addressed all aspects of the Supreme Court ruling, and agreed with the Supreme Court that the term 'amend' included 'repeal'. Additionally, the court argued that with the repealing of electoral boundaries there is an implicit and required redrawing of boundaries for an election to be held, and therefore the legislation constituted a repeal and simultaneous amendment of boundaries. In his dissenting judgment, Justice Kirby argued that the word 'amend' is usually used in reference to partial repeals, where words or sections of an Act may be deleted, whereas the total repeal of an Act should not be referred to as an amendment. The High Court decision brought to a conclusion the three-year battle that the first Gallop Government had waged to introduce the one vote, one value principle to Western Australia's electoral laws.

The Supreme Court and High Court deliberations necessarily concentrated on the constitutionality of the legislative process, and it should be noted that the High Court has been reluctant to interfere with the parliament's role of determining electoral distribution and administration. In a number of cases,[19] the High Court has supported deviations from voting equality on the basis that the Constitution provides for parliament to be the primary decision maker of the electoral system that provides representative government. In contrast, Labor argues that the US Supreme Court provides more relevant interpretations of the

---

17  Redistributions are held after every second election. The 2003 redistribution reduced mining and pastoral assembly seats from six to five, and increased south-west seats from 10 to 11.

18  *Attorney-General (WA) v Marquet* [2003], High Court of Australia, 2003.

19  For example, *Attorney-General (Cwlth) ex rel McKinlay v Commonwealth* (1975); and *McGinty v Western Australia* (1996).

meaning of election 'by the people'.[20] The US examples are, however, based on explicit constitutional rights, such as the Fourteenth Amendment, which provides equal rights. Such protections and rights are absent in the Australian Constitution.

In June 2004, Alan Cadby, a Liberal member of the legislative council, resigned from his party as a result of a preselection process that placed him in an unwinnable position for the upcoming State election. This breathed new life into the electoral reform debate, with the possibility that Labor could obtain Cadby's vote, thereby achieving an absolute majority for its legislation, with the Greens' support. Alternatively, it was suggested that Cadby could be offered the president's position, giving Labor an absolute majority, again with the Greens' support. The Greens stated that they would support the legislation if it were reintroduced; however, the premier ruled out this option in response to media questioning, and apparently without consulting his party, as explained by the Greens:

> That's why we were really dirty on Gallop when Cadby resigned, there it was, on a plate…and it would have gone through…we've seen Gallop do this before, he gets put on the spot, he doesn't consult because at that stage we'd been talking for about a week with [council president] Cowdell, and McGinty through Cowdell, and we had been relayed Cadby's position and there it was…the Labor Party was devastated.

The premier's statement brought an end to Labor's efforts for reform prior to the 2005 general election (held on 26 February). While the Labor Party was easily returned to power, the overall legislative council result maintained the ideological balance that existed before the election.[21] This meant that Labor and the Greens could not achieve an absolute majority on the floor of the house; however, newly elected councillors do not take up their seats until 22 May every four years, so the government had a window of opportunity of almost three months to put through legislation if it could win the support of the Greens and former Liberal Alan Cadby.

During the election campaign, Labor promised that none of the five existing mining and pastoral assembly electorates would be lost in any redistribution brought about by its proposed electoral reforms. Following the election, however, the Greens insisted that the only exemption from voting equality for the assembly should be on the grounds of remoteness, as had been proposed in the earlier legislation. For the legislative council, the Greens maintained their

20   See Jim McGinty MLA. 2001. 'Electoral Amendment Bill 2001—Second Reading Speech.' *Hansard*, 1 August 2001. Perth: Parliament of Western Australia.
21   Labor won an additional three seats, while the Greens lost three seats. The Liberal Party won a further three seats, while One Nation lost three seats.

position of enlarging the chamber to six six-member regions, giving metropolitan and non-metropolitan regions a total of 18 members each. The government was in a difficult position. It had to either break its election promise to protect the five seats or find an alternative to retain them. Labor also had to defend itself against accusations of acting out of self-interest, protecting seats where they had strong support, while removing seats from the Nationals' heartland in the agricultural region.

Labor introduced its reform Bill[22] on 30 March 2005, which included the provision for five guaranteed seats in the Mining and Pastoral region. The Bill also increased the size of the council from 34 to 36, and aimed to reduce malapportionment by having 21 metropolitan and 15 non-metropolitan members (this was later amended to 18/18, due to the Greens' insistence). Without the guarantee, the Mining and Pastoral region stood to lose one of its five assembly seats. The legislation's passage in the council was slowed due to the differences between Labor and the Greens (and Cadby); however, Labor negotiated an agreement by suggesting a small increase in the number of assembly seats. Simply by enlarging the size of the assembly from 57 to 59 seats, the average electorate enrolment (based on 2005 election figures) reduces by almost 10 per cent, from 22 092 to 21 343. Combined with the special provision for geographically large electorates, this ensures that the Mining and Pastoral region retains five assembly seats. This satisfied the Greens' demands while keeping Labor's election commitment intact.

The 'one vote, one value' legislation progressed, passing its final parliamentary stage on 17 May 2005, only five days before the newly elected council members took their seats. On 4 May, the government had introduced separate legislation[23] to increase the assembly numbers, which was also passed in the old council's final week of sitting.

Once the electoral distribution commissioners conducted the redistribution process, the metropolitan area had gained eight seats (from 34 to 42), while the Agricultural and South West regions each lost three seats (seven to four, and 11 to eight, respectively). Under a system of full 'one vote, one value', the Mining and Pastoral region would have been reduced to three assembly seats; however, it retained its five seats, as intended (and promised) by Labor.

It is no surprise that the electoral impacts of these reforms, based on 2005 election results, clearly advantage Labor. In the non-metropolitan regions, which lost a total of six seats, Labor would only lose two seats, while the Liberals would lose one or two. The major loser was the National Party, who stood to lose two or three seats and, as a result, parliamentary party status. In the metropolitan area,

---

22   One Vote One Value Bill 2005, later renamed the Electoral Amendment and Repeal Bill 2005.
23   Constitution and Electoral Amendment Bill 2005.

Labor notionally gained an additional five seats, while the Liberals picked up another three seats. The impacts for the assembly are summarised in Table 8.4. It can be seen that in overall terms Labor picked up three seats while the Coalition parties lost one seat.

**Table 8.4 Legislative Assembly: Seats by Party, 2005 Election—Post reform**

| Party | Metropolitan | Non-metropolitan | | | Total |
|---|---|---|---|---|---|
| | | Mining and Pastoral | Agricultural | South West | |
| Labor | 24–9 | 4–4 | 1–0 | 3–2 | 32–5 |
| Liberal | 8–11 | 1–1 | 2–2 | 7–6 | 18–20 |
| Nationals | - | - | 4–2 | 1–0 | 5–2 |
| Independents | 2–2 | - | - | - | 2–2 |
| Total | 34–42 | 5–5 | 7–4 | 11–8 | 57–9 |

Note: 2005 election results are shown first. Post-reform figures are estimates based on 2005 election results and are subject to the results of the redistribution process.

In the legislative council, it is theoretically easier for minor parties to win seats, on the basis that the quota reduces from 16.7 to 14.3 per cent in four regions (but increases from 12.5 to 14.3 per cent in the other two regions). Once again, however, based on 2005 election results, the council reform will benefit Labor, giving the party an increased chance of winning half of the council seats. The Greens will struggle to retain or win seats, and will continue to rely on preferences, especially from any unused Labor overflow.

Of course, the above estimations are based on the 2005 election result. In reality, at the 2008 general election, there was a significant swing of 6 per cent away from Labor, most of which went to the Coalition. As a result, Labor lost government, losing four assembly seats and five council seats.

# Conclusion

It can be seen that an ingenious solution to the impasse between Labor and the Greens was found, one that had nothing to do with voting equality principles and everything to do with political expediency and self-interest. There are reasonable arguments for (and also arguments against) making special provisions for remote electorates, and in this sense the new WA legislation largely replicates that of Queensland, which has similar issues of remoteness; however, increasing the size of the parliament to accommodate political self-interest makes a mockery of consultation processes and principles of representation. In the past 105 years, the assembly has increased in size only from 50 to 59 seats. It is a pity that a rational public debate (as occurred with the Commission on Government inquiry in the 1990s, then subsequently ignored) on the appropriate size of parliament was not held prior to this legislation being passed.

In assessing the merits of the Gallop Government's electoral reforms, it is definitely a major step towards voting equality for the legislative assembly. Malapportionment of about 2:1 will continue to exist—however, this will only be in relation to the five Mining and Pastoral region seats—compared with a similar degree of malapportionment for the 23 non-metropolitan seats under the previous system. Unfortunately, the inherent soundness of the new system is tainted by the political self-interest that was the driver of change.

It is not possible to argue, however, that the reform of the legislative council is in the best interests of voting equality, as the reform actually increases the previous level of malapportionment. Because the new legislation retains geographically distinct non-metropolitan council regions irrespective of population, the level of malapportionment increased in the worst-case scenario from 4.1:1 to 4.6:1.[24] It is remarkable that this legislation, which Labor purports is based on voting equality, actually increases inequality for one house of parliament. Labor has, however, repeatedly made it clear that it is the reform of the assembly, the house of government, that it is really concerned about.

Labor is the clear political winner in these electoral reforms, despite the 2008 election result. It has been able to protect its assembly seats in the Mining and Pastoral region, while severely weakening the Nationals in their areas of support. The Liberal Party will also benefit from the increase in the number of metropolitan seats, and by having a weaker Coalition partner in the Nationals. The Greens have probably been neither big winners nor big losers, but are responsible for increasing the council's level of malapportionment. While political scientists and theorists might lament the lack of democratic principle applied to these reforms, until such electoral reforms can be determined by impartial and independent processes, the political realities of partisanship and self-interest will be the prime movers of reform.

---

24  Based on the number of voters enrolled per member, comparing the Mining and Pastoral region (68 240 enrolled, increasing from five to six members) with the North Metropolitan region (388 999 enrolled; this will change as metropolitan regions will be approximately the same size—about 311 142, decreasing from seven to six members).

# 9. Postal Voting

Australia's major political parties regularly use their numbers in parliament to change electoral laws. Often such amendments are made in line with modern electoral administrative practice, with no obvious partisan benefits. There are, however, several occasions when either Labor or the Coalition ignore electoral 'best practice' and fairness and use their powers over the *Commonwealth Electoral Act 1918* to bring about a political advantage—either for a direct partisan advantage over opposition parties or when opposition numbers are needed for passage of the reforms, for mutual benefit and acting as a party cartel. Usually these reforms have at least the tacit support of the Australian Electoral Commission (AEC). There are times, however, when the Labor and Coalition parties' cartel is united in opposing the AEC's efforts to operate a fairer and more independent electoral administration regime. One such area of electoral management that has been subject to legislative reforms throughout the past 30 years, since the major Commonwealth reforms of 1983, is the administration of postal voting application (PVA) forms. The Australian administration of this aspect of the voting process highlights the conflict between internationally accepted norms for fair elections and governing-party self-interest.

In recent times postal voting has become more prominent in many modern democracies. It is seen as a way of encouraging and increasing voter turnout, especially among travellers, the elderly and the infirm. Postal voting therefore promotes fairer elections by increasing the opportunity for participation by all groups in society. Typically, as with other aspects of electoral administration, the electoral management body is responsible for providing postal vote application forms and processing applications; however, a search of the ACE Electoral Knowledge Network database did not reveal any instances where political parties are as intricately involved in the promotion and administration of the postal voting process as in Australia. In the United Kingdom, however, when postal voting rules were relaxed in 2001 (but not to the extent that allowed party involvement as in Australia), it was accompanied by significant fraud by Labour and Conservative candidates who saw the advantages in controlling postal ballots.[1]

While there is little in the way of specific direction on this aspect of electoral administration, international best-practice literature consistently refers to the need for parties and candidates not to interfere with election processes. The handbook of electoral standards of the International Institute for Democracy and Electoral Assistance (International IDEA), while concentrating on polling-

---

1   Richard Mawrey. 2010. 'Easy Voting Means Fraudulent Voting.' *Quadrant* 54(4).

day behaviour, also refers to the need for parties not to 'handle any official election material'.[2] The emphasis is on parties observing rather than being involved in the conduct of an election.

It is also widely accepted that, to ensure free and fair elections, electoral management bodies should be independent, both of the government of the day and of any political partisan connections. In IDEA's handbook on electoral management design, Wall et al. identify seven aspects of independent electoral management. Particularly pertinent to the discussion on postal voting applications are the three aspects of: *institutional arrangements*—is the electoral management body institutionally independent from the executive branch of government; *implementation*—does the electoral management body exercise full responsibility for implementation of election processes; and *powers*—does the electoral management body have powers to develop the electoral regulatory framework independently under the law?

IDEA goes on to argue that the legitimacy of election results is enhanced if electoral authorities are perceived to be impartial and not subject to political interference or control.[3] This argument stresses the importance of a 'perception' of independence, irrespective of the organisational framework that an electoral management body operates in.

## The increased use of postal voting

There has been a steady increase in the use of postal voting in Australian federal elections during the study period, from 2.83 per cent in 1993 to 6.15 per cent at the 2010 election.[4] There have been a number of reasons for this increase. The 1983 reforms to the *Commonwealth Electoral Act 1918* introduced a category of 'general postal voter'; a 1990 amendment allowed employment reasons as grounds to apply for a postal vote; parties and candidates were allowed to include PVAs in their campaigning material following a 1998 amendment; and further amendments in 2000 and 2001 facilitated the electronic provision of postal voter information to parties.

The growth in postal voting raises three important questions in regard to the integrity of elections. First, are there sufficient safeguards to ensure that postal votes (which are, by their nature, cast in an uncontrolled environment) have been made freely, without coercion or undue influence? Second, can election

---

2  IDEA [Institute for Democracy and Electoral Assistance]. 2002. *International Electoral Standards: Guidelines for Reviewing the Legal Framework of Elections*. Stockholm: International IDEA, pp. 85–6.

3  Alan Wall et al. 2006. *Electoral Management Design: The International IDEA Handbook*.

4  Senate figures. Prior to the 1993 election, postal voting was about 4–6 per cent; however, pre-poll voting was introduced for the 1993 election, resulting in a significant initial drop in the rate of postal voting.

officials have confidence that a postal vote has been cast by the person stated on the accompanying application forms (and has that person had a legitimate reason for applying for the postal vote)? Finally, because of the ability for political parties to be intricately involved in the distribution and collection of PVA forms, does this corrupt the process and increase the possibility of also disenfranchising some voters?[5]

In answer to the first two questions, it is impossible to ascertain or control the conditions in which postal voters cast their votes, and whether an application has been forged. With an accurate electoral roll, however, and the electronic availability of signatures from enrolment forms for crosschecking PVA signatures, there can be a good degree of confidence that identities are correct. The answer to the question of whether voters have legitimate reasons to lodge a postal vote is less clear. Schedule 2 of the *Commonwealth Electoral Act 1918* specifies several circumstances when an application for a postal vote may be made—namely, when the voter: will be outside the State or Territory; will not be within 8 km of a polling booth; will be travelling throughout polling hours; is ill, infirm or approaching childbirth (or caring for someone in these conditions); is in a hospital without polling facilities; has religious beliefs that preclude attending a polling booth; is in prison; is a silent elector; or has work conditions preventing attendance at a polling booth. In 2010, eligibility was further broadened to anyone who will be outside their electorate on polling day.[6]

As applicants only need to specify that they are eligible for a postal vote, without indicating the particular reason (at least, at the federal level), there is a relaxed onus of proof. Electoral commissions understandably do not investigate applicants' eligibility in the middle of conducting an election, but a doubling of applicants in recent years suggests that more voters are using postal voting as a convenience rather than a necessity. If voters were required to provide the reason they were applying for a postal vote, it would not only strengthen the onus of proof, it would also provide the AEC with valuable data on how it could better adapt to voters' needs.

## Party involvement in postal voting

Part XV of the Act details the process of applying for a postal vote. As a result of the amendments in the past 30 years, political parties can now actively solicit for electors to lodge postal votes. Such solicitation is commonly carried out by the parliamentary representatives of the major parties, who can use both taxpayer-

---

5   Norm Kelly. 2011. 'Australian Electoral Administration and Electoral Integrity.' In *Electoral Democracy: Australian Prospects*, eds Tham, Costar and Orr. Melbourne: Melbourne University Press.
6   Schedule 8 of the *Electoral and Referendum (Modernisation and Other Measures) Act 2010*.

funded and party resources, such as elector databases and printing allowances, to mail postal vote applications to enrolled voters. It is also standard practice for the mail-outs to include a return envelope to the member or party, which then forwards the application on to the AEC. AEC figures show that of all PVAs received indirectly from electors (that is, through party agents and others), 98.7 per cent were forwarded by the Labor and Coalition parties (see Table 9.1). This is an indication that the governing or major parties have an advantage over less-resourced parties in influencing electors.

**Table 9.1 PVAs Received by the AEC for the 2010 Election: Period Between Witness Signature and AEC Receipt of PVA**

| Source | Sent directly to the AEC | Sent via Labor | Sent via Nationals | Sent via Liberal[1] | Other |
|---|---|---|---|---|---|
| Same day | 15 013 | 792 | 24 | 607 | 212 |
| 1 day later | 36 619 | 6094 | 299 | 9222 | 228 |
| 2 days later | 33 215 | 9572 | 594 | 13 896 | 237 |
| 3 days later | 28 152 | 10 268 | 639 | 13 664 | 334 |
| 4 days later | 22 955 | 10 793 | 773 | 13 433 | 305 |
| 5 days later | 14 581 | 9529 | 758 | 10 962 | 270 |
| 6 days later | 9214 | 7478 | 638 | 8987 | 257 |
| 7 days later | 5884 | 5883 | 610 | 6942 | 219 |
| 8 days later | 3391 | 4258 | 417 | 4309 | 92 |
| 9 days later | 2020 | 2842 | 287 | 2964 | 57 |
| 10 days later | 1616 | 2508 | 315 | 2636 | 67 |
| 11 days later | 1399 | 2371 | 281 | 2429 | 39 |
| 12 days later | 1120 | 2109 | 350 | 2360 | 18 |
| 13 days later | 947 | 1914 | 314 | 2304 | 15 |
| 14 + days later | 3996 | 6315 | 392 | 5016 | 50 |
| Total | 180 122 | 82 726 | 6691 | 99 371 | 2400 |

[1] Includes Country Liberal Party

Source: AEC submission to JSCEM, 21 February 2011, p. 84.

The AEC's figures also show that 49 per cent of all PVAs are returned by electors directly to the AEC. This leaves more than 51 per cent being returned via a third party (usually Labor or the Coalition, as shown above). For the 2010 election, this amounted to more than 191 000 applications that were delayed in being received by the AEC due to them being sent on a circuitous route. This is a substantial number, roughly equivalent to two House of Representatives seats, and is an increase of more than 87 000 on 2007 figures.

Over the past 20 years, the AEC has consistently criticised the practice of such overt party involvement in the conduct of an election. The AEC's arguments include the following:

- There is a potential for voters to become confused, thinking that the parties are the ones who are responsible for postal voting, rather than the AEC.

- Delays occur, due to applications not being returned directly to the AEC, resulting in possible disenfranchisement.

- Electors often receive more than one PVA, sometimes resulting in multiple applications being received by the AEC, adding to its administrative burden.

- There is unnecessary use of postal voting, increasing costs and delaying the finalisation of results.

- Political parties stockpile PVAs before sending them to the AEC, resulting in processing delays and, at times, disenfranchisement. Stockpiling is an offence under Section 197 of the Act.

- The secrecy and integrity of the ballot might be compromised, as votes are cast in an uncontrolled environment.

- Parties attempt to obscure the fact that the PVA is returned to a party address, by using terms such as 'Returning Officer'.

- Party officials 'correct' details on PVAs before sending them to the AEC.

Despite the AEC's ongoing concerns, the JSCEM and successive governments have chosen to support the continued involvement of parties in the PVA process. At times, the JSCEM has shifted blame to the AEC for some of the problems, stating that it 'is possible that some [voters] were disenfranchised as a result of administrative errors by the AEC'.[7] The general thrust of JSCEM reports is that the parties are providing a public service in distributing PVA material—for example:

> The Committee is of the view that distribution of PVAs by candidates provides an important and now well-established service to electors, and that it is important for candidates and political parties to be confident that a service initiated by them has been successfully concluded. The relatively high rate of return experienced in many electorates demonstrates the helpfulness and popularity of the service. Breaking with this practice at future elections may lead to significant voter inconvenience and possibly disenfranchisement.[8]

---

7   JSCEM [Joint Standing Committee on Electoral Matters]. 2000. *The 1998 Federal Election: Report of the Inquiry into the Conduct of the 1998 Federal Election and Matters Related Thereto*. Canberra: Commonwealth of Australia, p. 60.

8   JSCEM [Joint Standing Committee on Electoral Matters]. 2003. *The 2001 Federal Election: Report of the Inquiry into the Conduct of the 2001 Federal Election and Matters Related Thereto*. Canberra: Commonwealth of Australia, p. 149.

This view was supported by both Labor and Liberal party members during a 2008 JSCEM hearing:

> We are liaising with a number of voters about their rights to vote. We are making sure that, if they have not got their postal ballot, they ring us— they do not ring [the AEC]...Their relationship is with their political party, not the AEC.[9]

> The elector who has dealt with the party does not ring [the AEC], the elector rings us...These [PVAs] go out with big Labor Party and Liberal Party stamps on them. I do not think they are confused where this information is coming from.[10]

> Thanks to the parties, most voters, within a couple of days of the election being called, have got a PVA in their hot little hands. If the parties have no incentive to send that out they probably will not, therefore voters probably will not have the PVA in their hot little hands in that first week of the election.[11]

Under the Commonwealth system, parties can, either accidentally or deliberately, delay a PVA from reaching the AEC, meaning that eligible voters might be prevented from casting a vote. During JSCEM's inquiry into the 1998 election, the AEC identified 174 electors who were disenfranchised through apparent delays in parties returning PVAs. In reporting this, JSCEM attempted to spread the blame by stating in their report that:

> It is not entirely clear from the evidence that the political parties are wholly responsible for the 174 disenfranchised postal voters. It is possible that some were disenfranchised as a result of administrative errors by the AEC. In the absence of further evidence, the Committee urges both the AEC and the political parties to improve their processing of postal vote application forms.[12]

The AEC has raised its concerns since at least 1993 about the delays created by parties stockpiling PVAs, and evidence in its 2008 submission to JSCEM suggests the practice is continuing, with a surge in the number of applications being received more than 14 days after the witness signature on the PVA (see Table 9.1). The proportion of all PVAs received was far higher for the parties

---

9 Jon Sullivan MP. 2008. *Official Committee Hansard*. Joint Standing Committee on Electoral Matters, Friday, 27 June 2008. Canberra: Parliament of Australia, p. 11.

10 Scott Morrison MP. 2008. *Official Committee Hansard*. Joint Standing Committee on Electoral Matters, Friday, 27 June 2008. Canberra: Parliament of Australia, p. 14.

11 Senator Simon Birmingham. 2008. *Official Committee Hansard*. Joint Standing Committee on Electoral Matters, Friday, 27 June 2008. Canberra: Parliament of Australia, p. 13.

12 JSCEM [Joint Standing Committee on Electoral Matters]. 2000. *The 1998 Federal Election: Report of the Inquiry into the Conduct of the 1998 Federal Election and Matters Related Thereto*, pp. 59–60.

(Labor, 7.6 per cent; Liberal, 5.1 per cent) for this category (more than 14 days after signing) than for those sent directly to the AEC (2.2 per cent of all PVAs). This indicates delays from the double mailing involved in sending a PVA to the AEC via a party address, and possibly from the parties stockpiling PVAs prior to sending them to the AEC. In both cases, the possibility of voters being disenfranchised increases.

A test was conducted during the 2007 election period to gauge the service from the parties and their attitude to dealing with PVAs. The author received PVAs in the mail from the Labor and Liberal parties, as outlined below.

## Labor

The Labor package (see excerpt at Figure 9.1) was received in an envelope marked 'Important Voter Information Enclosed—From Bob McMullan MP Federal Member for Fraser'. On one side of a folded A3-size pamphlet was the PVA and early voting information from the AEC. The other side contained party campaign material (including three photos of Bob McMullan and Labor mentioned 11 times). On three panels, reference is made to a 'Postal Voting Hotline—6257 7575'. The number is that of McMullan's campaign office. A reply-paid envelope was enclosed for the voter to send the PVA: it was addressed to Bob McMullan MP.

Figure 9.1 Labor Postal Voting Information Leaflet (excerpt)

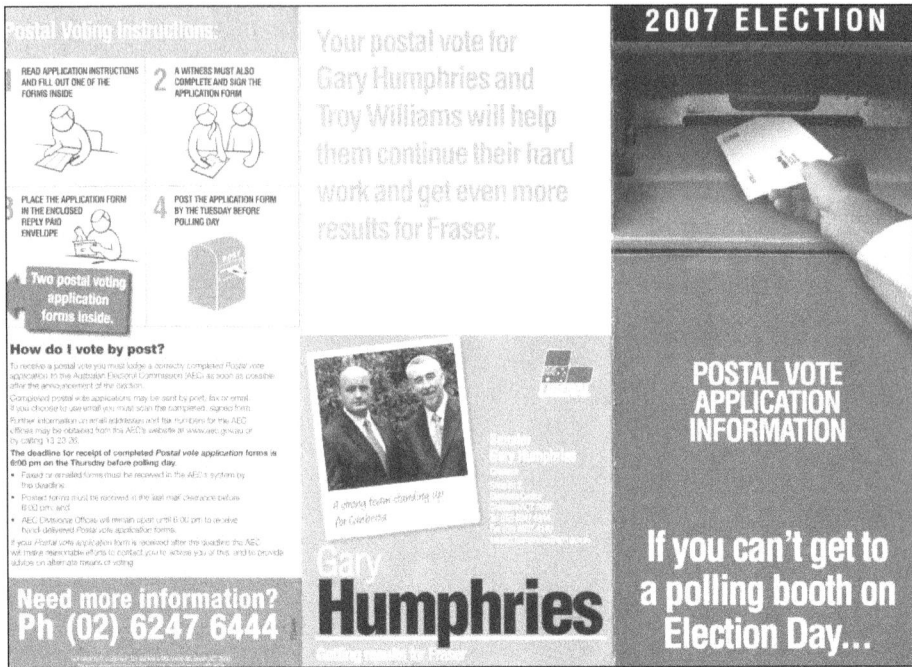

**Figure 9.2 Liberal Postal Voting Information Leaflet (excerpt)**

## Liberal

The Liberal Party's Senator Gary Humphries sent a personally addressed A4-size campaign letter, at the end of which was the text: 'PS: I enclose a postal vote application in case you are unable to vote on polling day.' The enclosed PVA (see excerpt at Figure 9.2) was on a slightly larger than A4 folded pamphlet. The PVA and associated AEC information were displayed on seven of the eight panels, with the remaining panel containing party campaign material. At the bottom of one panel of AEC material was a message in large font: 'Need more information? Ph (02) 6247 6444.' This is Senator Humphries' electorate office number. A reply-paid envelope was enclosed, addressed to the Canberra Liberals.

In both cases, the parties provided official AEC information, including the AEC's phone number (in small font), while promoting their own phone numbers in a much larger font. To gauge how willing the parties were to give out AEC contact details, a call was made to each of the printed party numbers, asking for the address to send the PVA directly to the AEC. The responses were:

> Labor: You want to send it straight to them, OK. It's GPO Box 2867, Canberra City.

Liberal: I'll just grab it for you. Here it is. It's GPO Box 2867, Canberra City.

A call was made to the AEC information line, also seeking their postal address:

AEC: What is your postcode?

Caller: 2602.

AEC: So you're in New South Wales.

Caller: No, I'm in the ACT.

AEC: There's only one electorate in Canberra, isn't there?

Caller: [Explained that there are two electorates in the ACT.]

After a pause, the postal address was given. The call took three minutes.

These calls give the impression that the parties are better equipped to respond to electors' inquiries. It appears, however, that the parties' proficiency in dealing with PVA inquiries has developed in response to the fact that a significant number of electors probably believe that it is the parties' responsibility to deal with these matters—a perception that is encouraged by the parties themselves. In terms of fairness and equity, it is apparent that the Coalition and Labor parties are the only ones that have the financial and database resources to engage in mass mail-outs to electors.

With the incumbency benefit of having electronic databases of electors, these mail-outs can be designed in a personalised format. The databases and tracking systems that have been developed by the major parties also include information that indicates whether an elector is a possible party supporter. Although there is no evidence that this practice occurs, it is conceivable that a party might delay forwarding a completed PVA to the AEC if the elector is identified as a non-supporter. For example, in 2009 the Australian National Audit Office (ANAO) observed a political party lodging PVAs the day prior to a by-election— too late for postal ballots to be issued—despite these being completed by the applicant and received by the party well before the election.[13] The question is whether this was a case of party administration incompetency or deliberate disenfranchisement of non-party supporters. The ANAO recommended that all PVAs should be required to be delivered directly to the AEC.

---

13   Australian National Audit Office. 2010a. *The Auditor-General Audit Report No. 28 2009–10 Performance Audit: The Australian Electoral Commission's Preparation for and Conduct of the 2007 Federal General Election.* Canberra: Australian National Audit Office, p. 154.

# Australian Electoral Commission action

Despite continuing evidence of voters being disenfranchised due to the delays in parties returning PVAs to the AEC, the AEC has been reluctant to initiate prosecutions against the parties.[14] This reluctance might be due in part to the AEC's need to keep the parties 'on side', as the parties' support is needed if legislative change is to occur. While the AEC is limited by its legislation, the recent history of the PVA issue indicates that the AEC does not operate as an independent body, and that it falls short in terms of IDEA's criteria on institutional arrangements, implementation and powers.

The fact that the AEC in its submission to JSCEM in 2008 did not argue for the removal of political party PVAs suggests that the commission is aware of the political realities and has chosen not to fight the main issue, instead concentrating on administrative problems related to this political involvement in the election process. In particular, the AEC reiterated its previous concerns that political party PVAs were delayed in reaching the AEC, due to them being sent to a party address for forwarding. The AEC provided a simple solution to this problem, suggesting that the Commonwealth Act could be amended by adding a provision that already exists for postal voting applications in the Australian Capital Territory. The Australian Capital Territory's *Electoral Act* provides for an offence to induce a person 'to return the completed form to an address that is not an address authorised by the Commissioner' (Section 143[2] of the *Electoral Act 1992 [ACT]*). The JSCEM, however, chose to reject the AEC's recommendation, stating that delays were 'relatively minor' and 'may be influenced by other factors'.[15] The JSCEM's report did not explain what 'other factors' might be involved.

The JSCEM's 2009 report into the conduct of the 2007 election also identified that the receipt of political party PVAs resulted in multiple voting in 'quite a few' cases, where voters used a postal vote and then voted again on election day. This was particularly common with voters from culturally and linguistically diverse backgrounds. This seemingly critical aspect of the impacts of political party involvement in the PVA process is not discussed in any greater detail anywhere in the committee's report; however, the parties' knowledge of which electors have applied for a postal vote allows for possible electoral fraud. If a

---

14 JSCEM [Joint Standing Committee on Electoral Matters]. 2000. *The 1998 Federal Election: Report of the Inquiry into the Conduct of the 1998 Federal Election and Matters Related Thereto*, pp. 59–60; JSCEM [Joint Standing Committee on Electoral Matters]. 2003. *The 2001 Federal Election: Report of the Inquiry into the Conduct of the 2001 Federal Election and Matters Related Thereto*, pp. 147–8.
15 JSCEM [Joint Standing Committee on Electoral Matters]. 2009. *Report on the Conduct of the 2007 Federal Election and Matters Related Thereto*. Canberra: Commonwealth of Australia, p. 213.

party official is aware that someone is unlikely to attend a polling booth (in this case, because they have applied for a postal vote), it becomes easier to fraudulently vote for them at a polling station on election day.

An added advantage for parties in government is the ability to send out PVAs (with campaigning material) to coincide with the announcement of the election date. As Australia does not have fixed dates for its general elections, it is the prime minister who recommends the election date to the governor-general. This provides a strategic advantage for governing parties to plan their election campaigns and book their advertising, while opposition and minor parties need to be prepared for several possibilities. According to the author's sources, in 2007, with Labor in opposition, it took three days after Prime Minister John Howard announced the election date to send out their PVAs. In 2010, with Labor in government, PVAs were sent out on Friday 16 July, prior to the formal announcement of the election the following day. The Liberal Party had mailed 90 per cent of their PVAs by the Sunday night.

As stated earlier, a search of an international electoral law database failed to find other instances of party involvement in the PVA process. This does not mean that there are not cases where this does occur, simply that an initial search has failed to identify examples. It does appear, however, that where the availability of postal voting increases, through the relaxation of rules for attending a polling booth, parties see benefits in increasing and influencing the use of postal voting. This has been evident in the increase in postal voting in Australia since the 1980s.

More recently in the United Kingdom, electoral laws have been amended to allow postal voting 'on demand', leading a British electoral commissioner to state that postal voting on demand is 'lethal to the democratic process'.[16] The British reforms have led to a significant increase in electoral offences and other allegations of fraud.

# Recent developments

In 2010, the Rudd Labor Government proposed several changes to postal voting regulations.[17] Several of these could be considered relatively non-contentious, such as allowing for the electronic lodgement of PVAs. In addition, the Rudd Government was not suggesting that political parties be removed from the postal voting process entirely, but did put forward amendments to require

---

16  Stuart Wilks-Heeg. 2008. *Purity of Elections in the UK: Causes for Concern*. York: The Joseph Rowntree Reform Trust Limited.
17  The Electoral and Referendum Amendment (Modernisation and Other Measures) Bill 2010.

PVAs to be returned directly to the AEC—as had been recommended by the AEC (repeatedly) and the ANAO—and to prohibit written material from being attached to PVAs. These two reforms were, however, opposed by the Liberal–Nationals Coalition. In opposing these reforms, the Coalition argued that

> it strongly suspects that this has been done in a cynical attempt to undermine the extremely successful Postal Voting processes of the Coalition parties. Even a simple reading of the voter returns shows that the Coalition consistently polls higher with postal votes than with any other type of declaration vote.[18]

Opposition Shadow Minister Andrew Robb argued in a similar vein, and chose to ignore the AEC's and ANAO's arguments:

> This is a totally cynical move and the motives of the Labor Party on these aspects of the bills need to be very seriously questioned…which appear to have no merit other than that of being an attack on the coalition…it is very clear that without any arguments, good or bad, being advanced in support of it, the Labor government has sought to sneak this measure in.

These arguments highlight the political nature of the postal voting issue, and suggest that both sides of politics might be more interested in the political advantage that can be gained from the regulation of postal voting, rather than issues of fairness and equity. The Bill was debated in June 2010, and the Labor government (coincidentally, the first day of the Gillard Labor Government) agreed to the removal of these provisions, arguing that it would forgo these reforms for the sake of achieving the other measures contained in the legislation. As Independent Senator Nick Xenophon stated, 'this is an opportunity lost'. Following the passing of the legislation, the AEC again recommended that PVAs be required to be returned directly to the AEC.

The fact that Labor and the Coalition combine application forms with their own campaigning literature is indicative of the political advantage in being the source of 'official' information. By requiring these applications to be sent to a party office rather than directly to the AEC, the parties are provided with information that is added to their databases on individual constituents (which, incidentally, constituents are not able to access, due to the parties' exemption under the *Privacy Act 1988*). Political parties are not altruistic by nature; there is a political advantage in undertaking this work. With the knowledge of the date

---

18  Senate Finance and Public Administration Legislation Committee. 2010. *Report into the Electoral and Referendum Amendment (How-to-Vote Cards and Other Measures) Bill 2010 and the Electoral and Referendum Amendment (Modernisation and Other Measures) Bill 2010*. Canberra: Parliament of Australia.

they lodge PVAs with the AEC, parties are able to calculate when electors will receive their ballot papers and will send party campaign material to coincide with this.

There is strong and ongoing evidence in Australia that political parties' involvement in the PVA process leads to delays in the AEC sending out ballot papers. This inevitably means that some intending electors will miss out on making a vote. This, combined with the stated instances of multiple voting, might easily lead to a British-style scandal in a tight contest at a future election. What is assured is that while political parties continue to be allowed to be involved in the postal voting process, the integrity of Australia's 'independent' electoral administration is undermined.

In addition, there is significant waste of human and physical resources. For the 2007 general election, MPs and senators printed 16.5 million PVAs, which is 2.9 million more PVA forms than the number of voters enrolled for the election. At least 97.6 per cent of these forms were not used. In two cases, MPs printed four times as many PVAs as the number of people enrolled in their electorates.[19]

Finally, it should be remembered that Section 219 of the *Commonwealth Electoral Act 1918* states that '[a] candidate shall not in any way take part in the conduct of an election'. While this part of the Act relates to 'The Polling', meaning election-day activities, why should postal voting, which is part of the polling, be treated any differently?

---

19   Australian National Audit Office. 2009. *Auditor-General Report no. 3 2009–10 Audit Report: Administration of Parliamentarians' Entitlements by the Department of Finance and Regulation*. Canberra: Australian National Audit Office, pp. 147–8.

# 10. The Size of Parliament

One of the concepts of the fairness of electoral systems is equality of representation—sometimes defined as 'one vote, one value'. Another aspect of fairness is that citizens have reasonable access to their elected representatives. In 1983, the incoming Hawke Labor Government established the Joint Select Committee on Electoral Reform (JSCER) to progress Labor's substantial electoral reform agenda. Following its first inquiry, the JSCER put forward equality of representation and accessibility as reasons why the size of parliament should be increased. On the first issue of representativeness, the committee argued that due to the constitutional guarantee of a minimum of five House of Representatives seats for each State, Tasmania's seats were malapportioned in their favour, and an increase in the overall number of seats would dilute this disparity. On the second issue—accessibility of members—the committee noted that the number of voters had grown considerably since the last significant increase in seats, which had occurred in 1949. As a result, a decrease in voters per electorate was required so that members could more effectively serve their electorates. The parliament supported the committee's view.

## The 1983 Federal Parliament increase in size

An interesting question in relation to the 1983 increase in the size of the House of Representatives, from 125 to 148 seats, is whether it had an impact on the representativeness of the House in proportional terms. While acknowledging that voting behaviour influences results, Table 10.1 indicates that there has been little, if any, impact on proportionality based on the increase in seats. Using Gallagher's Least Squares Index (LSI), there was an average index score of 10.98 for the six elections prior to the increase (1972–83), and a similar average score of 10.37 in the 10 elections since the change (1984–2010). This is understandable as the reform was primarily a correction for the growth in the number of voters enrolled in each electorate, rather than a change in the majoritarian, single-member voting system. Therefore, the single-member majority system, combined with the strong two-party system that exists across Australia, makes it difficult for the proportionality of the House to be significantly improved by providing opportunities for lesser parties that gain small but significant levels of support, such as, in the past, the Democrats and One Nation and, currently, the Greens.

## Table 10.1 Proportionality in the House of Representatives

| Election | Major party support (%) | Gallagher's Least Squares Index |
|---|---|---|
| 1972 | 92.1 | 6.96 |
| 1974 | 94.2 | 6.08 |
| 1975 | 95.9 | 14.22 |
| 1977 | 87.8 | 15.16 |
| 1980 | 91.6 | 12.94 |
| 1983 | 93.1 | 10.54 |
| 1984 | 92.6 | 7.87 |
| 1987 | 91.9 | 10.57 |
| 1990 | 82.9 | 12.94 |
| 1993 | 89.2 | 9.08 |
| 1996 | 86.1 | 11.23 |
| 1998 | 79.6 | 11.34 |
| 2001 | 80.8 | 9.80 |
| 2004 | 84.3 | 9.00 |
| 2007 | 85.5 | 10.50 |
| 2010 | 81.6 | 11.32 |

Notes: The smaller the index figure, the more proportional is the result. Data in Appendix D.

What is more significant in terms of the representative nature of the House is the increase in support for geographically dispersed minor parties, for whom winning seats is extremely difficult under the single-member electorate system. Table 10.1 shows the levels of support for the major parties (Labor and the Coalition) prior to and throughout the study period. Although major-party support has recovered in recent elections from its low of 79.6 per cent in 1998, it remains significantly lower than the levels experienced in the 1970s and 1980s. This is largely a reflection of voting behaviour rather than the impact of reforms. As WA political scientist David Charnock notes, the impact of the increase in the number of seats has diminished over time as enrolment numbers have steadily increased. In comparison, Charnock argues that the redistribution methods introduced in 1983 are possibly a more significant factor in terms of any partisan bias from the reforms.[1]

Section 24 of the Australian Constitution requires that for every seat in the House of Representatives there 'shall be, as nearly as practicable, twice the number of senators'. An increase in the size of the House of Representatives requires an increase in the size of the Senate to retain the approximate 2:1 ratio. The 1983–

---

1 David Charnock. 1994. 'Electoral Bias in Australia 1980–1993: The Impact of the 1983 Electoral Amendments.' *Australian Journal of Political Science* 29(3): 498–9.

84 reforms therefore included an increase in the size of the Senate from 64 to 76 seats. As the Senate is based on a proportional representation voting system, an increase in seat magnitude has the potential to impact on the ability of minor parties to win seats, and therefore on the proportionality of representation. The increase in seats resulted in a reduction in the quota required to win a State Senate seat in an ordinary half-Senate election from 16.7 per cent (for five seats) to 14.3 per cent (six seats). For the less-common full-Senate elections, the quota reduced from 9.1 per cent (10 seats) to 7.7 per cent (12 seats). The impacts of this change on proportionality are shown in Table 10.2.

**Table 10.2 Proportionality in the Senate**

| Election | Major party support (%) | Gallagher's Least Squares Index |
|---|---|---|
| 1970 | 80.4 | 3.18 |
| 1974[1] | 91.2 | 4.23 |
| 1975[1] | 92.6 | 3.34 |
| 1977 | 82.3 | 8.49 |
| 1980 | 85.7 | 2.05 |
| 1983[1] | 85.5 | 3.94 |
| 1984[2] | 81.7 | 5.71 |
| 1987[3] | 84.8 | 2.93 |
| 1990 | 85.4 | 5.01 |
| 1993 | 87.3 | 3.54 |
| 1996 | 80.2 | 5.53 |
| 1998 | 75.0 | 7.24 |
| 2001 | 76.1 | 8.45 |
| 2004 | 80.1 | 8.33 |
| 2007 | 80.2 | 6.05 |
| 2010 | 73.7 | 6.30 |

[1] Full-Senate election: 10 seats per State.

[2] Seven senators elected from each State to increase the overall size of the Senate to 76.

[3] Full-Senate election: 12 seats per State.

Note: Data in Appendix E.

It can be seen from these figures that proportionality has actually decreased since 1983, although there was greater proportionality in the only double-dissolution election since the increase in seats—2.93 in 1987—than the average of 3.84 in the three double-dissolutions in the decade prior to the change (in 1974, 1975 and 1983). The most obvious impact has been the decreased proportionality in the five most recent elections (1998–2007)—a period that has also seen the highest non–major-party vote in history. The voting figures suggest that the increased disproportionality is a combination of the major parties becoming more over-represented and some minor parties winning significant support without winning seats. In fairness terms, the reduced quotas required to win Senate seats improve the ability for the Senate to be more representative of voters' choices; however, while the reform is an improvement on the fairness of election outcomes, voter behaviour (that is, who voters actually choose) has resulted in less proportional results.

As for the reasons behind the increase in the size of the parliament, current ACT Electoral Commissioner, Phillip Green, noted in 1986 that a major concern of the JSCER was how an increase in the Senate size would impact on the possibility of a major party having control of the Senate. Green suggests that the committee might have preferred to increase the Senate to 88 (14 senators per State, plus four from the Territories) to maintain the pattern of each State electing an odd number of senators at half-Senate elections (seen by some as advantageous for the major parties). Such an increase was, however, considered to be too extreme, especially with the 2:1 requirement for the House of Representatives.[2]

Green goes on to argue that the real impetus for reform came from the National Party, which had suggested the increase to the JSCER as a way to consolidate and possibly expand their House of Representatives seats in rural Australia. Meanwhile, the Labor Party thought such an increase might be a way to reduce the impact of the Democrats, who had gained the balance of power in the Senate in 1981. The reforms were passed by Labor with National Party support, with the Liberals and Democrats opposing the measure.

# The Tasmanian case: reform for political advantage

Tasmania's *Parliamentary Reform Act 1998* was the culmination of almost two decades of public debate on reducing the size of the legislative assembly. From the early 1980s—virtually from the time the Greens first won representation in the Tasmanian Parliament in 1982—there had been suggestions that the house of assembly should be reduced in size from 35 members. Associated with this debate were calls for a complementary reduction in the size of the 19-member legislative council, in keeping with the tradition of having the upper house roughly half the size of the lower house. Table 10.3 details the various attempts to bring about change during this period. It is interesting to note that the Greens

---

2   Phillip Green. 1986. 'The Australian Labor Party and the Commonwealth Electoral System 1972–1986.' Unpublished Litt. B. sub-thesis. Canberra, p. 96.

held the balance of power in the assembly from 1989 to 1992, and again from 1996 to 1998. It can be seen in the table that it was during this second period of balance of power, when the Liberal Party was in minority government, that efforts to reduce the size of the assembly increased.

**Table 10.3 Reduction in Size of Tasmanian Parliament: Reform Process**

| Year | Reform action | Proposal and outcome | Election outcome (assembly) Liberal–Labor–Greens |
|------|---------------|----------------------|---------------------------------------------------|
| 1982 | General election | | 19–14–1 (Independent Green) (+ 1 Democrats) |
| 1983 | Advisory Committee— Ogilvie Report (1984) | Recommends against any reduction | |
| 1986 | General election | | 19–14–2 (Independent Greens) |
| 1989 | General election | | 17–13–5 |
| 1992 | General election | | 19–11–5 |
| 1993 | Liberal government legislation | Recommends bicameral parliament with reduction from 35 to 30 MHAs. Proposal lapses | |
| 1994 | Board of inquiry— Morling Report | Recommends against a reduction but, if size is to be reduced, it should be a unicameral parliament of 44: four x seven-member electorates; 16 x single-member electorates | |
| 1995 | Labor opposition legislation | Recommends bicameral parliament of 25 MHAs and 15 MLCs. Proposal lapses | |
| 1996 | General election | | 16–14–4 (+ 1 Independent) |
| 1997 | Tasmanian Chamber of Commerce and Industry proposal | Recommends unicameral parliament of 40: five x five-member electorates; 15 single-member electorates | |
| 1997 | Commonwealth–State inquiry—Nixon Report | Recommends unicameral parliament of 27: three x nine-member electorates | |

| Year | Reform action | Proposal and outcome | Election outcome (assembly) Liberal–Labor–Greens |
|------|---------------|----------------------|----------------------------------------------------|
| 1997 | Liberal government proposes referendum | Recommends unicameral parliament of 40: four x seven-member electorates; 12 single-member electorates. Proposal lapses | |
| 1997–98 | Various attempts at reducing the size of parliament | Nixon Report not supported; Liberal government wants 28 MHAs, based on Morling Report, Labor opposition wants 25 MHAs | |
| May 1998 | Labor opposition introduces Bill; Liberal Premier Rundle recalls parliament in July to debate Bill | Proposal for bicameral parliament: 25 MHAs and 15 MLCs. Bill passes in two days with Labor and Liberal support | |
| 1998 | General election Assembly size reduced to 25 members | | 10–14–1 |
| 2002 | General election | | 7–14–4 |
| 2006 | General election | | 7–14–4 |
| 2010 | General election | | 10–10–5 |

Note: Greens were first elected in 1982.

The reduction in assembly electorates in 1998 from seven to five members increased the required quota from 12.5 per cent to 16.7 per cent, making it far more difficult for minor parties such as the Greens to win seats. This was evident in the election held a month after the reform was implemented, in which the Greens managed to retain only one of their four seats. In the subsequent elections of 2002 and 2006, however, the Greens recovered to win four seats on both occasions. Political commentary at the time of the reform made it clear that the change was primarily designed by the two major parties to remove, or at least reduce, the influence of the Greens. Comments from interviewees support this popular view. Comments from Tasmanian politicians included:

[NK: Was that simply a matter of diminishing the role of the Greens?]

Yep, that's my view—to increase the quota from about 11 per cent to 16. It worked the first time and didn't work the second. It was politically expedient at the time.

The real reason was that some idiot had told [Premier] Rundle and [Opposition Leader] Bacon that this would be the way to make it very difficult for the Greens to win seats. We've got a ridiculously small parliament. It's not working. It hasn't got the numbers to work.

The impact of the reduction in size of the assembly can be observed using Gallagher's Least Squares Index, as illustrated in Table 10.4. The proportionality index for the five general elections prior to the reform averaged 4.14, while the average increased to 5.65 at the four elections since the reform. This indicates that the reform has had a negative impact on representation.

**Table 10.4 Tasmanian Legislative Assembly: Gallagher's Least Squares Index**

| Election | Gallagher's Least Squares Index |
|---|---|
| 1982 | 6.71 |
| 1986 | 4.25 |
| 1989 | 3.02 |
| 1992 | 2.82 |
| 1996 | 3.88 |
| 1998 | 9.93 |
| 2002 | 3.79 |
| 2006 | 5.73 |
| 2010 | 3.14 |

Note: Data in Appendix F.

While voter behaviour will also have an impact on proportionality, an increase in the quota makes it more likely that such negative impacts will occur. Furthermore, as noted in an interviewee's comment earlier, this partisan-driven reform has reduced the capacity of the parliament to effectively carry out its functions of legislative review and executive scrutiny, and to act as a channel for community participation—a result of the 26 per cent overall decrease in the size of the parliament from 54 to 40 members.

# The Australian Capital Territory

Since the inception of the ACT Assembly, there has been regular debate on its size. Partisan advantage is at the heart of these debates on whether, and to what level, the size of the assembly should be increased. A 1998 governance inquiry, the Pettit Review, recommended that the assembly be increased from 17 to 21 members. Democratic arguments put forward in support of an increase included that 'an increase in the size of the Assembly is important just to provide a greater pool of people for the Ministry and the non-executive element'.[3] In the following year, an assembly committee inquiry recommended against an increase, noting that the proposed change was unpopular with the public. Proposals to increase the size of the assembly—implying more politicians and therefore increased costs—always tend to be unpopular with the wider public, and the tone of the committee report indicates concern for a voter backlash if such an increase occurred.

The dominance of partisan advantage is more clearly expressed in a dissenting report from a 2002 inquiry: 'It is painfully obvious that Members who support this minor increase [to 21 members] do so from an ill-conceived intention to protect personal and party interests.'[4] The Australian Democrats, Greens and the Liberal Party all supported a model of 21 members (three electorates of seven members). Labor, however, supported an increase to 25 members (five electorates of five members). There is a clear advantage for Independents and minor parties such as the Greens and Democrats in having electorates with a greater magnitude, as this increases proportionality and improves their chances of winning seats. Labor sees advantages in having five-member electorates. The political reasons for this were explained by one interviewee:

> Labor thinks it has a much better chance of getting three out of five seats than it has of getting four out of seven seats, so it thought it had a better chance of getting majority government with a five-by-five than three-by-seven and the Liberals probably thought that, more so, and thought that's why they'd rather have three-by-seven. The Greens and Democrats would prefer seven than five because they're more likely to get seats so that's where it potentially bogged down, because they couldn't agree.

Due to the constraints of the Commonwealth self-government legislation, any increase in the size of the assembly needs to be approved by the Federal Government. This was a restriction for the Stanhope Labor Government. Despite enjoying an absolute majority in the assembly from 2004 to 2008, the Stanhope Government was unable to get support from the Liberal federal minister, possibly due to the Liberal Party's concerns that an increase could advantage Labor. The recommendation of the 1998 Pettit Review, and the acknowledgment that the current size of the assembly creates logistical problems for cabinet and committee structures, appears to be overlooked in the concern about partisan advantage.

---

3   Philip Pettit, Tim Keady and Bill Blick. 1998. *Review of the Governance of the Australian Capital Territory*. Canberra: Chief Minister's Department, p. 39.

4   Standing Committee on Legal Affairs. 2002. *The Appropriateness of the Size of the Legislative Assembly for the ACT and Options for Changing the Number of Members, Electorates and Any Other Related Matter*. Report no. 4. Canberra: Legislative Assembly for the Australian Capital Territory, p. 63.

# 11. Conclusion

It should be clear, and unsurprising, that political parties will endeavour to adjust the electoral rules to their own advantage. Political parties are not altruistic entities; they compete in a highly contested arena, and it is natural that they will seek whatever advantage they can get. Parties in control of a legislature, either in their own right or by acting as a cartel, have benefited from having control over Australia's electoral systems, as these chapters have shown.

The institutional structure for electoral administration in Australia—primarily the relationships between parliaments, political parties and commissions—allows governing parties to control the electoral system to their own benefit. This power to control arises from the ability to legislate, and from having majorities on committees inquiring into electoral matters. Legislation is typically heavily prescriptive, providing commissions with little scope to independently adopt reforms based on non-partisan ideals of fairness and equity.

The analysis of the independence of electoral management bodies demonstrates that Australian electoral commissions are non-partisan, or neutral, rather than being truly independent in the internationally accepted meaning of the concept. While Australian electoral commissions have a good degree of autonomy in carrying out their functions of enrolling voters, registering parties and conducting elections, they lack the true independence that would enable them to structure the regulatory framework in accordance with international standards for fair elections and independent electoral management.

A frequently occurring theme in interviews conducted with commissioners was that they lacked the power to publicly criticise weaknesses in their governing legislation. This was largely due to the ongoing need to carry out the functions of their commissions as dictated by parliament. Electoral commissions are, therefore, only able to make suggestions for reform, rather than being advocates for specific changes to occur. Accordingly, the commissions are servants of their political masters—administering the laws they are given—rather than being truly independent and ensuring the electoral system is regulated on the basis of fairness principles.

The emerging body of inquiry by parliamentary committees is important in providing a forum for public debate of electoral matters issues; however, the value of the committees' work is severely limited by the partisan approach that is often taken by committee members, particularly at the Commonwealth level. This is evident in the approach the JSCEM has consistently taken on postal voting processes, despite the protestations of the AEC. Although not as extreme as the Commonwealth example, evidence of partisan behaviour on committee inquiries was also found at the State and Territory levels.

The findings of this research provide evidence of party cartelisation. While the Labor/Coalition cartel is the dominant relationship, formation of other cartels occurs when it is in the interests of the participants to collude. Evidence of the dominant cartel is apparent in JSCEM's approach to postal voting, and the lack of action from both Labor and the Coalition to address the concerns of the AEC. These findings support the Australian party cartelisation theory, as promoted by Ian Marsh, Ian Ward, Sally Young and others,[1] that Labor and the Coalition collude to prevent other parties and candidates from being able to compete on equal terms. At the State level, Labor/Liberal cartel behaviour was clearly apparent in reducing the size of the Tasmanian Parliament in an attempt to limit growth of the Greens party.

Interestingly, however, the Australian party cartel does not involve only Labor and the Coalition. The Australian party cartel is more fluid, with members joining and leaving the cartel on an issue-by-issue basis. For example, the National Party joined with Labor to further its own interests by agreeing to the increase in seats for the Federal House of Representatives in 1983. Also, while the Democrats have opposed electoral reforms such as party involvement in postal voting, they combined with Labor to support the introduction of public funding, against opposition from both Coalition parties. It is understandable that the Democrats would oppose the former measure, which it could not participate in equally due to a lack of resources, while supporting the latter, which would provide resources to the party.

Is this cartelisation at work or is it better described as shifting 'marriages of convenience', with partisan self-interest acting as the primary driver of temporary coalescence? The evidence over the past 30 years suggests that, where possible, parties will act alone in instigating reform in their own interests. An example is Labor's treatment of party registration in the Northern Territory, where it increased the membership threshold from the recommended 20 to its preferred 200, to limit electoral competition. The Coalition's reform agenda at the federal level, which was supported by JSCEM's acquiescence and passed in 2006, provides another example of parties acting in their own self-interest.

Australian party cartelisation behaviour is comparable with what has been found in other countries. In their study of party cartelisation, looking primarily at European and North American democracies, Katz and Mair identified the

---

1  Marsh, I., ed. 2006. *Political Parties in Transition*. Sydney: The Federation Press; Sally Young. 2003. 'Killing Competition: Restricting Access to Political Communication Channels in Australia.' *AQ Journal of Contemporary Analysis* 75(3): 9–15.

'emergence of a new model of party, the cartel party, in which colluding parties become agents of the state and employ the resources of the state (the party state) to ensure their own collective survival'.[2] This definition fits neatly with the Australian scenario. After much debate in the academic community over their original findings, Katz and Mair went on to assert that while political parties 'might be disinclined to rely heavily on overt deals with one another, their mutual awareness of shared interests [indicates] cartel-like behavior'.[3]

Katz and Mair go on to identify that a country's constitutional provisions can be a limiting factor in the ability of parties to form cartels. They cite the example of the Federal Constitutional Court of Germany expanding access to public funding of political parties. Instead of such funding being available only to parties that obtain more than 5 per cent of the vote, the court extended funding to parties achieving more than 0.5 per cent. Similarly, in Canada, the Supreme Court overturned legislation that would have restricted party registration (and therefore the benefits that come with registration) to major parties that could field at least 50 electorate candidates.[4]

The examples of Germany and Canada stand in stark contrast to public funding and party registration in Australia, where such constitutional safeguards do not exist. In fact, the first mention of political parties in the Australian Constitution occurred only after an amendment was passed in 1977, in relation to Senate casual vacancies. With governing parties having firm control of the constitutional amending process (through parliament), the likelihood of constitutional amendments that enhance the rights of smaller parties and independent candidates is minimal.

With many of the reforms discussed in this book, the main difficulty is separating self-interest from genuine reform based on principles of fairness and international best practice. In Australia, fierce partisan divisions exist on a number of electoral issues, such as the timing of roll closures, donation disclosure and the prisoner franchise. The lack of an independent decision-making body with the power to implement reform means that such issues will continue to be fought on partisan lines, with fairness remaining a secondary consideration. In the context of democratic outcomes, partisan advantage has been shown to be a far stronger driver of reform than the desire to improve the fairness of elections. Any advantages to voters or non-governing parties tend to be an incidental, or even accidental, outcome of reform rather than a motivating

---

2   Richard Katz and Peter Mair. 1995. 'Changing Models of Party Organization and Party Democracy.' *Party Politics* 1(1): 5–28.

3   Richard Katz and Peter Mair. 2009. 'The Cartel Party Thesis: A Restatement.' *Perspectives on Politics* 7(4): 753–66.

4   Richard Katz and Peter Mair. 2009. 'The Cartel Party Thesis: A Restatement', p. 759.

Directions in Australian Electoral Reform

consideration. While some reforms have benefited other (minor) parties, this has largely occurred in situations where governing parties have required minor-party support to pass legislation.

Voters are able to express their opinions about a government's or a party's policy direction at the ballot box; however, it is electoral law that determines how these citizens vote, and if they can vote at all. When governing parties have control over such laws, this raises concerns about the legitimacy of a democracy. In Australia, governing-party control highlights the need for greater independence in the management and conduct of Australian elections. Despite the growth of issue-specific parliamentary committees, these do not provide a sufficiently powerful policy process to bring about electoral reforms based on international norms for electoral management and fair elections. This problem is not specific to Australia. Many other countries that are considered to have independent electoral management, such as Canada, India, Indonesia and South Africa, still rely on their national parliaments to provide the legislative framework to conduct elections. Electoral commissions in these countries have an advocacy role (either overt or covert) when it comes to electoral reform.

An alternative approach would be to establish an agency independent of both government and parliament that has the power to regulate the manner and conduct of elections. Such a truly independent agency could only be achieved, however, if the governing parties were willing to cede their law-making powers. An example of the devolution of electoral law-making responsibilities can be found in the area of electoral boundary redistributions. Responsibility for this aspect of electoral law has generally been transferred in recent decades from parliaments (usually initiated by Labor governments) to independent boundary commissions (typically including an electoral administrator and government statistician, among others). While parliaments (and, by extension, political parties) retain the legislative power to change these arrangements, it would be a brave government that would run the gauntlet of public opprobrium to remove or reduce existing and established independent processes.

The evidence provided in this book indicates that voluntary relinquishment of further aspects of electoral law and administration is unlikely to occur. Indeed, such a proposal might not be viable in terms of principles of responsible government and accountability. A more achievable alternative might be to establish a public forum to inquire into the conduct of elections. Such a forum, referred to in Chapter 2, could include political parties, electoral administrators, academics and civil society organisations, and would replace the politically biased work of the various electoral-matters parliamentary committees. Parties and other political players would still have input (and representation), but the voices of non-political interests would have a stronger voice on how Australians' views convert to political representation. With sufficient funding for research, and conducting inquiries and hearings, the forum could become the primary catalyst for electoral reforms.

Pressure external to the existing electoral institutional structure is required. Another source of such pressure is the media. There is evidence of growing media interest in party donations, incumbency benefits and the political finance system in recent times, and it might be that the media becomes a louder voice in broader areas of electoral reform.

# Appendix A

Joint Select Committee on Electoral Reform and Joint Standing Committee on Electoral Matters (Commonwealth) Reports

| Year | Report Name |
|---|---|
| 1983* | First report |
| 1984* | Second report |
| 1986* | Determining the Entitlement of Federal Territories and New States to Representation in the Commonwealth Parliament |
| 1987* | The Operation During the 1984 General Election of the 1983–84 Amendments to Commonwealth Electoral Legislation |
| 1988# | One Vote, One Value: Inquiry into the Constitution Alteration (Democratic Elections) Bill 1987 |
| 1988 | 'Is this where I pay the electricity bill?': Inquiry into Report on Efficiency Scrutiny into Regionalisation within Australian Electoral Commission |
| 1989 | Inquiry into the Conduct of the 1987 Federal Election and 1988 Referendums |
| 1989 | Who Pays the Piper Calls the Tune: Minimising the Risks of Funding Political Campaigns—Inquiry into Conduct of the 1987 Federal Election and 1988 Referendums |
| 1989 | Inquiry into the ACT Election and Electoral System |
| 1990 | The 1990 Federal Election |
| 1991 | Aboriginal and Islander Electoral Information Service |
| 1992 | The Conduct of Elections: New Boundaries for Cooperation |
| 1992 | Counting the Vote on Election Night: Conduct of the 1990 Federal Election, Part II, and Preparations for the Next Election |
| 1992 | Ready or Not: Refining the Process for Election '93—Conduct of the 1990 Federal Election, Part II, and Preparations for the Next Election |
| 1994 | Women, Elections and Parliament |
| 1994 | Financial Reporting by Political Parties: Interim Report of the Inquiry into the 1993 Election and Matters Related Thereto |
| 1994 | Conduct of the 1993 Federal Election |
| 1996 | Electoral Redistribution: Report on the Effectiveness and Appropriateness of the Redistribution Provisions of Part III and IV of the Commonwealth Electoral Act 1918 |
| 1997 | The 1996 Federal Election: Report of an Inquiry into the Conduct of the 1996 Federal Election and Matters Related Thereto |
| 1997 | Industrial Elections: Report of the Inquiry into the Role of the Australian Electoral Commission (AEC) in Conducting Industrial Elections |
| 2000 | The 1998 Federal Election: Inquiry into the Conduct of the 1998 Federal Election and Matters Related Thereto |
| 2001 | User Friendly, Not Abuser Friendly: Inquiry into the Integrity of the Electoral Roll |
| 2002 | Audit Report No. 42 of 2001–2002, Integrity of the Electoral Roll |

| Year | Report Name |
|------|-------------|
| 2003 | 2001 Federal Election: Report of the Inquiry into the 2001 Federal Election and Matters Related Thereto |
| 2003 | Inquiry into Representation of the Territories in the House of Representatives |
| 2005 | The 2004 Federal Election: Report of the Inquiry into the Conduct of the 2004 Federal Election and Matters Related Thereto |
| 2006 | Funding and Disclosure: Inquiry into Disclosure of Donations to Political Parties and Candidates |
| 2007 | Civics and Electoral Education |
| 2007 | Review of Certain Aspects of the Administration of the Australian Electoral Commission |
| 2008 | Advisory Report on Schedule 1 of the Tax Laws Amendment (2008 Measures No. 1) Bill 2008 |
| 2008 | Advisory Report on the Commonwealth Electoral Amendment (Political Donations and Other Measures) Bill 2008 |
| 2009 | Report on the 2007 Federal Election Electronic Voting Trials: Interim Report of the Inquiry into the Conduct of the 2007 Election and Matters Related Thereto |
| 2009 | Report on the Conduct of the 2007 Federal Election and Matters Related Thereto |
| 2009 | Advisory Report on the Commonwealth Electoral (Above-the-Line Voting) Amendment Bill 2008 |
| 2010 | Inquiry into the Implications of the Parliamentary Electorates and Elections Amendment (Automatic Enrolment) Act 2009 (NSW) for the Conduct of Commonwealth Elections |
| 2010 | Report on the 2007 Federal Election—Events in the Division of Lindsay |
| 2011 | Report on the Conduct of the 2010 Federal Election and Matters Related Thereto |

* JSCER reports

# First JSCEM report

# Appendix B

Northern Territory Turnout and Informality: 2005 General Election

| Electorate | Indigenous population (%) | Turnout rate (%) | Informality rate (%) | Number of candidates |
|---|---|---|---|---|
| Port Darwin | 4.7 | 78.2 | 4.3 | 2 |
| Wanguri | 6.2 | 87.7 | 3.3 | 2 |
| Nelson | 6.3 | 83.4 | 2.3 | 3 |
| Nightcliff | 6.3 | 84.2 | 2.5 | 5 |
| Fannie Bay | 7.4 | 85.0 | 4.7 | 3 |
| Casuarina | 8.6 | 86.6 | 2.6 | 4 |
| Sanderson | 8.9 | 89.4 | 3.8 | 4 |
| Goyder | 9.5 | 88.8 | 3.3 | 5 |
| Johnston | 9.7 | 86.9 | 3.1 | 5 |
| Drysdale | 10.4 | 82.1 | 4.7 | 2 |
| Brennan | 11.3 | 84.4 | 3.2 | 3 |
| Greatorex | 12.4 | 86.3 | 2.5 | 3 |
| Karama | 13.3 | 89.1 | 5.1 | 2 |
| Blain | 13.4 | 86.0 | 3.5 | 4 |
| Millner | 14.0 | 83.1 | 2.8 | 5 |
| Braitling | 15.9 | 84.0 | 2.7 | 3 |
| Araluen | 16.5 | 82.1 | 3.0 | 3 |
| Katherine | 24.0 | 81.8 | 3.5 | 2 |
| Daly | 45.4 | 77.6 | 5.0 | 4 |
| Nhulunbuy | 51.7 | 65.1 | 4.1 | 2 |
| Barkly | 60.3 | 69.4 | 3.8 | 3 |
| MacDonnell | 67.7 | 67.7 | 7.8 | 5 |
| Arafura | 77.2 | 66.2 | 4.9 | 3 |
| Arnhem | 82.8 | 64.2 | 6.4 | 3 |
| Stuart | 84.3 | 59.3 | 4.6 | 2 |

Source: NTEC.

# Appendix C

Gallagher's Least Squares Index: NSW Legislative Council

**1984 NSW Legislative Council**

| Party | % votes | No. seats | % of seats | % seats– % votes | Sqd |
|---|---|---|---|---|---|
| Australian Labor Party | 46.88 | 7 | 46.67 | −0.2133 | 0.05 |
| Coalition | 42.61 | 7 | 46.67 | 4.0567 | 16.46 |
| Call to Australia | 6.09 | 1 | 6.67 | 0.5767 | 0.33 |
| Democrats | 3.15 | 0 | 0.00 | −3.1500 | 9.92 |
| Independents & Others | 1.27 | 0 | 0.00 | −1.2700 | 1.61 |
| | 100.00 | 15 | | | 28.37 |
| | | | | Halve | 14.19 |
| | | | | Sq. root | 3.77 |

**1988 NSW Legislative Council**

| Party | % votes | No. seats | % of seats | % seats– % votes | Sqd |
|---|---|---|---|---|---|
| Australian Labor Party | 37.51 | 6 | 40.00 | 2.4900 | 6.20 |
| Coalition | 46.15 | 7 | 46.67 | 0.5167 | 0.27 |
| Democrats | 2.70 | 1 | 6.67 | 3.9667 | 15.73 |
| Call to Australia | 5.71 | 1 | 6.67 | 0.9567 | 0.92 |
| Independent Enterprise, Freedom and Family | 2.42 | 0 | 0.00 | −2.4200 | 5.86 |
| Environment Group | 1.60 | 0 | 0.00 | −1.6000 | 2.56 |
| Independents & Others | 3.91 | 0 | 0.00 | −3.9100 | 15.29 |
| | 100.00 | 15 | | | 46.82 |
| | | | | Halve | 23.41 |
| | | | | Sq. root | 4.84 |

**1991 NSW Legislative Council**

| Party | % votes | No. seats | % of seats | % seats– % votes | Sqd |
|---|---|---|---|---|---|
| Australian Labor Party | 37.29 | 6 | 40.00 | 2.7100 | 7.34 |
| Coalition | 45.34 | 7 | 46.67 | 1.3267 | 1.76 |
| Greens | 3.32 | 0 | 0.00 | −3.3200 | 11.02 |
| Democrats | 6.70 | 1 | 6.67 | −0.0333 | 0.00 |
| Call to Australia | 3.58 | 1 | 6.67 | 3.0867 | 9.53 |
| Independents & Others | 3.77 | 0 | 0.00 | −3.7700 | 14.21 |
| | 100.00 | 15 | | | 43.87 |
| | | | | Halve | 21.93 |
| | | | | Sq. root | 4.68 |

## 1995 NSW Legislative Council

| Party | % votes | No. seats | % of seats | % seats– % votes | Sqd |
|---|---|---|---|---|---|
| Australian Labor Party | 35.25 | 8 | 38.10 | 2.8452 | 8.10 |
| Coalition | 38.49 | 8 | 38.10 | −0.3948 | 0.16 |
| Greens | 3.72 | 1 | 4.76 | 1.0419 | 1.09 |
| Democrats | 3.21 | 1 | 4.76 | 1.5519 | 2.41 |
| Call to Australia | 3.01 | 1 | 4.76 | 1.7519 | 3.07 |
| A Better Future For Our Children | 1.28 | 1 | 4.76 | 3.4819 | 12.12 |
| Shooters | 2.84 | 1 | 4.76 | 1.9219 | 3.69 |
| Independents & Others | 12.20 | 0 | 0.00 | −12.2000 | 148.84 |
| | 100.00 | 21 | | | 179.47 |
| | | | | Halve | 89.74 |
| | | | | Sq. root | 9.47 |

## 1999 NSW Legislative Council

| Party | % votes | No. seats | % of seats | % seats– % votes | Sqd |
|---|---|---|---|---|---|
| Australian Labor Party | 37.27 | 8 | 38.10 | 0.8252 | 0.68 |
| Coalition | 27.39 | 6 | 17.14 | −10.2471 | 105.00 |
| One Nation | 6.34 | 1 | 4.76 | −1.5781 | 2.49 |
| Democrats | 4.01 | 1 | 4.76 | 0.7519 | 0.57 |
| Christian Democratic Party | 3.17 | 1 | 4.76 | 1.5919 | 2.53 |
| Greens | 2.91 | 1 | 4.76 | 1.8519 | 3.43 |
| Shooters | 1.67 | 0 | 0.00 | −1.6700 | 2.79 |
| Progressive Labor Party | 1.58 | 0 | 0.00 | −1.5800 | 2.50 |
| Marijuana Smokers Rights | 1.24 | 0 | 0.00 | −1.2400 | 1.54 |
| Reform Legal System | 1.00 | 1 | 4.76 | 3.7619 | 14.15 |
| Independents & Others | 13.42 | 2 | 9.52 | −3.8962 | 15.18 |
| | 100.00 | 21 | | | 150.86 |
| | | | | Halve | 75.43 |
| | | | | Sq. root | 8.69 |

## 2003 NSW Legislative Council

| Party | % votes | No. seats | % of seats | % seats– % votes | Sqd |
|---|---|---|---|---|---|
| Australian Labor Party | 43.54 | 10 | 47.62 | 4.0790 | 16.64 |
| Coalition | 33.30 | 7 | 33.33 | 0.0333 | 0.00 |
| Greens | 8.60 | 2 | 9.52 | 0.9238 | 0.85 |
| Christian Democratic Party | 3.03 | 1 | 4.76 | 1.7319 | 3.00 |
| One Nation | 1.49 | 0 | 0.00 | −1.4900 | 2.22 |
| Democrats | 1.57 | 0 | 0.00 | −1.5700 | 2.46 |
| Shooters | 2.05 | 1 | 4.76 | 2.7119 | 7.35 |
| Hanson | 1.92 | 0 | 0.00 | −1.9200 | 3.69 |
| Unity | 1.42 | 0 | 0.00 | −1.4200 | 2.02 |
| Fishing-Horse-4WD | 1.06 | 0 | 0.00 | −1.0600 | 1.12 |
| Independents & Others | 2.02 | 0 | 0.00 | −2.0200 | 4.08 |
| | 100.00 | 21 | | | 43.44 |
| | | | | Halve | 21.72 |
| | | | | Sq. root | 4.66 |

## 2007 NSW Legislative Council

| Party | % votes | No. seats | % of seats | % seats– % votes | Sqd |
|---|---|---|---|---|---|
| Australian Labor Party | 39.14 | 9 | 42.86 | 3.7171 | 13.82 |
| Coalition | 34.22 | 8 | 38.10 | 3.8752 | 15.02 |
| Greens | 9.12 | 2 | 9.52 | 0.4038 | 0.16 |
| Christian Democratic Party | 4.42 | 1 | 4.76 | 0.3419 | 0.12 |
| Democrats | 1.78 | 0 | 0.00 | −1.7800 | 3.17 |
| Unity | 1.21 | 0 | 0.00 | −1.2100 | 1.46 |
| Shooters | 2.79 | 1 | 4.76 | 1.9719 | 3.89 |
| Fishing | 1.53 | 0 | 0.00 | −1.5300 | 2.34 |
| Australians Against Further Immigration | 1.64 | 0 | 0.00 | −1.6400 | 2.69 |
| Independents & Others | 4.15 | 0 | 0.00 | −4.1500 | 17.22 |
| | 100.00 | 21 | | | 59.89 |
| | | | | Halve | 29.94 |
| | | | | Sq. root | 5.47 |

**2011 NSW Legislative Council**

| Party | % votes | No. seats | % of seats | % seats– % votes | Sqd |
|---|---|---|---|---|---|
| Australian Labor Party | 24.05 | 5 | 23.81 | −0.24 | 0.06 |
| Coalition | 48.57 | 11 | 52.38 | 3.81 | 14.52 |
| Greens | 11.11 | 3 | 14.29 | 3.18 | 10.11 |
| Christian Democratic Party | 3.01 | 1 | 4.76 | 1.75 | 3.06 |
| Shooters | 3.64 | 1 | 4.76 | 1.12 | 1.25 |
| Fishing | 1.30 | 0 | 0.00 | −1.30 | 1.69 |
| No Parking Meters | 1.18 | 0 | 0.00 | −1.18 | 1.39 |
| Family First | 1.41 | 0 | 0.00 | −1.41 | 1.99 |
| Independents & Others | 5.73 | 0 | 0.00 | −5.73 | 32.83 |
| | 100.00 | 21 | | | 66.90 |
| | | | | Halve | 33.45 |
| | | | | Sq. root | 5.78 |

# Appendix D

Gallagher's Least Squares Index: House of Representatives

### 2007 House of Representatives

| Party | % votes | No. seats | % of seats | % seats– % votes | Sqd |
|---|---|---|---|---|---|
| Australian Labor Party | 43.38 | 83 | 55.33 | 11.9533 | 142.88 |
| Liberal–Country Liberal Party | 36.60 | 55 | 36.67 | 0.0667 | 0.00 |
| The Nationals | 5.49 | 10 | 6.67 | 1.1767 | 1.38 |
| The Greens | 7.79 | 0 | 0.00 | −7.7900 | 60.68 |
| Family First | 1.99 | 0 | 0.00 | −1.9900 | 3.96 |
| Independents & Others | 4.75 | 2 | 1.33 | −3.4167 | 11.67 |
| | 100.00 | 150 | | | 220.59 |
| | | | | Halve | 110.29 |
| | | | | Sq. root | 10.50 |

### 2004 House of Representatives

| Party | % votes | No. seats | % of seats | % seats– % votes | Sqd |
|---|---|---|---|---|---|
| Australian Labor Party | 37.64 | 60 | 40.00 | 2.3600 | 5.57 |
| Liberal/Country Liberal Party | 40.81 | 75 | 50.00 | 9.1900 | 84.46 |
| The Nationals | 5.89 | 12 | 8.00 | 2.1100 | 4.45 |
| The Greens | 7.19 | 0 | 0.00 | −7.1900 | 51.70 |
| Family First | 2.01 | 0 | 0.00 | −2.0100 | 4.04 |
| Democrats | 1.24 | 0 | 0.00 | −1.2400 | 1.54 |
| Independents & Others | 5.22 | 3 | 2.00 | −3.2200 | 10.37 |
| | 100.00 | 150 | | | 162.12 |
| | | | | Halve | 81.06 |
| | | | | Sq. root | 9.00 |

### 2001 House of Representatives

| Party | % votes | No. seats | % of seats | % seats– % votes | Sqd |
|---|---|---|---|---|---|
| Australian Labor Party | 37.84 | 65 | 43.33 | 5.4933 | 30.18 |
| Liberal/Country Liberal Party | 37.40 | 69 | 46.00 | 8.6000 | 73.96 |
| The Nationals | 5.61 | 13 | 8.67 | 3.0567 | 9.34 |
| The Greens | 4.96 | 0 | 0.00 | −4.9600 | 24.60 |
| Democrats | 5.41 | 0 | 0.00 | −5.4100 | 29.27 |
| One Nation | 4.34 | 0 | 0.00 | −4.3400 | 18.84 |
| Independents & Others | 4.44 | 3 | 2.00 | −2.4400 | 5.95 |
| | 100.00 | 150 | | | 192.14 |
| | | | | Halve | 96.07 |
| | | | | Sq. root | 9.80 |

**1998 House of Representatives**

| Party | % votes | No. seats | % of seats | % seats– % votes | Sqd |
|---|---|---|---|---|---|
| Australian Labor Party | 40.10 | 67 | 45.27 | 5.1703 | 26.73 |
| Liberal/Country Liberal Party | 34.21 | 64 | 43.24 | 9.0332 | 81.60 |
| The Nationals | 5.29 | 16 | 10.81 | 5.5208 | 30.48 |
| The Greens | 2.14 | 0 | 0.00 | -2.1400 | 4.58 |
| Democrats | 5.13 | 0 | 0.00 | -5.1300 | 26.32 |
| One Nation | 8.43 | 0 | 0.00 | -8.4300 | 71.06 |
| Independents & Others | 4.70 | 1 | 0.68 | -4.0243 | 16.20 |
| | 100.00 | 148 | | | 256.97 |
| | | | | Halve | 128.48 |
| | | | | Sq. root | 11.34 |

**1996 House of Representatives**

| Party | % votes | No. seats | % of seats | % seats– % votes | Sqd |
|---|---|---|---|---|---|
| Australian Labor Party | 38.75 | 49 | 33.11 | -5.6419 | 31.83 |
| Liberal/Country Liberal Party | 39.04 | 76 | 51.35 | 12.3114 | 151.57 |
| The Nationals | 8.21 | 18 | 12.16 | 3.9522 | 15.62 |
| The Greens | 1.74 | 0 | 0.00 | -1.7400 | 3.03 |
| Democrats | 6.76 | 0 | 0.00 | -6.7600 | 45.70 |
| Independents & Others | 5.50 | 5 | 3.38 | -2.1216 | 4.50 |
| | 100.00 | 148 | | | 252.25 |
| | | | | Halve | 126.12 |
| | | | | Sq. root | 11.23 |

**1993 House of Representatives**

| Party | % votes | No. seats | % of seats | % seats– % votes | Sqd |
|---|---|---|---|---|---|
| Australian Labor Party | 44.92 | 80 | 54.42 | 9.5018 | 90.28 |
| Liberal/Country Liberal Party | 37.10 | 49 | 33.33 | -3.7667 | 14.19 |
| The Nationals | 7.17 | 16 | 10.88 | 3.7144 | 13.80 |
| Democrats | 3.75 | 0 | 0.00 | -3.7500 | 14.06 |
| Independents & Others | 7.06 | 2 | 1.36 | -5.6995 | 32.48 |
| | 100.00 | 147 | | | 164.81 |
| | | | | Halve | 82.41 |
| | | | | Sq. root | 9.08 |

**1990 House of Representatives**

| Party | % votes | No. seats | % of seats | % seats– % votes | Sqd |
|---|---|---|---|---|---|
| Australian Labor Party | 39.44 | 78 | 52.70 | 13.2627 | 175.90 |
| Liberal/Country Liberal Party | 35.04 | 55 | 37.16 | 2.1222 | 4.50 |
| The Nationals | 8.42 | 14 | 9.46 | 1.0395 | 1.08 |
| Democrats | 11.26 | 0 | 0.00 | −11.2600 | 126.79 |
| Independents & Others | 5.84 | 1 | 0.68 | −5.1643 | 26.67 |
| | 100.00 | 148 | | | 334.94 |
| | | | | Halve | 167.47 |
| | | | | Sq. root | 12.94 |

**1987 House of Representatives**

| Party | % votes | No. seats | % of seats | % seats– % votes | Sqd |
|---|---|---|---|---|---|
| Australian Labor Party | 45.83 | 86 | 58.11 | 12.2781 | 150.75 |
| Liberal/Country Liberal Party | 34.55 | 43 | 29.05 | −5.4959 | 30.21 |
| The Nationals | 11.52 | 19 | 12.84 | 1.3178 | 1.74 |
| Democrats | 6.03 | 0 | 0.00 | −6.0300 | 36.36 |
| Independents & Others | 2.07 | 0 | 0.00 | −2.0700 | 4.28 |
| | 100.00 | 148 | | | 223.34 |
| | | | | Halve | 111.67 |
| | | | | Sq. root | 10.57 |

**1984 House of Representatives**

| Party | % votes | No. seats | % of seats | % seats– % votes | Sqd |
|---|---|---|---|---|---|
| Australian Labor Party | 47.55 | 82 | 55.41 | 7.8554 | 61.71 |
| Liberal/Country Liberal Party | 34.38 | 45 | 30.41 | −3.9746 | 15.80 |
| The Nationals | 10.63 | 21 | 14.19 | 3.5592 | 12.67 |
| Democrats | 5.45 | 0 | 0.00 | −5.4500 | 29.70 |
| Independents & Others | 1.99 | 0 | 0.00 | −1.9900 | 3.96 |
| | 100.00 | 148 | | | 123.84 |
| | | | | Halve | 61.92 |
| | | | | Sq. root | 7.87 |

**1983 House of Representatives**

| Party | % votes | No. seats | % of seats | % seats– % votes | Sqd |
|---|---|---|---|---|---|
| Australian Labor Party | 49.48 | 75 | 60.00 | 10.5200 | 110.67 |
| Liberal/Country Liberal Party | 34.36 | 33 | 26.40 | –7.9600 | 63.36 |
| The Nationals | 9.21 | 17 | 13.60 | 4.3900 | 19.27 |
| Democrats | 5.03 | 0 | 0.00 | –5.0300 | 25.30 |
| Independents & Others | 1.92 | 0 | 0.00 | –1.9200 | 3.69 |
| | 100.00 | 125 | | | 222.29 |
| | | | | Halve | 111.15 |
| | | | | Sq. root | 10.54 |

**1980 House of Representatives**

| Party | % votes | No. seats | % of seats | % seats– % votes | Sqd |
|---|---|---|---|---|---|
| Australian Labor Party | 39.44 | 78 | 52.70 | 13.2627 | 175.90 |
| Liberal/Country Liberal Party | 35.04 | 55 | 37.16 | 2.1222 | 4.50 |
| The Nationals | 8.42 | 14 | 9.46 | 1.0395 | 1.08 |
| Democrats | 11.26 | 0 | 0.00 | –11.2600 | 126.79 |
| Independents & Others | 5.84 | 1 | 0.68 | –5.1643 | 26.67 |
| | 100.00 | 148 | | | 334.94 |
| | | | | Halve | 167.47 |
| | | | | Sq. root | 12.94 |

**1977 House of Representatives**

| Party | % votes | No. seats | % of seats | % seats– % votes | Sqd |
|---|---|---|---|---|---|
| Australian Labor Party | 39.65 | 38 | 30.65 | –9.0048 | 81.09 |
| Liberal/Country Liberal Party | 38.09 | 67 | 54.03 | 15.9423 | 254.16 |
| The Nationals | 10.01 | 19 | 15.32 | 5.3126 | 28.22 |
| Democrats | 9.38 | 0 | 0.00 | –9.3800 | 87.98 |
| Independents & Others | 2.87 | 0 | 0.00 | –2.8700 | 8.24 |
| | 100.00 | 124 | | | 459.69 |
| | | | | Halve | 229.84 |
| | | | | Sq. root | 15.16 |

**1975 House of Representatives**

| Party | % votes | No. seats | % of seats | % seats– % votes | Sqd |
|---|---|---|---|---|---|
| Australian Labor Party | 42.84 | 36 | 28.35 | -14.4935 | 210.06 |
| Liberal/Country Liberal Party | 41.80 | 68 | 53.54 | 11.7433 | 137.91 |
| National Country Party | 11.25 | 23 | 18.11 | 6.8602 | 47.06 |
| Democratic Labor Party | 1.32 | 0 | 0.00 | -1.3200 | 1.74 |
| Independents & Others | 2.79 | 0 | 0.00 | -2.7900 | 7.78 |
| | 100.00 | 127 | | | 404.56 |
| | | | | Halve | 202.28 |
| | | | | Sq. root | 14.22 |

**1974 House of Representatives**

| Party | % votes | No. seats | % of seats | % seats– % votes | Sqd |
|---|---|---|---|---|---|
| Australian Labor Party | 49.30 | 66 | 51.97 | 2.6685 | 7.12 |
| Liberal/Country Liberal Party | 34.95 | 40 | 31.5 | -3.4539 | 11.93 |
| Country Party | 9.96 | 21 | 16.54 | 6.5754 | 43.24 |
| Democratic Labor Party | 1.42 | 0 | 0.00 | -1.4200 | 2.02 |
| Australia Party | 2.33 | 0 | 0.00 | -2.3300 | 5.43 |
| Independents & Others | 2.04 | 0 | 0.00 | -2.0400 | 4.16 |
| | 100.00 | 127 | | | 73.89 |
| | | | | Halve | 36.95 |
| | | | | Sq. root | 6.08 |

**1972 House of Representatives**

| Party | % votes | No. seats | % of seats | % seats– % votes | Sqd |
|---|---|---|---|---|---|
| Australian Labor Party | 49.59 | 67 | 53.60 | 4.0100 | 16.08 |
| Liberal/Country Liberal Party | 32.04 | 38 | 30.40 | -1.6400 | 2.69 |
| Country Party | 9.44 | 20 | 16.00 | 6.5600 | 43.03 |
| Democratic Labor Party | 5.25 | 0 | 0.00 | -5.2500 | 27.56 |
| Australia Party | 2.42 | 0 | 0.00 | -2.4200 | 5.86 |
| Independents & Others | 1.26 | 0 | 0.00 | -1.2600 | 1.59 |
| | 100.00 | 125 | | | 96.81 |
| | | | | Halve | 48.40 |
| | | | | Sq. root | 6.96 |

# Appendix E

Gallagher's Least Squares Index: Senate

## 2007 Senate

| Party | % votes | No. seats | % of seats | % seats– % votes | Sqd |
|---|---|---|---|---|---|
| Australian Labor Party | 40.30 | 18 | 45.00 | 4.7000 | 22.09 |
| Coalition | 39.94 | 18 | 45.00 | 5.0600 | 25.60 |
| Democrats | 1.29 | 0 | 0.00 | –1.2900 | 1.66 |
| The Greens | 9.04 | 3 | 7.50 | –1.5400 | 2.37 |
| Family First | 1.62 | 0 | 0.00 | –1.6200 | 2.62 |
| Pauline's United Australia Party | 1.12 | 0 | 0.00 | –1.1200 | 1.25 |
| Independents & Others | 6.69 | 1 | 2.50 | –4.1900 | 17.56 |
|  | 100.00 | 40 |  |  | 73.16 |
|  |  |  |  | Halve | 36.58 |
|  |  |  |  | Sq. root | 6.05 |

## 2004 Senate

| Party | % votes | No. seats | % of seats | % seats– % votes | Sqd |
|---|---|---|---|---|---|
| Australian Labor Party | 35.02 | 16 | 40.00 | 4.9800 | 24.80 |
| Coalition | 45.09 | 21 | 52.50 | 7.4100 | 54.91 |
| Democrats | 2.09 | 0 | 0.00 | –2.0900 | 4.37 |
| The Greens | 7.67 | 2 | 5.00 | –2.6700 | 7.13 |
| Family First | 1.76 | 1 | 2.50 | 0.7400 | 0.55 |
| One Nation | 1.73 | 0 | 0.00 | –1.7300 | 2.99 |
| Independents & Others | 6.64 | 0 | 0.00 | –6.6400 | 44.09 |
|  | 100.00 | 40 |  |  | 138.84 |
|  |  |  |  | Halve | 69.42 |
|  |  |  |  | Sq. root | 8.33 |

## 2001 Senate

| Party | % votes | No. seats | % of seats | % seats– % votes | Sqd |
|---|---|---|---|---|---|
| Australian Labor Party | 34.32 | 14 | 35.00 | 0.6800 | 0.46 |
| Coalition | 41.84 | 20 | 50.00 | 8.1600 | 66.59 |
| Democrats | 7.25 | 4 | 10.00 | 2.7500 | 7.56 |
| The Greens | 4.94 | 2 | 5.00 | 0.0600 | 0.00 |
| One Nation | 5.54 | 0 | 0.00 | –5.5400 | 30.69 |
| Independents & Others | 6.11 | 0 | 0.00 | –6.1100 | 37.33 |
|  | 100.00 | 40 |  |  | 142.64 |
|  |  |  |  | Halve | 71.32 |
|  |  |  |  | Sq. root | 8.45 |

**1998 Senate**

| Party | % votes | No. seats | % of seats | % seats– % votes | Sqd |
|---|---|---|---|---|---|
| Australian Labor Party | 37.31 | 17 | 42.50 | 5.1900 | 26.94 |
| Coalition | 37.68 | 17 | 42.50 | 4.8200 | 23.23 |
| Democrats | 8.45 | 4 | 10.00 | 1.5500 | 2.40 |
| The Greens | 2.72 | 0 | 0.00 | −2.7200 | 7.40 |
| One Nation | 8.99 | 1 | 2.50 | −6.4900 | 42.12 |
| Christian Democratic Party | 1.09 | 0 | 0.00 | −1.0900 | 1.19 |
| Independents & Others | 3.76 | 1 | 2.50 | −1.2600 | 1.59 |
|  | 100.00 | 40 |  |  | 104.87 |
|  |  |  |  | Halve | 52.43 |
|  |  |  |  | Sq. root | 7.24 |

**1996 Senate**

| Party | % votes | No. seats | % of seats | % seats– % votes | Sqd |
|---|---|---|---|---|---|
| Australian Labor Party | 36.15 | 14 | 35.00 | −1.1500 | 1.32 |
| Coalition | 43.97 | 20 | 50.00 | 6.0300 | 36.36 |
| Democrats | 10.82 | 5 | 12.50 | 1.6800 | 2.82 |
| The Greens | 1.66 | 1 | 2.50 | 0.8400 | 0.71 |
| Call to Australia | 1.08 | 0 | 0.00 | −1.0800 | 1.17 |
| Australians Against Further Immigration | 1.26 | 0 | 0.00 | −1.2600 | 1.59 |
| Australian Shooters Party | 1.05 | 0 | 0.00 | −1.0500 | 1.10 |
| Independents & Others | 4.01 | 0 | 0.00 | −4.0100 | 16.08 |
|  | 100.00 | 40 |  |  | 61.15 |
|  |  |  |  | Halve | 30.57 |
|  |  |  |  | Sq. root | 5.53 |

**1993 Senate**

| Party | % votes | No. seats | % of seats | % seats– % votes | Sqd |
|---|---|---|---|---|---|
| Australian Labor Party | 43.50 | 17 | 42.50 | −1.0000 | 1.00 |
| Coalition | 43.04 | 19 | 47.50 | 4.4600 | 19.89 |
| Democrats | 5.31 | 2 | 5.00 | −0.3100 | 0.10 |
| The Greens | 2.96 | 1 | 2.50 | −0.4600 | 0.21 |
| Call to Australia | 1.02 | 0 | 0.00 | −1.0200 | 1.04 |
| Independents & Others | 4.17 | 1 | 2.50 | −1.6700 | 2.79 |
|  | 100.00 | 40 |  |  | 25.03 |
|  |  |  |  | Halve | 12.51 |
|  |  |  |  | Sq. root | 3.54 |

## 1990 Senate

| Party | % votes | No. seats | % of seats | % seats– % votes | Sqd |
|---|---|---|---|---|---|
| Australian Labor Party | 38.41 | 15 | 37.50 | –0.9100 | 0.83 |
| Coalition | 41.92 | 19 | 47.50 | 5.5800 | 31.14 |
| Democrats | 12.63 | 5 | 12.50 | –0.1300 | 0.02 |
| The Greens | 2.80 | 1 | 2.50 | –0.3000 | 0.09 |
| Independents & Others | 4.25 | 0 | 0.00 | –4.2500 | 18.06 |
| | 100.00 | 40 | | | 50.13 |
| | | | | Halve | 25.07 |
| | | | | Sq. root | 5.01 |

## 1987 Senate

| Party | % votes | No. seats | % of seats | % seats– % votes | Sqd |
|---|---|---|---|---|---|
| Australian Labor Party | 42.83 | 32 | 42.11 | –0.7247 | 0.53 |
| Coalition | 42.03 | 34 | 44.74 | 2.7068 | 7.33 |
| Democrats | 8.47 | 7 | 9.21 | 0.7405 | 0.55 |
| Nuclear Disarmament Party | 1.09 | 1 | 1.32 | 0.2258 | 0.05 |
| Independents & Others | 5.58 | 2 | 2.63 | –2.9484 | 8.69 |
| | 100.00 | 76 | | | 17.14 |
| | | | | Halve | 8.57 |
| | | | | Sq. root | 2.93 |

## 1984 Senate

| Party | % votes | No. seats | % of seats | % seats– % votes | Sqd |
|---|---|---|---|---|---|
| Australian Labor Party | 42.17 | 20 | 43.48 | 1.3083 | 1.71 |
| Coalition | 39.55 | 20 | 43.48 | 3.9283 | 15.43 |
| Democrats | 7.62 | 5 | 10.87 | 3.2496 | 10.56 |
| Nuclear Disarmament Party | 7.23 | 1 | 2.17 | –5.0561 | 25.56 |
| Independents & Others | 3.44 | 0 | 0.00 | –3.4400 | 11.83 |
| | 100.00 | 46 | | | 65.10 |
| | | | | Halve | 32.55 |
| | | | | Sq. root | 5.71 |

**1983 Senate**

| Party | % votes | No. seats | % of seats | % seats– % votes | Sqd |
|---|---|---|---|---|---|
| Australian Labor Party | 45.49 | 30 | 46.88 | 1.3850 | 1.92 |
| Coalition | 39.96 | 28 | 43.75 | 3.7900 | 14.36 |
| Democrats | 9.57 | 5 | 7.81 | –1.7575 | 3.09 |
| Independents & Others | 4.98 | 1 | 1.56 | –3.4175 | 11.68 |
| | 100.00 | 64 | | | 31.05 |
| | | | | Halve | 15.53 |
| | | | | Sq. root | 3.94 |

**1980 Senate**

| Party | % votes | No. seats | % of seats | % seats– % votes | Sqd |
|---|---|---|---|---|---|
| Australian Labor Party | 42.25 | 15 | 44.12 | 1.8676 | 3.49 |
| Coalition | 43.48 | 15 | 44.12 | 0.6376 | 0.41 |
| Democrats | 9.25 | 3 | 8.82 | –0.4265 | 0.18 |
| Independents & Others | 5.02 | 1 | 2.94 | –2.0788 | 4.32 |
| | 100.00 | 34 | | | 8.40 |
| | | | | Halve | 4.20 |
| | | | | Sq. root | 2.05 |

**1977 Senate**

| Party | % votes | No. seats | % of seats | % seats– % votes | Sqd |
|---|---|---|---|---|---|
| Australian Labor Party | 36.76 | 14 | 41.18 | 4.4165 | 19.51 |
| Coalition | 45.57 | 18 | 52.94 | 7.3712 | 54.33 |
| Democrats | 11.13 | 2 | 5.88 | –5.2476 | 27.54 |
| Independents & Others | 6.54 | 0 | 0.00 | –6.5400 | 42.77 |
| | 100.00 | 34 | | | 144.15 |
| | | | | Halve | 72.07 |
| | | | | Sq. root | 8.49 |

**1975 Senate**

| Party | % votes | No. seats | % of seats | % seats– % votes | Sqd |
|---|---|---|---|---|---|
| Australian Labor Party | 40.91 | 27 | 42.19 | 1.2775 | 1.63 |
| Coalition | 51.70 | 35 | 54.69 | 2.9875 | 8.93 |
| Democratic Labor Party | 2.67 | 0 | 0.00 | –2.6700 | 7.13 |
| Liberal Movement | 1.07 | 1 | 1.56 | 0.4925 | 0.24 |
| Independents & Others | 3.65 | 1 | 1.56 | –2.0875 | 4.36 |
| | 100.00 | 64 | | | 22.29 |
| | | | | Halve | 11.14 |
| | | | | Sq. root | 3.34 |

**1974 Senate**

| Party | % votes | No. seats | % of seats | % seats– % votes | Sqd |
|---|---|---|---|---|---|
| Australian Labor Party | 47.29 | 29 | 48.33 | 1.0433 | 1.09 |
| Coalition | 43.89 | 29 | 48.33 | 4.4433 | 19.74 |
| Democratic Labor Party | 3.56 | 0 | 0.00 | −3.5600 | 12.67 |
| Australia Party | 1.39 | 0 | 0.00 | −1.3900 | 1.93 |
| Independents & Others | 3.87 | 2 | 3.33 | −0.5367 | 0.29 |
| | 100.00 | 60 | | | 35.73 |
| | | | | Halve | 17.86 |
| | | | | Sq. root | 4.23 |

**1970 Senate**

| Party | % votes | No. seats | % of seats | % seats– % votes | Sqd |
|---|---|---|---|---|---|
| Australian Labor Party | 42.22 | 14 | 43.75 | 1.5300 | 2.34 |
| Coalition | 38.18 | 13 | 40.63 | 2.4450 | 5.98 |
| Democratic Labor Party | 11.11 | 3 | 9.38 | −1.7350 | 3.01 |
| Australia Party | 2.90 | 0 | 0.00 | −2.9000 | 8.41 |
| Independents & Others | 5.59 | 2 | 6.25 | 0.6600 | 0.44 |
| | 100.00 | 32 | | | 20.17 |
| | | | | Halve | 10.09 |
| | | | | Sq. root | 3.18 |

# Appendix F

Gallagher's Least Squares Index: Tasmanian Legislative Assembly

**1982 Tasmanian Legislative Assembly**

| Party | % votes | No. seats | % of seats | % seats– % votes | Sqd |
|---|---|---|---|---|---|
| Australian Labor Party | 36.86 | 14 | 40.00 | 3.1400 | 9.86 |
| Liberal | 48.52 | 19 | 54.29 | 5.7657 | 33.24 |
| Democrats | 5.39 | 1 | 2.86 | −2.5329 | 6.42 |
| Independents & Others | 9.23 | 1 | 2.86 | −6.3729 | 40.61 |
| | 100.00 | 35 | | | 90.13 |
| | | | | Halve | 45.07 |
| | | | | Sq. root | 6.71 |

**1986 Tasmanian Legislative Assembly**

| Party | % votes | No. seats | % of seats | % seats– % votes | Sqd |
|---|---|---|---|---|---|
| Australian Labor Party | 35.14 | 14 | 40.00 | 4.8600 | 23.62 |
| Liberal | 54.20 | 19 | 54.29 | 0.0857 | 0.01 |
| Democrats | 2.06 | 0 | 0.00 | −2.0600 | 4.24 |
| Independents & Others | 8.60 | 2 | 5.71 | −2.8857 | 8.33 |
| | 100.00 | 35 | | | 36.20 |
| | | | | Halve | 18.10 |
| | | | | Sq. root | 4.25 |

**1989 Tasmanian Legislative Assembly**

| Party | % votes | No. seats | % of seats | % seats– % votes | Sqd |
|---|---|---|---|---|---|
| Australian Labor Party | 34.71 | 13 | 37.14 | 2.4329 | 5.92 |
| Liberal | 46.92 | 17 | 48.57 | 1.6514 | 2.73 |
| Tasmanian Greens | 17.13 | 5 | 14.29 | −2.8443 | 8.09 |
| Independents & Others | 1.24 | 0 | 0.00 | −1.2400 | 1.54 |
| | 100.00 | 35 | | | 18.27 |
| | | | | Halve | 9.14 |
| | | | | Sq. root | 3.02 |

### 1992 Tasmanian Legislative Assembly

| Party | % votes | No. seats | % of seats | % seats– % votes | Sqd |
|---|---|---|---|---|---|
| Australian Labor Party | 28.85 | 11 | 31.43 | 2.5786 | 6.65 |
| Liberal | 54.11 | 19 | 54.29 | 0.1757 | 0.03 |
| Tasmanian Greens | 13.23 | 5 | 14.29 | 1.0557 | 1.11 |
| Advance Tasmania | 2.55 | 0 | 0.00 | −2.5500 | 6.50 |
| Independents & Others | 1.26 | 0 | 0.00 | −1.2600 | 1.59 |
| | 100.00 | 35 | | −100 | 15.88 |
| | | | | Halve | 7.94 |
| | | | | Sq. root | 2.82 |

### 1996 Tasmanian Legislative Assembly

| Party | % votes | No. seats | % of seats | % seats– % votes | Sqd |
|---|---|---|---|---|---|
| Australian Labor Party | 40.47 | 14 | 40.00 | −0.4700 | 0.22 |
| Liberal | 41.20 | 16 | 45.71 | 4.5143 | 20.38 |
| Tasmanian Greens | 11.14 | 4 | 11.43 | 0.2886 | 0.08 |
| Nationals | 2.20 | 0 | 0.00 | −2.2000 | 4.84 |
| Independents & Others | 4.99 | 1 | 2.86 | −2.1329 | 4.55 |
| | 100.00 | 35 | | | 30.07 |
| | | | | Halve | 15.04 |
| | | | | Sq. root | 3.88 |

### 1998 Tasmanian Legislative Assembly

| Party | % votes | No. seats | % of seats | % seats– % votes | Sqd |
|---|---|---|---|---|---|
| Australian Labor Party | 44.79 | 14 | 56.00 | 11.2100 | 125.66 |
| Liberal | 38.06 | 10 | 40.00 | 1.9400 | 3.76 |
| Tasmanian Greens | 10.18 | 1 | 4.00 | −6.1800 | 38.19 |
| Tasmanian First | 5.10 | 0 | 0.00 | −5.1000 | 26.01 |
| Independents & Others | 1.87 | 0 | 0.00 | −1.8700 | 3.50 |
| | 100.00 | 25 | | | 197.13 |
| | | | | Halve | 98.56 |
| | | | | Sq. root | 9.93 |

## 2002 Tasmanian Legislative Assembly

| Party | % votes | No. seats | % of seats | % seats– % votes | Sqd |
|---|---|---|---|---|---|
| Australian Labor Party | 51.88 | 14 | 56.00 | 4.1200 | 16.97 |
| Liberal | 27.38 | 7 | 28.00 | 0.6200 | 0.38 |
| Tasmanian Greens | 18.13 | 4 | 16.00 | −2.1300 | 4.54 |
| Independents & Others | 2.61 | 0 | 0.00 | −2.6100 | 6.81 |
| | 100.00 | 25 | | | 28.71 |
| | | | | Halve | 14.35 |
| | | | | Sq. root | 3.79 |

## 2006 Tasmanian Legislative Assembly

| Party | % votes | No. seats | % of seats | % seats– % votes | Sqd |
|---|---|---|---|---|---|
| Australian Labor Party | 49.26 | 14 | 56.00 | 6.7400 | 45.43 |
| Liberal | 31.81 | 7 | 28.00 | −3.8100 | 14.52 |
| Tasmanian Greens | 16.63 | 4 | 16.00 | −0.6300 | 0.40 |
| Independents & Others | 2.30 | 0 | 0.00 | −2.3000 | 5.29 |
| | 100.00 | 25 | | | 65.63 |
| | | | | Halve | 32.82 |
| | | | | Sq. root | 5.73 |

## 2010 Tasmanian Legislative Assembly

| Party | % votes | No. seats | % of seats | % seats–% votes | Sqd |
|---|---|---|---|---|---|
| Australian Labor Party | 36.88 | 10 | 40.00 | 3.12 | 9.73 |
| Liberal | 38.99 | 10 | 40.00 | 1.01 | 1.02 |
| Tasmanian Greens | 21.61 | 5 | 20.00 | 1.61 | 2.59 |
| Independents & Others | 2.52 | 0 | 0.00 | −2.52 | 6.35 |
| | 100.00 | 25 | | | 19.69 |
| | | | | Halve | 9.85 |
| | | | | Sq. root | 3.14 |

# Bibliography

ACE Electoral Knowledge Network. 2007. *EMB Independence and the Origin of Independent Election Administrations*. URL: <http://aceproject.org/electoral-advice/archive/questions/replies/156664001>

AEC [Australian Electoral Commission]. 2001. *Submission to the Senate Public Finance and Administration Inquiry into Bills Concerning Political Honesty and Accountability*. Submission no. 14. Canberra: Australian Electoral Commission.

AEC [Australian Electoral Commission]. 2004. 'Over 13 Million Australians Have the Right to Vote in the 2004 Federal Election.' Media release, 10 September. Canberra: Australian Electoral Commission.

AEC [Australian Electoral Commission]. 2008. *Submission to the Inquiry by the Joint Standing Committee on Electoral Matters into the 2007 Federal Election*. Canberra: Parliament of Australia.

AEC [Australian Electoral Commission]. 2011. *Analysis of Informal Voting: House of Representatives, 2010 Federal Election*. Research Report no. 12, 29 March. Canberra: Australian Electoral Commission.

Alport, Kate and Lisa Hill. 2008. 'Voting Attitudes and Behaviour Among Aboriginal Peoples: Reports from 29 Anangu Women.' Refereed paper delivered at the Australian Political Studies Association Conference, Brisbane, 6–9 July.

Austin, Reginald and Maja Tjernström, eds. 2003. *Funding of Political Parties and Election Campaigns*. Stockholm: International IDEA.

Australian Bureau of Statistics. 2007. '4705.0—Population Distribution, Aboriginal and Torres Strait Islander Australians, 2006.' Canberra: Australian Bureau of Statistics. URL: <http://www.abs.gov.au>

Australian Labor Party. 2002. *Joint Standing Committee on Electoral Matters Inquiry into the 2001 Federal Election: Submission by the Australian Labor Party*. Submission no. 153. Canberra: Parliament of Australia.

Australian National Audit Office. 2009. *Auditor-General Report no. 3 2009–10 Audit Report: Administration of Parliamentarians' Entitlements by the Department of Finance and Regulation*. Canberra: Australian National Audit Office.

Australian National Audit Office. 2010a. *The Auditor-General Audit Report no. 28 2009–10 Performance Audit: The Australian Electoral Commission's Preparation for and Conduct of the 2007 Federal General Election*. Canberra: Australian National Audit Office.

Australian National Audit Office. 2010b. *The Australian Electoral Commission's Preparation for and Conduct of the 2007 Federal General Election*. Report 28/10. Canberra: Commonwealth of Australia.

Bean, Clive. 2005. 'Young People's Voting Patterns.' Paper prepared for the Youth Electoral Study Workshop, Old Parliament House, Canberra, June.

Benoit, Ken. 2004. 'Models of Electoral System Change.' *Electoral Studies* 23(3): 363–89.

Byrne, N. F. 1959. 'A Historical Survey of the Western Australian Electoral System, 1917–1956.' Master of Arts thesis. Perth: University of Western Australia.

Campbell, Ian. 2006. 'Senate Finance and Public Administration Legislation Committee hearing.' *Hansard*, 7 March. Canberra: Parliament of Australia.

Charnock, David. 1994. 'Electoral Bias in Australia 1980–1993: The Impact of the 1983 Electoral Amendments.' *Australian Journal of Political Science* 29(3): 484–500.

Costar, Brian. 2006. *Submission to the Senate Finance and Public Administration Committee Inquiry*. Submission no. 2. Canberra: Parliament of Australia.

Costar, Brian. 2009. 'Democracy Under Siege for the Sake of a Few Pennies.' *The Age*, 29 May.

Dacey, Paul. 2005. 'What do "Impartiality", "Independence" and "Transparency" Mean?—Some Thoughts from Australia.' Paper delivered at the Improving the Quality of Election Management Conference of Commonwealth Chief Election Officers, New Delhi, India.

Dario, Gina. 2005. *Analysis of Informal Voting During the 2004 House of Representatives Election*. Research Report no. 7. Canberra: Australian Electoral Commission. URL: <http://www.aec.gov.au/pdf/research/papers/paper7/research_paper7.pdf>, retrieved 24 June 2007.

Dundas, Carl W. 1994. *Dimensions of Free and Fair Elections: Frameworks, Integrity, Transparency, Attributes and Monitoring*. London: Commonwealth Secretariat.

Duverger, Maurice. 1951. *Political Parties: Their Organization and Activity in the Modern State*. New York: Wiley.

Election Funding Authority. 2007. *Annual Report 2006–2007*. Sydney: Election Funding Authority.

Electoral Matters Committee. 2008. *Inquiry into the Conduct of the 2006 Victorian State Election and Matters Related Thereto: Report to Parliament Electoral Matters Committee*. Melbourne: Victorian Government Printer.

Elkins, David J. 1992. 'Electoral Reform and Political Culture.' In *Comparative Political Studies: Australia and Canada*, eds M. Alexander and B. Galligan. Melbourne: Pitman.

Ellis, Andrew, Maria Gratschew, Jon H. Pammett and Erin Thiessen. 2006. *Engaging the Electorate: Initiatives to Promote Voter Turnout from Around the World—Including Voter Turnout Data from National Elections Worldwide 1945–2006*. Stockholm: International IDEA.

Ewing, Keith and Navraj Singh Ghaleigh. 2006. 'Donations to Political Parties in the United Kingdom.' Paper prepared for the Political Finance and Government Advertising Workshop, The Australian National University, Canberra, 25 February.

Garber, Larry. 1994. 'Election Commissions: Responsibilities and Composition.' Paper presented at the NDI-sponsored African Election Colloquium, Victoria Falls, Zimbabwe.

Goot, Murray. 1985. 'Electoral Systems.' In *Surveys of Australian Political Science*, ed. D. Aitken. Sydney: George Allen & Unwin.

Green, Antony. 2003. *Prospects for the 2003 Legislative Council Election*. Background Paper no. 3/03, NSW Parliamentary Library Research Service. Sydney: Parliament of New South Wales.

Green, Phillip. 1986. 'The Australian Labor Party and the Commonwealth Electoral System 1972–1986.' Unpublished Litt. B. sub-thesis. Canberra.

Harris, Paul. 1997. *An Electoral Administration: Who, What and Where*. Paper prepared at IDEA for the South Pacific Electoral Administrators' Conference in Fiji, October.

Harvey, Ben. 2002. 'Greens Sink Votes Bid.' *West Australian*, 18 November 2002.

Harwin, D. 2007. 'Select Committee on Electoral and Political Party Funding: Establishment.' *Hansard*, 27 June. Sydney: Parliament of New South Wales, p. 1807. URL: <http://www.parliament.nsw.gov.au>

Hasen, Richard L. 2004. *Ending Felon Disenfranchisement in the United States: Litigation or Legislation?* Canberra: Democratic Audit of Australia, The Australian National University. URL: <http://democratic.audit.anu.edu.au/papers/20040913_hasen_felon_disenfranch.pdf>, retrieved 23 September 2007.

Hill, Lisa and Cornelia Koch 2011. 'The Voting Rights of Incarcerated Australian Citizens.' *Australian Journal of Political Science* 46(2): 213–28.

House of Assembly. 1986. *General Elections 1985*. Adelaide: Government Printer.

Hughes, Colin. 1977. *A Handbook of Australian Government and Politics 1965– 1974*. Canberra: Australian National University Press.

Hughes, Colin. 1986. *Handbook of Australian Government and Politics 1975– 1984*. Canberra: Australian National University Press.

Hughes, Colin. 2001. 'Institutionalising Electoral Integrity.' In *Elections: Full, Free & Fair*, ed. Marian Sawer. Sydney: The Federation Press.

Hughes, Colin. 2007. *The Importance of Boundaries*. Research Paper 1. Canberra: Democratic Audit of Australia, The Australian National University. URL: <http://democratic.audit.anu.edu.au/papers/20071102hughesrespapredist. pdf>, retrieved 5 December 2007.

Hughes, Colin and Brian Costar. 2005. 'Fiddling the Ballot Books.' *The Age*, 3 November.

Hughes, Colin and Brian Costar. 2006. *Limiting Democracy: The Erosion of Electoral Rights in Australia*. Sydney: UNSW Press.

IDEA [Institute for Democracy and Electoral Assistance]. 2002. *International Electoral Standards: Guidelines for Reviewing the Legal Framework of Elections*. Stockholm: International IDEA.

Johnston, Michael. 2005. *Political Parties and Democracy in Theoretical and Practical Perspectives: Political Finance Policy, Parties, and Democratic Development*. Washington, DC: National Democratic Institute for International Affairs.

JSCEM [Joint Standing Committee on Electoral Matters]. 1994. *Financial Reporting by Political Parties: Interim Report from the Joint Standing Committee on Electoral Matters on the Inquiry into the Conduct of the 1993 Election and Matters Related Thereto*. Canberra: Parliament of Australia.

JSCEM [Joint Standing Committee on Electoral Matters]. 2005. *Official Committee Hansard, Joint Standing Committee on Electoral Matters, Wednesday 6 July, Brisbane.* Canberra: Commonwealth of Australia.

JSCEM [Joint Standing Committee on Electoral Matters]. 2009. *Report on the Conduct of the 2007 Federal Election and Matters Related Thereto.* Canberra: Commonwealth of Australia.

JSCEM [Joint Standing Committee on Electoral Matters]. 2011. *Report on the Funding of Political Parties and Political Campaigns.* Canberra: Commonwealth of Australia.

Jupp, James and Marian Sawer. 2001. 'Political Parties, Partisanship and Electoral Governance.' In *Elections: Full, Free & Fair*, ed. M. Sawer. Sydney: The Federation Press.

Katz, Richard S. and Peter Mair. 1995. 'Changing Models of Party Organization and Party Democracy.' *Party Politics* 1(1): 5–28.

Katz, Richard S. and Peter Mair. 2009. 'The Cartel Party Thesis: A Restatement.' *Perspectives on Politics* 7(4): 753–66.

Kelly, Norm. 2006. 'The Howard Government's Electoral Reforms—A Blight on Democratic Principles.' Paper delivered at the Australasian Political Studies Association Conference, Newcastle.

Kelly, Norm. 2011. 'Australian Electoral Administration and Electoral Integrity.' In *Electoral Democracy: Australian Prospects*, eds Tham, Costar and Orr. Melbourne: Melbourne University Press.

Lijphart, Arend. 1994. *Electoral Systems and Party Systems: A Study of Twenty-Seven Democracies 1945–1990.* Oxford: Oxford University Press.

López-Pintor, Rafael. 2000. *Electoral Management Bodies as Institutions of Governance.* New York: Bureau for Development Policy, United Nations Development Programme. URL: <www.undp.org/governance/docs/Elections-Pub-EMBbook.pdf>, retrieved 3 July 2008.

McAllister, Ian, Toni Makkai and Chris Patterson. 1992. *Informal Voting in the 1987 and 1990 Australian Federal Elections.* Canberra: Australian Government Publishing Service.

Mackenzie, William James Millar. 1967. *Free Elections.* London: George Allen & Unwin.

Marsh, Ian, ed. 2006. *Political Parties in Transition.* Sydney: The Federation Press.

Mason, Anthony. 2001. 'The Constitutional Principle of Representative Government.' In *Speaking for the People: Representation in Australian Politics*, eds Sawer and Zappala. Melbourne: Melbourne University Press.

Massicotte, Louis, André Blais and Antoine Yoshinaka. 2004. *Establishing the Rules of the Game: Election Laws in Democracies*. Toronto: University of Toronto Press.

Mawrey, Richard. 2010. 'Easy Voting Means Fraudulent Voting.' *Quadrant* 54(4).

Medew, Rod. 2003. *Informal Vote Survey, House of Representatives, 2001 Election*. Research Report no. 1. Canberra: Australian Electoral Commission. URL: <http://www.aec.gov.au/pdf/research/papers/paper1/res_rep_01.pdf>, retrieved 16 April 2007.

Minter Ellison Consulting. 2003. *Independent Review of the Northern Territory Electoral System: Final Report and Recommendations*. Canberra: Minter Ellison Consulting.

Miskin, Sarah and Greg Baker. 2006. *Political Finance Disclosure under Current and Proposed Thresholds*. Research Note 27, 2005–06. Canberra: Parliamentary Library, Parliament of Australia.

Mozaffar, Shaheen and Andreas Schedler. 2002. 'The Comparative Study of Electoral Governance—An Introduction.' *International Political Science Review* 23(1): 5–27.

Nelson, Paul. 2007. *Electoral Division Rankings: Census 2006 First Release*. Research Paper 12 2007–08. Canberra: Parliamentary Library, Parliament of Australia.

Northern Territory Electoral Commission. 2007. *2005 Legislative Assembly General Election Report: Part 1 of 2*. Darwin: Northern Territory Electoral Commission.

Offe, Claus. 1996. 'Designing Institutions in East European Transitions.' In *The Theory of Institutional Design*, ed. R. E. Goodin. Cambridge: Cambridge University Press.

Orr, Graeme. 1998. 'Ballotless and Behind Bars: The Denial of the Franchise to Prisoners.' *Federal Law Review* 26(1): 56–82.

Orr, Graeme. 2007. *Constitutionalising the Franchise and the Status Quo: The High Court on Prisoner Voting Rights*. Discussion Paper 19/07. Canberra: Democratic Audit, The Australian National University.

Orr, Graeme. 2010. *The Law of Politics: Elections, Parties and Money in Australia*. Sydney: The Federation Press.

Orr, Graeme, Bryan Mercurio and George Williams. 2003. 'Australian Electoral Law: A Stocktake.' *Election Law Journal* 2(3): 383–402.

Parliament of Australia. 2004. 'Referendum Results 1974.' Parliamentary Handbook of the Commonwealth of Australia. Parliament of Australia web site, URL: <http://www.aph.gov.au/library/handbook/referendums/r1974.htm>

Pettit, Philip, Tim Keady and Bill Blick. 1998. *Review of the Governance of the Australian Capital Territory*. Canberra: Chief Minister's Department.

Phillips, Harry. 1991. 'The Modern Parliament, 1965–1989.' In *The House on the Hill: A History of the Parliament of Western Australia 1832–1990*, ed. Black. Perth: Parliament of Western Australia.

Phillips, Harry and Kirsten Robinson. 2006. *The Quest for 'One Vote One Value' in Western Australia's Political History*. Perth: Western Australian Electoral Commission.

Public Accounts and Estimates Committee. 2006. *Report On—A Legislative Framework for Independent Officers of Parliament*. Melbourne: Parliament of Victoria.

Rae, Douglas. 1967. *The Political Consequences of Electoral Laws*. Clinton, Mass.: Colonial Press.

Reilly, Benjamin. 2002. 'Political Engineering and Party Politics in Papua New Guinea.' *Party Politics* 8(6): 701–18.

Reilly, Benjamin, Per Nordlund and Edward Newman. 2008. *Political Parties in Conflict-Prone Societies: Encouraging Inclusive Politics and Democratic Development*. Policy Brief no. 2. Tokyo: United Nations University.

Reynolds, Andrew and Benjamin Reilly. 2002. *The International IDEA Handbook of Electoral System Design*. Stockholm: International IDEA.

Sawer, Marian, ed. 2001. *Elections: Full, Free and Fair*. Sydney: The Federation Press.

Sawer, Marian. 2006. *Damaging Democracy? Early Closure of Electoral Rolls*. Canberra: Democratic Audit of Australia, The Australian National University. URL: <http://democratic.audit.anu.edu.au/papers/20060308_sawer_dam_dem.pdf> Retrieved 16 June 2007.

Sawer, Marian, Norman Abjorensen and Phil Larkin. 2009. *Australia: The State of Democracy*. Sydney: The Federation Press.

Select Committee on Electoral and Political Party Funding. 2008a. *Electoral and Political Party Funding in New South Wales*. Report no. 1. Sydney: Legislative Council, Parliament of New South Wales.

Select Committee on Electoral and Political Party Funding. 2008b. Hearing Transcript, 3 March. Sydney: Parliament of New South Wales, p. 21. URL: <http://www.parliament.nsw.gov.au/prod/parlment/committee.nsf/0/02C2 B246F4664981CA2573D8000D1077>

Senate Finance and Public Administration Legislation Committee. 2002. *Charter of Political Honesty Bill 2000*. Canberra: Parliament of Australia.

Senate Finance and Public Administration Legislation Committee. 2010.*Report into the Electoral and Referendum Amendment (How-to-Vote Cards and Other Measures) Bill 2010 and the Electoral and Referendum Amendment (Modernisation and Other Measures) Bill 2010*. Canberra: Parliament of Australia.

Senate Legal and Constitutional References Committee. 2004. *State Elections (One Vote, One Value) Bill 2001 [2002]*. Senate Legal and Constitutional References Committee. Canberra: Parliament of Australia.

Snowdon, Warren. 2004. 'Senate Victory Used to Silence Voters.' Media release, 20 December.

Standing Committee on Legal Affairs. 2002. *The Appropriateness of the Size of the Legislative Assembly for the ACT and Options for Changing the Number of Members, Electorates and Any Other Related Matter*. Report no. 4. Canberra: Legislative Assembly for the Australian Capital Territory.

State Electoral Office. 2007. *Election Report: South Australian Election: 18 March 2006*. Adelaide: State Electoral Office.

Tham, Joo-Cheong. 2010. *Money and Politics: The Democracy We Can't Afford*. Sydney: UNSW Press.

Wall, Alan, Andrew Ellis, Ayman Ayoub, Carl W. Dundas, Joram Rukambe and Sara Staino. 2006. *Electoral Management Design: The International IDEA Handbook*. Stockholm: International IDEA.

Whitlam, Gough. 2003. 'One Vote One Value.' The Whitlam Institute web site, URL: <http://www.whitlam.org/collection/2000/20000406_ onevoteonevalue/index.html>

Wilks-Heeg, Stuart. 2008. *Purity of Elections in the UK: Causes for Concern.* York: The Joseph Rowntree Reform Trust Limited.

Young, Sally. 2003. 'Killing Competition: Restricting Access to Political Communication Channels in Australia'. *AQ Journal of Contemporary Analysis* 75(3): 9–15.

Young, Sally and Joo-Cheong Tham. 2006. *Political Finance in Australia: A Skewed and Secret System.* Canberra: Democratic Audit of Australia, The Australian National University.

www.ingramcontent.com/pod-product-compliance
Lightning Source LLC
Chambersburg PA
CBHW061240270326
41927CB00035B/3450